To Father Franz Hessler

In memory of a
very happy friendship.

God bless you and
keep you, always

Oct. 1, 1951.

The Early Days of Maryknoll

THE
Early Days OF
Maryknoll

———◆———

RAYMOND A. LANE, M.M., D.D.

———◆———

David McKay Company

NEW YORK

Contents

Acknowledgments

Excerpt from *Ave Maria,* reprinted from "The Collected Poems of John Jerome Rooney" by permission of Dodd, Mead & Company. Copyright 1938, by Marie Collins Rooney.

Excerpt from *He Whom a Dream Hath Possessed,* by Shaemus O'Sheel, reprinted by permission of Liveright Publishing Corporation, New York.

Excerpts from two poems of Father Abram Ryan, reprinted from "Poems of Abram J. Ryan" by permission of P. J. Kenedy and Sons.

Foreword

When Father Considine asked me to write a book on the early years of Maryknoll, frankly I was pleased. I felt I knew a bit about the beginnings. Some of our men have a better memory of those early days, and others are good writers, but I liked the idea and consented on the condition that I provide the material and that someone put it into shape. This assurance given, I ventured into realms heretofore unfamiliar—recording reminiscences.

This book has been written under difficulties, and some of it in the most out of the way places as is befitting, I suppose, a volume treating of men who go far and wide for the spread of Christ's kingdom. The notes on Father Walsh's personality were written in Tripoli. I had been dropped there by the Italian Air Lines after flying over Stromboli, Messina, Mt. Aetna, Catania, and Malta. In a sort of barracks I waited for the British plane to Nairobi. The place was conducive to reminiscence. I never even bothered to drive into Tripoli.

Some chapters were written in Rome while convalescing from a broken leg sustained aboard ship. Five were written on the return trip from Naples to New York. The remainder had to be squeezed in here and there during a busy period, following a long absence from Maryknoll during which I visited our mission in Tanganyika.

I wish to dedicate this volume to our Immaculate Mother, Patron of America and of Maryknoll. The radio has just mentioned the Holy Father's proclamation of the Dogma of the Assumption on November the first. This year is the thirty-seventh anniversary of my arrival at Maryknoll, and the fifth anniversary of my release from a wartime internment camp.

The writing of this book has given me much joy for it brought back to my mind many happy experiences. May it bring some joy to the reader. The book is intended for a wide variety of readers. The younger generation may wonder why I have gone to such pains to mention many persons who have long since passed to their reward. The clergy will have to be patient with some of my detailed explanations about the seminary and sacred orders. It is a family book, and the Maryknoll Family includes young and old, the learned and the unlearned, the great and the small.

. . Were I to fail to acknowledge the help of others who have co-operated, I should be indeed ungrateful. My sincere thanks, then, to Father Mark Kent for having patiently gone over source material, to Father Considine for the layout and chapter headings and other helpful advice, to Father George Powers and Father John Murrett for their excellent works on which I have drawn, and to Sister Raphael Marie and her Sister companions of the General Secretariat at Maryknoll for having patiently interpreted my hieroglyphics and typed them into something readable, to Father Frederick Dietz, Sister Just and to Miss Amy English for having read the manuscript and made important corrections.

Finally, my special thanks to Father Edward McGurkin, companion for many years in Manchuria and in concentration camp during the War, for having given my rather inarticulate and roaming remarks the proper literary flavor.

May this book serve as evidence to all who read it of what can be done when men set themselves to a task with the singleness of purpose and love of an ideal possessed by James Anthony Walsh and Thomas Frederick Price—*Auspice Maria.*

Maryknoll   ✠ RAYMOND A. LANE, M.M., D.D.
                                                  Superior General of Maryknoll

The Early Days of Maryknoll

August 15th, 1913

"Lady, thy sailor I would be
This day I sign my name
To sail the high seas of the earth
For glory of thy fame. . . . ."

Ave Maria—John Jerome Rooney

Sixty-five minutes from the Grand Central, the Hudson River Local shot out of a short dark tunnel and screeched to a halt. Through my window I read "Ossining." This was my stop. With other passengers I got off and started across the station plaza. A trolley car would be there in a minute, I was told, to bring me on towards my journey's end.

It was August 15th, 1913. Like August 15th of nearly every year, the day was hot. The new black suit made me warm and uncomfortable. With the tip of my finger I tested the high stiff collar to gauge the degree of the wilting process. I took my handkerchief and mopped around the ears and neck and brow, wondering whence came the superstition that hard straw sailor hats are cool. It was Lady Day, and all good Christians were at the seaside, lakes, or riverside. I thought of the cool waters of the Spicket and the Merrimack, but consoled myself that I, too, was on a pilgrimage, on a big errand for Our Lady.

I picked up my bags and started again in the direction of the trolley tracks. A huge white horse, harnessed to a shiny carriage with brass and nickel fittings and clean linen seat covers, was hitched in front of Rigney's Hotel. Entrance to the hotel from the station street was made through swinging doors, flanked on either side by rich glass plaques which carried the comforting news that Budweiser's was best for you, and Old Scotch was aged in the wood, or something like that. I saw that the hotel could be entered also at the rear from a road that ran along the side of the hill propped up by a heavy masonry wall. Entering from that direction the visitor would find himself on the fifth floor.

Thus I learned that Ossining rises abruptly from the waters of the Hudson and I calculated the odds in making the ascent and continuing my journey aboard the Toonerville Trolley which was now rolling to a stop at the end of the line. The car was hardly big enough to display the elaborate title, "The Hudson River and Eastern Traction Company."

If you can imagine yourself sitting in an old-time rocking chair which has been mounted on a roller skate, you may experience somewhat the sensation I had as the trolley car started up through the town and on to higher places. Up Secor Road, on and up through the shops of Main Street. We passed Young's Hardware Store, Kipp's Furniture Shop, the Bank, Secor's Grocery Store, and all the rest. I noticed a couple of churches too. We coasted along a very brief stretch of the Albany Post Road and then zoomed again up Croton Avenue, up and up, swaying and rocking all the time.

The trolley line had been started with the best of intentions of continuing on to Pleasantville, six miles away. A mile or two from the river's edge, however, after climbing several hundred feet, it seemed to lose heart and made a sudden spur off to the left. This led it past the Camp Meeting Woods where business was good, especially during the summer months. The tracks ended abruptly half way down an incline, like a man alerted in the midst of a doodle. The motorman got off to swing the trolley pole around. I pulled my bags together and disembarked on terra firma.

A horse and wagon stood in the shade at the side of the road. What a contrast with the high-stepping steed and the elegant carriage I had just left hitched in front of Rigney's Hotel. This horse showed long wear and harder fare. Mentally I noted several safe places to hang my straw hat where his skeleton protruded prominently. The carriage was a high-wheeled open-air rig, neither a buckboard nor a droshky, but a sort of combination of both. The driver was looking at me: "Are you Mr. Lane?" I identified myself and climbed aboard and we started.

Brother Frederick had been sent down to fetch me. He had heard I was coming, Father Walsh had said something about it that morning. Father Walsh was back again, had been away for a few days, an awfully busy man. Father Price was home. The place was not quite settled, Brother Fred said, and he hoped I wouldn't mind roughing it a bit. The house needed some repairs, there was lots of work to do, everyone seemed happy though. "You're from Lawrence? I'm from Newton," he said. "Giddap, Billy!"

Brother Fred's words were few, chiefly brief replies to my questions. His fingers were black with printer's ink. "Have a little press up there," he explained. "Do some leaflets and things for Father Walsh." He turned to look me over once again as he spoke. His glasses were perched down below the bridge of his nose.

The carriage rolled noisily down the hill from the Camp Meeting Woods, rattled over the planks that bridged a beautiful little brook. Then we started up the hill. It was a dirt road climbing abruptly and laboriously up the side of Sunset Hill. I found myself leaning forward and holding my breath as Billy slipped on the loose gravel, strained at the lines, and made the leather creak against the shafts. Finally, the road leveled off and made a partial turn. I looked back and got my first glimpse of a view which I have never tired of seeing.

The hill dropped steeply to the green knolls at the edge of the village. Clumps of foliage were bunched here and there on the landscape. A white colonial homestead stood out clearly, and here and there a steeple. Two or three miles to the west, the Hudson, wide and beautiful and majestic, filled the panorama north and south for thirty miles, beginning at a bend below Bear Mountain and disappearing in the Palisades near Yonkers. The rocky cliffs on the far side of the river stood out sharply, and beyond them the forests and hills of the Hudson Highlands rolled away as far as the eye could see.

When I came back to the world about me, Brother Frederick was turning the carriage through a grove of evergreens and into what looked like an abandoned farm. I had tried many times to visualize

Maryknoll. Here it was now before my eyes, an old wooden farm-house with a new name, "Seminary." The entire student body was on the front porch; all six members were there to welcome the new arrival.

Father Walsh shook my hand and brought me in. I cannot remember now what he said. Then I was turned over to the students. It was almost time for supper. I had my first meal at Maryknoll and thereupon became a member of the family. The dining room was extremely simple; to me, it seemed bare. There were three tables and no table cloths. The tables were arranged like a U, with Father Walsh sitting at the head, Fathers Price and Lane at either side of him, and the rest of us on the outside edge of the two side tables, so that everyone was practically facing everyone else; at least, you looked at no one's back.

That first night I learned my fellow students' names and learned much more about them during the days that followed. They were Daniel McShane, James Walsh, Francis Ford, Alphonse Vogel, William O'Shea and William Lambert. After Night Prayers everyone seemed to keep quiet, and I was told that the "Great Silence" would continue until after breakfast the next morning.

There was a scarcity of everything about the farmhouse. Packing boxes served in some of the rooms as desks and bookcases. There was no electricity. Someone told me to pick up a kerosene lamp and carry it to my room. I started to undress and then knelt down to say a few prayers, I tried to think what they would be doing at home just at that moment. One thing was certain: they didn't have to keep quiet with any "Great Silence." I guess maybe I was homesick, though I was nineteen years old. Something gave way inside, and I broke down like a baby and cried for I don't know how long. It had been harder leaving than I had expected.

As I knelt and dozed, my mind traveled back over the years and I thought of my many childhood dreams and the varied incidents which led to my coming to Maryknoll.

Seven years before, in 1906, when I was in the seventh grade at St. Mary's School, I had seen Father James Anthony Walsh for the first time. He told us about Blessed Theophane Venard, a young priest of the Paris Foreign Missions who had been martyred for the

Faith in Indo-China. Father Venard was a classmate of Father Hogan who was a professor at the Brighton Seminary in Boston when Father Walsh was there as a student. The Xaverian Brothers who taught us bigger boys at St. Mary's, wanted us to know about the missions. Three years later, when I was at St. John's in Danvers, Mass., the Brothers were still my teachers, and there I again heard Father Walsh speak.

I thought of the good old days in Lawrence. All the things that had happened at St. Mary's: the day I threw the apple at Pee Wee Barry, missed and hit Brother Robert. It was during morning classes. Brother was at the blackboard, and the apple hit him square between the shoulders. I could still see him turning and demanding that the culprit come forward. I was ready to obey, but John Shine, the gang boss, told me to keep quiet—he'd break every bone in my body if I confessed. Hours of agony followed and I'll never forget the look of astonishment on Brother's face when, at four-thirty p.m., I went up to plead guilty.

The baseball teams, with our victories and defeats, all came back. I thought of the night my brother and myself challenged my father to a race, how he took off his shoes, ran with us and beat us, and how my mother upbraided the three of us for putting on such an undignified show for the neighbors. Then there was the old swimming hole in the Spicket above the mills, always delightfully cool and refreshing.

One day Father Conrardy who had been a helper of Father Damien at Molokai came to our school and talked about lepers. He was a Belgian Father, a little man with a long white beard, and he showed us a map of the world and pointed to an island in the West River in South China where he now lived with his lepers.

The *Annals of the Propagation of the Faith* used to come to our home. I found myself computing the numbers of the various missionary orders in foreign fields, trying to figure out what chance I should have of getting overseas if I joined one of them. I was really greatly interested, and almost afraid to admit it even to myself. I toyed with the idea of getting a job on a transatlantic liner and then in London or Paris joining one of these orders. There were no foreign mission societies in America.

My daydreams brought me pictures of myself as a missioner, a great missioner, of course, another Xavier, leading thousands and thousands into the fold. Doctors had been my heroes for a time. I thought of myself as a surgeon, a great surgeon, naturally, and pictured myself after saving someone's life in the operating room. There I was in my spotless white smock, standing in the hospital corridor, while I chatted with the grateful relatives, twiddling the stethoscope or perhaps trimming my nails with a scalpel. Our boyhood dreams usually give us the stage front and center under the spotlight. It is only later, when we grow up a little and begin to get sense, that we back off and grow small and yield the leading role to God.

Once the Dominican Fathers gave a mission in our parish. After that I thought of becoming a great preacher. I saw myself in my white habit, leaning from the pulpit, holding the people spellbound with my dramatic gestures and eloquence.

At an earlier age policemen and firemen had their attractions. From my father I learned that, when just beginning to talk, I had been so carried off by the shiny red hose cart and the galloping horses that one day, sitting in my high chair, I repeated snatches of the charm words I had heard Jerry O'Leary, the driver, heap on his fiery steeds. My poor mother was so shocked, she could have fainted. She told all to my father when he arrived from work that night, and after a council of war, he, in practical wisdom, decreed: "We won't say anything now because he might think he was smart. But, if he ever says it again, then knock the blazes out of him!"

So, the idea of the missions, rather than coming as a lightning flash, grew upon me gradually. One day in my senior year at St. John's, Danvers, I was browsing around the library and picked up the Boston *Pilot*. My heart gave a hop, skip and a jump, when my eye caught a heading on the editorial page: "American Priests to Start Foreign Mission Seminary." I tried to read the whole article in one glance, and then from start to finish I read it slowly over and over again. Breaking the rules of the library, I cut out the article and carried it in my pocket for a long time. The society had not yet been organized, the word, "Maryknoll" was still to be thought of; the work was just a blueprint and no more, and still I felt I was to be there. I did not even consider the possibility of being rejected. I began to read *The Field Afar*, read every line of it, and then one day without a word to anyone at home, I wrote to Father Walsh and told him what was in my mind.

At St. Mark's Church, in Dorchester, I met Father John I. Lane. When Father Walsh answered my letter he had told me to see Father Lane, who was joining the new foreign mission seminary. Father Lane, a star in sports at Holy Cross in the early eighties, was a big man, handsome, with a smile and a way about him that made you feel good. Too bad the movie producer who likes to show the world that "Priests are People" didn't know Father John Lane. A combination of Father O'Malley and Joe DiMaggio, this big boys' hero in flesh and blood would have put the box offices on easy street for months and years. When I walked out of St. Mark's and started back to Lawrence, I was saying to myself: "If he's going to be there, and any more like him, then—Boys! Count me in!"

Next came the job of telling my pastor. This was going to be hard. There was an old pastor near Boston who used to tell about the time, some few years back, when he caught a youngster high in the limbs of a tree that stood in the yard of the Sacred Heart rectory, looking down into the priest's house. "What were you doing up there?" he asked with all the severity of his position, when he got the little ape back on the sidewalk. "I had a date with Father Tom," he explained. "He didn't show up and when I whistled he didn't come, so I climbed up the tree to see if he was up yet."

My pastor, Father O'Reilly, an Augustinian, was too venerable in my eyes to be this kind of friend, but there was a real affection between us. He was the biggest man in Lawrence, and yet he would take time out to listen to me, a very small person. Even as a youngster I could go into the priest's house, knock at his door, be asked in, sit down and talk. He would listen with attention and sympathy and ponder my words carefully as if I really had something important to say. He was my hero.

In those days, if a boy in Lawrence wanted to be a priest, the usual procedure was to go to Villanova College and then study to be an Augustinian. Now I had to go and tell him that I wanted to be a priest, but I wasn't going to be an Augustinian; in fact, I was signing up with an outfit that just barely existed and wasn't even heard of.

I wondered what he was going to say. Honestly, my chief fear was that I might hurt him, not what he might say to me.

"Good, good, my boy. I'm glad that St. Mary's is going to have a boy at the new mission seminary. God bless you!" You could have bowled me over with a toothpick. I had underestimated Father O'Reilly. He knew more about the new seminary than I did. He was pleased, because he himself was an apostle.

Looking back now, I suppose there was hardly any time in my boyhood life that really deep down I didn't feel I ought to be a priest. At times, I thought of other things—doctor, policeman, baseball star, but being so close to priests made me follow along naturally with them. When I served Mass, when I went to the First Mass of one of the Lawrence boys, when I went with the priest on a sick call and minded the horses for him, when I saw the priest at a wake, I imagined myself doing all this some day. Of course, I liked to think of myself too, dressed neatly in black suit and straw hat, strolling out to see my altar boys practicing on the sand lot, stepping up to the plate and walloping the ball out of sight over the tops of the houses. We're all that way, I think: hero in our childhood musings.

Yet, if we were actually cornered and pressed to give the real reason why we wanted to be priests, I think the answer would be about the same: "I want to get to Heaven, and I want to help other people get to Heaven."

When you talked about going to the missions in those days, the reaction was not always flattering. People would look at you with a sort of pity, wondering whether you were intellectually immature, emotionally unstable, or whether you just couldn't make it in the seminary at home and had to get in out of the rain by going to a place where all they asked was that you observe the Ten Commandments and be able to write your baptismal name without too many mistakes. He's not too smart, poor boy, he would never do in our parishes here; but he'll be all right away off in some heathen land. That was the idea.

Sooner or later I had to tell my mother and father. My mother began to notice letters coming with a strange postmark, "Ossining, N. Y." Finally, one day I told her all. There was a big lump in my throat and tightening in my chest. I felt mean. All she said was: "Why do you want to go so far away?"

The biggest hurdle would be to get permission from my Dad, I thought. Time was getting short. Father Walsh's letter said that I should come to Maryknoll on August 15th. My father had asked me to work for two years, after leaving High School. A few weeks more and that time would be up. Finally, when only two weeks separated us from the fifteenth, I came back from work one night and found my Dad as usual in the garden reading the newspaper. I told myself it was now or never. I said a prayer, sat down beside him and said: "Dad, I'm going away soon."

"Where?"

"To New York to enter a seminary for the foreign missions."

"That's good. God bless you, son."

My parents' generosity and faith made me feel small. I had expected an argument; yet here they were—so much bigger and better than I had thought. How much better it would have been not to have held back from my parents, but to have opened up to them immediately. It would have been easier for me and would have been an expression of confidence which they well deserved.

The time came to say good-bye. It was going to be hard, I knew, and I had hoped to get it all over within our own home. My mother was brave and was as always the valiant woman of faith, but anyone could see that for her it was a heartbreaking farewell. My sister and brother, both younger, were unusually quiet.

My father insisted on coming with me as far as Boston. The ride on the Boston and Maine takes about an hour. It seemed a terribly long ride that day. Hardly a word was spoken. My father looked out one window; I looked out the opposite one. At the South Station we parted. He had some words of farewell ready, but they were choked in his throat. I couldn't do any better.

Pictures of home kept coming back to my mind during the ride to New York. It seemed so happy and attractive now that I was leaving it forever. I figured that it would take about seven years to complete my training. Then I would be ordained, return home for a brief visit and then depart for far away places. Thoughts of home began to alternate with images of what lay ahead—New York, the Hudson, Maryknoll, China. . . . .

I jumped up from beside the bed where I had been kneeling and dreaming and dozing I don't know how long. I was choking with smoke. The kerosene lamp had burnt itself out, the wick was smoldering, and the room was filled with acrid smoke. It was after midnight. I should have had the light out and been in bed hours ago. The frightening thought struck me that I might be expelled for this grave infraction of the rule, on the very first night after my arrival! I rubbed out the smoking wick and jumped into bed, hoping and praying that I had not been detected. First of all, I had left my light burning long after the time allowed, and then, too, I had been careless and might have started a serious fire. Actually, vocations were coming so slowly in those days that, as we used to joke later, hardly anything short of murder or highway robbery would be considered sufficient reason for sending a student home. When I opened my eyes again, it was daylight. There was a rooster crowing near by, and a bell somewhere about the house was making a terribly unpleasant noise.

2

First Days

"Learn to dream when thou dost wake,
Learn to wake when thou dost sleep;
Learn to water joy with tears,
Learn from fear to vanquish fears. . . ."
—— Francis Thompson

A battle was raging beside me when I sat down in the dining room the next morning. History does not record who fired the first shot. It could have started when the O'Shea boy shouldered up to Alphonse Vogel, coming out of Chapel, and whispered belittling words about the east side and west side of Tammany's broken sidewalks. Master Alphonse, no doubt, looked down his nose and dropped spiky disparagement about a hobo from Hoboken, or perhaps about the sea-faring prowess of "Cap" O'Shea.

In the refectory, this cold war deteriorated quickly into a hot shooting war. The Captain aimed a kick at the enemy. His range-finder was faulty. He missed by a millimeter and struck the bottom of the table with a resounding thwack that sent sugar bowl, cups and saucers dancing in the air. This drew the attention of all neutrals and brought frowns and stern looks from the Powers. Father Walsh seemed worried lest the new student from Lawrence should be scandalized by this early morning horse play. Far from scandalized, the new student from Lawrence began to feel right at home.

At breakfast it seemed that I had been up half a day already. After the bell at 5:30, or 6:00, we went to Chapel. Morning prayers were led by one of the students. There were certain parts where everyone joined in and other parts where everyone kept quiet, except the reader. This meant that you had to be alert; dreaming would not do. Opening your mouth at the wrong moment would startle the others and humiliate yourself. All this while we were kneeling up straight against the rough wooden kneeling benches.

Then we sat down for twenty minutes and meditated. I was too new and too curious to fall asleep, but my neighbors felt otherwise. Some nodded slowly with their eyes closed as if in solemn thought and assenting to the truth of a deep, consoling dogma. One lad, also wrapped in rhythmic recollection, was leaning dangerously off his chair, and I wondered how soon the center of gravity would shift enough to tumble the thinker.

The Angelus rang at the end of Meditation, and then came the Mass. Everyone had a missal to follow the prayers with the priest. Being such a small group we were all near the altar, which was placed in a bay window of the old farmhouse. Somehow the Mass seemed different, more intimate. After Mass there were several minutes of thanksgiving, and by the time we got to breakfast we had been up for two hours.

The house was still on vacation schedule. The students were just back from a month at home. Reading at meals would not start until the retreat in September, just before classes began again, and so at breakfast that morning I picked up more information on the life history of each one in the little group.

Alphonse Vogel had come from Cathedral College in New York. He was a quiet peaceful lad, in between battles with his pal from Hoboken, but he had a strong and public antipathy for a big sign-board that stood by the road halfway up Sunset Hill, "*Ossining— High and Dry—No Malaria.*" He had come down with malaria shortly after arriving at Maryknoll. Brought up on the sidewalks of 42d street, he had learned to love the friendly bustle and noise of the big city. Here in the country, he used to say, you could hear the silence. The stillness kept him awake at night. The malaria gave him a lot of trouble and left him permanently affected. After some years of hard work in South China, he returned to the States and later transferred to the New York diocesan clergy. He died in 1944, in New York City.

The student near him was William O'Shea. He came from Hoboken, was older than the rest, a deferred vocation. He had worked in the Brooklyn Navy Yard for a time, as secretary to an admiral, and had been skipper of his own little motor boat. Everyone called him "Cap." He had a number of stories of his Navy Yard days and told about one of his bosses who had a theory that water rusts your pipes. To safeguard his own the Commandant used lots of alcohol. One of the Cap's duties was to sound the "Slow Down" signal when the Boss started to list from an overload of John Barleycorn.

He had dipped into politics before turning towards the priesthood and had a battery of platform slogans always on the tip of his tongue. His persistence was an example to all of us, starting Latin and Greek as he did so late in life. In no time he was speaking many languages. His later life was a full one. He was a missioner in South China, held administrative positions back in this country, was made a mission superior in Korea, was consecrated in Rome by the Holy Father Pope Pius XII, and was sent back to Korea as a bishop. He returned to the States during World War II and died from a heart attack in the Grand Central Station, in 1945, while hurrying to catch a train for Ossining.

Francis Ford also came from Cathedral College. In those days everyone knew the Fords. His father, Austin Brendan Ford, was the editor of the *Irish World* and the *Freeman's Journal*. His mother had written a life of Joan of Arc. His sister Una was known too, and Frank himself could always write. He was the first student to reach Maryknoll. His arrival may have coincided with the graying process of Father Walsh's hair. He was forever on the move, a genius for tricks, a jack-in-the-box in perpetual motion. Right now he is Bishop of Kaying, in China.

James Walsh, who, I learned at breakfast, was Manual Labor boss, came from Maryland and had been at Mount St. Mary's, Emmitsburg. He came from a family of refined southern gentry, and we thought he did his best to live it down, going about in all sorts of bizarre attire. He might be seen on the coldest day of winter pushing a wheelbarrow with only a light jacket on, without hat or overcoat. One day Father Walsh called him and lectured him on the importance of keeping sewed up. He punctuated his points by plucking at Jimmy's cassock which had large rips under the sleeves and showed patches of white beneath.

James Edward gets the credit for introducing the title "Bro" to replace "Brother," which Father Walsh had inaugurated with the first arrivals. "Brother" was to be a convenient designation that would steer clear of nicknames and the formality of Mister, and would also avoid the crudity of using simply the last name. Obviously, Father Walsh was annoyed when he discovered that his dignified innovation had been streamlined to an abrupt "Bro."

Jimmy Walsh, years later, was consecrated Maryknoll's first bishop, on an island off the China coast where St. Francis Xavier died. He was Superior General for ten years, immediate successor to his namesake, James Anthony, the co-founder of Maryknoll and first Superior General. He is now back in China, directing the Catholic Central Bureau.

There was another boy there that morning. They called him "Luke," but this was a nickname, given perhaps because of his particular interest in scriptural studies and his readiness to discuss them. His name was William Lambert. He gave up his seminary studies later, and has since passed away, killed by a motorcar while hiking along the highway.

Daniel McShane was the sixth student. He seemed more mature than the rest, was further advanced in his studies, and I would easily have taken him to be a priest already. He was dignified, just a bit remote. They said he would be ordained the next year. I still remember that day when we all went to St. Patrick's Cathedral and saw Cardinal Farley ordain Father McShane, the first Maryknoll student raised to the priesthood.

It was that same year, 1913, that Father Walsh had written a long, interesting page for his *Field Afar*, of which the theme was "the missioner must not mind getting the worst of it." When he gets a mission, and when he starts to preach, when he wants to build a shelter for his horse, and so on, the missioner will usually get the worst of it. He continues: "Again he will get the worst of it when in the midst of his attempts to start things, his catechist catches smallpox, and the catechist's assistant's baby goes and dies, and it will die for a certainty, little angel though it be, just at the moment when heaven and earth will fall if you are left with no one to help you . . ." This was near prophecy for Daniel McShane. Fourteen years later, in South China, he died from smallpox contracted when he took in a dying infant at his orphanage in Loting.

There were three Brothers at Maryknoll in 1913. Brother Thomas McCann was a New Yorker, neatly dressed, alert, pleasant, a good talker, a walking example and living lesson of How to Make Friends and Influence People. He was very useful to Father Price and Father Walsh.

Brother Frederick McGuire, who had brought me up in the buggy pulled by Billy, was a printer. He had a little press in the corner of *The Field Afar* office where he turned out leaflets and various printed forms and otherwise helped Father Walsh.

Brother Ernst had come from the Tyrol where he had met Father Walsh on one of the latter's visits to the Mill Hill Junior Seminary at Brixen. He had quit his studies there on account of poor health. After a time with us he left to take up again his seminary course, hoping to exercise his ministry in the homeland.

The Manual Labor list was posted outside the dining room. Among the several assignments these caught my eye: Care of the Chapel, Care of the Bathrooms, Superintendent of Lamps, Fire Chief, Store Keeper, Water Superintendent, Infirmarian, Carpenter Gang, Paint Squad, Upkeep. This latter, as I soon learned, included what we called the "Wet and Dry Men," designated as the boys with the strong backs and the weak minds, they who really deserved an M. L. on their jerseys for long hours of hard useful toil.

Listed also were the Head Waiter, Manager of the Barber Shop, Forester, Road Supervisor. I wondered how six students and three brothers could hold so many and such important positions. The mystery has never been fully explained.

Father McCabe was in charge of Manual Labor. He was loaned to Maryknoll by the Mill Hill Fathers and he came shortly after ordination. In class he taught us how to split hairs. At Manual Labor he showed us how to clip them. That became my part-time job. With nine heads to practice on, I gradually acquired a certain facility, if not finesse, as a tonsorial artist. Most of my time at Manual Labor was with the "Wet and Dry Men."

Before I was quite qualified to plant a red and white pole outside my door, Frank Ford had been one of my victims. Father Mc-Cabe tried to show me how to graduate the trim, beginning somewhere at the back of the neck and working gradually upwards and outwards with the comb and scissors. My attempts to "graduate" Frank's jet black locks ended in an upside down version of the stone steps on the tombs of the Incas. While still looking like an escaped prisoner of the Iroquois, Frank received a telegram to go home to Brooklyn for his grandmother's funeral. Eye witnesses may testify that the family shed more tears over little Frankie's shearing than they did over dear old Granny. Undoubtedly, he had a hard time convincing them all that Maryknollers did not live in wigwams.

The largesse of our benefactors was near to spoiling those early students. They even sent us their old clothes. Such gifts included long discarded, but still magnificent, frock coats, silk hats and spats. It was common to see a student at Manual Labor on some gusty fall day pushing a wheelbarrow along the road, dressed in khaki trousers, a baseball cap, and a swallow-tail coat much too big for him. Walking up and down the boardwalk during recreation, the students produced a picture resembling the ambulatory at the House of Parliament. Frock coats, surely the envy of Disraeli and Lord Plushbottom, tall silk hats, white gloves, velvet collars, and bearskin overcoats were all on parade. The only puzzling element was to combine all this high brow haberdashery with khaki pants, overalls, and white sailor hats.

Sometimes Manual Labor brought the squads down to St. Teresa's Lodge where *The Field Afar* offices were located. The Teresians staffed the offices, or rather office, for there was at that time one big room, a real beehive of activity.

The Teresians, or Secretaries, as they were called at first, were the young women who on reading about the new foreign mission movement, had written to Fathers Price and Walsh, volunteering their services for *The Field Afar* clerical work or wherever they might be needed. There were six in the group when I arrived.

Later they became the Maryknoll Sisters, now numbering more than a thousand, scattered all over the world.

They lived upstairs and had their chapel, kitchen and dining room downstairs. Carpenters were always in demand there, and sometimes painters, too. I was a barber, and my professional skill was never requisitioned at St. Teresa's, but sometimes I had to fill in as a carpenter's helper or just ordinary day laborer.

You had to watch your step when you walked around that house. George Washington once stopped there, someone said. If you were fixing something outside and unwittingly put the ladder in the wrong place, a window went up with a bang and you heard a shout: "Look out for those rose bushes!" And you would look up to see Betsy Ross leaning out the window and giving you a severe once-over. It wasn't really Betsy Ross but it looked like her, especially leaning from the window of that old colonial farmhouse. She had a real 1776 hair-do, parted in the middle and pulled back tight to either side. A Buster Brown collar topped the shoulder cape, which was something like the Archbishop's, except that it was gray and the east side missed the west by about four inches, and the buttons were on both sides and were farther apart and didn't reach all the way to the bottom edge. She had a needle and thread in one hand, something under her arm that could have been an American flag, and maybe there was a spare common pin or two tucked in the corner of her lips. I knew it wasn't Betsy Ross, because for months I had been reading every word of *The Field Afar*, and felt I knew the complete history of the Secretaries, or Teresians, as they were then called.

I can never forget the impression I got when I walked into that little *Field Afar* office for the first time. The whole place seemed to smile on you, such a genuine, awfully-glad-to-see-you sort of smile, that made you feel good and made you want to thank God for producing such a place and making you part of it.

It must have been on the very first day that I discovered the seminary bell. The sound of it depressed me, and I had a grudge against it especially after it ended so abruptly that first short night. Someone had bought it at a wholsale crockery house down in the city and paid something over a dollar for it—not much over. It roused the community at morning, rang out the Angelus, started devotions, Manual Labor and the classes. As Father Walsh used to say, it called us to time.

After many a handshake it was cracked and became nothing but a piece of thick crockery and filled the house with its terrible ringless noise, until a kind benefactor released it from active service by sending us a new bell, shiny and bigger, with a silver tone. This new bell was installed on the roof, after Msgr. John Edwards, Vicar General of New York, blessed it and called it "Paul" after the Apostle of the Gentiles.

A boardwalk, not so elegant as Atlantic City's, but much more picturesque, ran from the farmhouse down through the trees as far as St. Teresa's. It had two planks. At the first bend, about fifty feet from the house, it ran by St. Michael's. This was a coachman's cottage with stable and carriage shed attached. St. Michael's still had a bucolic face when I arrived, and the stable doors still let you in and out. It became too small for two horses, so they were moved out. Fifteen students and farm hands moved in.

The conversation around me included occasional reference to "Caspar" and "Starlight" and "Prima." These names meant more to me when I began to learn my way around the farm. "George" had come with a surrey and run-about, or as they say in New England, a carry-all and buggy. He came from friends in Brooklyn who had him for eight years, having bought him from Terry McGovern, the famous prize-fighter. "George" must have been genuinely humble. With such an illustrious career behind him, he was still willing to settle down to the unexciting existence of Ossining and Sunset Hill.

"Billy," the horse that brought me up the first day, made the routine trips for supplies. He had become too dignified to run any more, although one day at the gate of the Camp Meeting Woods he backed up with so much pep that he spilled one of our visitors.

"Caspar" and "Starlight" were the two farm horses, nice looking animals. Perhaps they should have been "Castor and Pollux," but Charlie Grant or somebody may have been unable to spell or pronounce "Pollux," like the policeman who had the dead horse dragged to the corner of White Street, because White was easier to spell in his report than Llewellyn Terrace.

Charlie was our farmer. Like the Chinese he had some superstitions. Don't sit on the fence posts by moonlight, he would say; it causes early rotting. If you eat a little poison ivy every day, you won't catch it. He said he could eat more oysters than anyone he ever met. He used to drop down to the village tavern now and then for a little something to bolster his courage and prevent early rotting.

One night he listened to the keeper tell about a neighbor's wife, a sort of domesticated wildcat, who was always beating up the poor husband. Charlie, feeling strong with the Kentucky corn coursing through his veins, elaborated with many words and gestures on how he would handle such a partner. Meanwhile, the fair lady in question had been listening unseen through the window, and the next instant she was in the room glowering at Charlie, with arms akimbo. Fortunately, Charlie then and there bethought himself of the cows which had been left standing at the fence, and he hurried home to let down the bars.

We had several good orchards. At the end of the summer there were barrels of cider. A common stunt was to fix a long straw and draw the cider right from the barrel. One day Frank Ford challenged Thomas O'Connor, a visiting relative of Father Walsh, to a cider-drinking contest. It was pitiful to see the visitor. He was the victor, perhaps, but had turned a sickly green and was very droopy and clammy looking. Frank took a severe dressing down from Father Walsh, who had an excellent command of English and he showed unusual skill in the choice of his words.

The favorite cow, "Hibernia," and her offspring, "Patricia," were so called because they came from a good friend named Pat. There had been a bull. He was in cold storage, however, and was being served up to the community in bits.

We also had a ram, a fellow with a fiery temper. A favorite sport of the boys was to go into the yard, get the ram's goat, and then run for their lives, closing the gate in the nick of time to let him butt it amidship, just where he aimed to butt them.

The ram used to pick on the oxen in a playful way, pawing the ground and then going for them at full tilt. One day he got fresh with the wrong man, or rather the wrong ox. "Dan," the ox, let his head and horns drop with a majestic sweep, caught ramsy in his toss and sent him flying into the air. Next day we had ram chops for dinner. The rambunctious ram was just as tough in death as he had been in life.

The lambs were always the pets of the Teresians. Perhaps, as time went on and their numbers grew and they were herded from one packed sheepfold to another, they felt a kindred sympathy, one for the other and likewise vice versa.

Everyone liked the "merenda." This was a lunch about 4:00 in the afternoon, consisting of left-overs from dinner plus milk or coffee. It was a fine old European custom, one of several that Father Walsh had imported from the Tyrol and elsewhere.

One Sunday, a guest at merenda was John Heemskerk, a boy from Holland who was then working in a florist's hot house near Ossining. He had always wanted to be a missioner. In Holland, as a boy, he once made his pastor lift his eyebrows when he told him that he wanted to go to the missions because the life of a parish priest at home was too easy. As soon as John Heemskerk heard of Maryknoll, he came up to apply for admission.

On this day, while he was waiting to see Father Walsh, the boys took him in for merenda. He was up to his ears in apple pie and milk, when word came that Father Superior would see him. John replied in his best transliterated Dutch: "Let him vait," meaning of course "I vill come at vonce." The difficulty of idiom, and the difficulty of correctly rendering one's thoughts in a new language, may result at times in unfortunate misunderstandings.

John came to Maryknoll, was ordained and has been a missioner in China for more than twenty-five years; but the incident was the legal end of our merendas. O happy memory!

3

The Secretaries

"Fair Maid, nigh bending 'neath the weight of roses,
Which May from corbels rich and gay discloses
And showers on thy golden hair,
What sudden flash hath crossed thy peaceful mind?
Why dost thou hasten, leaving all behind?—
The sunlit skies are blue and fair. . . ."

— Victoria Larmour

A Park and Tilford candy box lay on the table, spilling out old stamps, tin foil, bits of jewelry, gold washed cuff links, broken rosaries, and a gleaming gold tooth in someone's discarded plate. Beside the box was a pile of unopened letters, there were packages on the floor, and in a square wire basket on the table were more letters flattened out open with little colored tags clipped to a corner. A waste basket was overflowing with opened envelopes and bits of wrapping paper. Odds and ends of string, coiled and neatly tied, partly filled a shoe box. I edged my way across the threshold to see the rest of the room. It was one of my first visits to St. Teresa's Lodge and *The Field Afar* office.

Six young women, all dressed alike in gray, were opening letters, closing letters, licking stamps, and tapping away at typewriters. One was writing in a big ledger. All were busy, very busy. If they looked up and saw you, you got a smile, a big happy smile. This was St. Teresa's that I had read about, and these were the Secretaries, or Teresians, and this one room was the heart of *The Field Afar*, the General Headquarters of Father Walsh's campaign to bring America to the foreign missions. The atmosphere of that little room was a mingling of kindliness, interest and hard work, and you said to yourself: here they are truly on the job.

Letters on the Director's desk were from all parts of the world. There were letters in abundance from New York and Massachusetts, others from Pennsylvania, New Jersey, the other New England states, and so on as far as California. Odd shaped envelopes with strange stamps came from China, India, Belgium and Italy. Austria and France were represented. Several were from Africa. Of these latter, more than one, I was told, was from a Father Peter Rogan. I remember one of his letters in particular that Father Walsh had in *The Field Afar* just at the time I reached Maryknoll.

"I have been quite quiet for quite a long time," went the letter, "but 'silence is golden' and so is my opinion of your Maryknoll Seminary and everything connected with it—landslips, cowslips, pigs, piglets, farm, students, pumps, Secretaries, Auxiliaries, plates, dishes, dental chairs, etc. . . . .

"Like many another curious *Field Afar* reader I have often wondered what those famous landslips were . . . One thing is certain, you are not going to let people 'give you the slip,' for after squeezing as much as you can out of them during their lives, you calmly inform them on their death beds, when they are making out their wills, that your 'legal title is . . . .'

"I admire your pluck, and I'd love to help, but right now the only piece of old jewelry about me is a set of artificial teeth. These I might bequeath to your 'legal title,' provided you retain the dental chair. Besides, melted down, they would come in handy to make Roman-collar studs for some poor missioner. . . .

"But joking aside, I must thank God for the zeal with which He has inflamed the hearts of American Catholics. *You* must have a heart as light as a lunatic's head, seeing the way they are supplying the wants of their first Foreign Mission Seminary. . . .

"Right now I am going through the 'dry season,' as far as gifts from home are concerned . . Recently I sent an appeal to the 'Peters' and 'Pats' of Ireland. All the 'Peters' and 'Pats' must be on a holiday or gone off to America. There doesn't seem to be a single 'Pat,' or a married one either, left in all Ireland. The only 'Pat' who answered my appeal was an Englishman named 'George,' and he promised to help me if his certain prayer was granted. Yes, you guessed it: his prayer must be still unanswered. Now I think I will write to all the 'Marys' and 'Bridgets' . . . Sincerely. . . . ."

At St. Teresa's Lodge I noticed that all the Secretaries were "Marys." They addressed one another as "Mary Sara," "Mary Nora," "Mary Louise," and so on. Father Walsh called them Teresians, because they looked to St. Teresa of Avila as their special patroness.

Their gray garb, I learned, with its particular cut and the short shoulder cape of dungaree or some similar coarse cotton, the Buster Brown collar and white wrist bands, was suggested by Cardinal Farley. It was the Cardinal, too, who gave them the little chapel alongside of the office quarters and permitted them to have the Blessed Sacrament there. They were not Sisters, not yet, but they followed a regular community life. Individually they had written to Fathers Price and Walsh, offering their services for the mission movement that was beginning.

One day, during that summer of 1913, Father Walsh remarked: "Some day the Teresians will multiply so that Maryknoll cannot hold them, and we shall send them out over the country to establish branches of our work from here to the Pacific Coast. Will that day be soon?"

Certainly, there was never a dull moment for the Secretaries. In those first days we had difficulty keeping a cook for any length of time. When a cook would leave, Father Walsh would send an SOS to Mary Rogers at St. Teresa's, or "Mary Joseph" as she was being called, and then she and the other Secretaries would have to shuttle back and forth between their desks and our kitchen. Knowing that this would be the usual procedure, we generally greeted a cook's departure with fervent cheers. The interims were much more toothsome.

Mary Rogers understood a boy's need of extra nourishment. Everyone said that she could cook, and cook well. In fact, they bestowed their highest tribute and agreed unanimously that "she could cook just like nobody's business." She understood too the value of two desserts. We heartily approved, of course, but Father Walsh did not. As often as possible he saw to it that she was kept busy in more important and less costly projects. Thirty-seven years later, Mary Rogers, now Mother Mary Joseph, cooked a "snack" for my Thirtieth Anniversary of Ordination. After this festive celebration, we sat content and smiling like a cat that's had a nice fat mouse, and testified from the heart that Mary Rogers' master hand in the culinary arts has lost none of its refined precision.

In those days Father Walsh admitted that he, too, liked the cook-less periods. He called them eras of peace,—peace for us, that is, not for the long-suffering Marys of Maryknoll. He wrote to some friends: "The 'best cook ever' left the camp recently. She had an eye like a Maxim gun and was trained to the queen's taste in her art. She never failed us and she used her brains as well as her hands. Nor would she accept any recompense for her five months of hard work. God reward her!

"She came from that place where the only kind of baked beans can be successfully grown. That was her misfortune, or rather ours, for it meant that she could not live long away from Boston. It did not matter that here her station was more elevated, that she could enjoy a sweeping view of the Hudson River while she was grinding out our hash or softening up the prunes. She left it all for Boston.

"Well, she's gone. We can only hope that she may have a change of heart and return or that someone just as acceptable may come to us before our subscribers send a sheriff after us. . . ." Meanwhile, the Marys of Maryknoll kept the pot boiling.

In the kitchen the gray uniform sometimes disappeared under a Mother Hubbard. That kept their outfit smokeless and greaseless and medal-less and always ready for public appearances. Public appearances—my, what a headache, especially if it meant going to town. They were new arrivals, very new but without the new look, not even with a normal old look. When you sat down in a trolley car, they said, and looked across the aisle, you were sure someone was stealing a look across at you and wondering what in the world you were, or thought you were, or thought you would like to be.

Two of them hurried down the long steps of the Ossining station one day, each balancing two armfuls of bundles. Trips to

New York were not a picnic. A kindly lady approached: "May I help you, Deaconess?" she asked. She was the wife of an elderly doctor at Croton-on-Hudson. She still likes to tell about the first time she met the ladies from Maryknoll.

But the topknot was the problem. Before they were organized as Sisters they wore no bonnet. In chapel they used a mesh veil. The Secretaries antedated the wind-blown bob and the Frankenstein bangs. The correct coiffure of the period called for "rats," and perhaps a chignon if you could afford it. Father Walsh was death on "rats." Out they must go, he said, and out they went. The fair maidens bending 'neath the exuberance of rich, wavy locks didn't suffer so much, but the poor damsels with the skimpy tresses had a problem.

"When my sister saw me," moaned one of them, "she was mortified. 'Where are your "rats"?' she wanted to know. 'You are a sight! I don't care if you're not a social whirly-whirly; at least you could look presentable!' She said she was humiliated. Honestly, that little hat of mine: you could just touch it and it would spin around on the top of my head like a pinwheel. When we were coming back from my father's funeral, she was so ashamed of me, she had the coachman drive through the back streets hoping that no one would see us."

Much of the spirit of the Maryknoll Sisters can be traced to the influence of Mary Rogers. Miss Rogers was a graduate of Smith College and was teaching there when she decided to drop her career and join the pioneer group that had volunteered to help Father Price and Father Walsh. All of our first students looked on Miss Rogers as a second mother, a sort of fairy godmother, though she was only a few years older than the students themselves.

The Secretaries were but a handful, only six, but they did everything. They handled all the office work, they took care of the kitchen, the laundry, and then found extra moments for mending, canning, and what not. Mary Rogers was the natural leader. There was also Nora Shea, who had already shown an interest in the work when she was secretary to Father Walsh in the Propagation of the Faith Office in Boston. Later she became Sister Mary

Theophane, and died in 1940, after a life filled with priceless service.

Mary Louise Wholean, a graduate of Wellesley College, was the first volunteer to arrive, she and two others coming when the work was just getting started at Hawthorne. She became Sister Mary Xavier. She died in 1917 and was the first Maryknoller buried in our little cemetery.

Sara Sullivan, our present Sister Mary Teresa, who had been in the Dean's Office at Harvard Medical School, and Mary Augustine Dwyer, were also among the pioneers, and were at Hawthorne. Both of these, with an excellent knowledge and experience of office organization, started the early *Field Afar* office which has continued on till now. Miss Dwyer's health was poor and before long she had to return to her home.

The youngest of the group was Margaret Shea. She came with Miss Rogers and was only sixteen at the time. Later, as Sister Mary Gemma, she worked in the missions of Japan, Korea, Manchuria, and on the West Coast. The Japanese often told me they wished they could speak their own language as well as Sister Gemma spoke it. Since the war, she has been back in Kyoto, hard at work. A Miss Foylan, also in that first group, was unable to continue at the work.

It was like a big family. Father Walsh told Frank Ford to hitch "George" to the buggy one day and meet Miss Rogers at the end of the trolley line. Frank was going to show off and prove that "George" could still pace. Sunset Hill was not a race track, particularly going up. Poor "George's" better days were long past. He was already spavined and had a "pull" to the right, like a motor car that's been in a collision. When he reached the front door, "George" was wheezing like a locomotive, his eyes were half closed and he was ready to lean against anything that would hold him up.

Father Walsh, just coming out of the house, saw what had taken place. He looked at the horse, looked at Miss Rogers, looked at Frank and then turned to the latter with a flow of the King's English that has been handed down through the years as a classic in Maryknoll's history. Of course, Miss Rogers too was partly to blame. They call it guilt by association. She was always on our side.

We were having a play one evening. It wasn't grand opera. There was nothing grand about it at all, in fact, no matter how you looked at it. But it was funny—at least we thought so. Chiefly, it was a string of vaudeville acts. A lad came out on the stage with a cage. Inside the cage was another of the crowd, done up as the Wild Man of Borneo. The circus barker started up his cry: "Ladies and Gentlemen! We have with us to-night the ter-ri-bul vicious man-eating Wi-ild Man! The Very, very wild-est Crea-ture in Cap-ti-vi-ty! Hurry—Hurry—Hurry! Come and see the jump-ing climb-ing man-eating Wild Man from Borneo! Who will come up he-ah to tame the terribul wild man?" Just then, Mary Rogers, with muscles well in evidence from hours of toil in the kitchen and laundry, walked calmly up the aisle: "Where is he?" she asked. "I'll tame him." This was too much for the Wild Man and his barker. Completely disorientated by these lines not in the original script, they stood open-mouthed in dismay, until the lady went back to her place. But I am running ahead and getting off the track. This is supposed to be about St. Teresa's Lodge and *The Field Afar* office.

St. Teresa's was a roomy place in its own old-fashioned way. Like many old farmhouses, it gave the impression of having been expanded away beyond the original idea of the builder. It was neither Georgian in style, nor French colonial. Father Walsh said it belonged to the "box" type of architecture. It had started off as a two-story building with an attic. There must have been at least two additions before we got it, and a couple more afterwards.

As you entered the old house there was a big room at your right. Mail desks, filing cabinets, bookkeeping equipment filled this room. Here you found everything connected with the editing and publishing of a magazine, including the address files and benches for mailing. How did all that office furniture, with incoming mail and outgoing magazines, fit in that small space and still leave room for the Teresians to move about? I don't know: it's a mystery.

I can see them now, that first group, on Monday mornings, turning out the laundry in a small basement room filled with steam. It's another mystery how in the world they ever fitted into that tiny cubbyhole, which was already overcrowded with tubs. Again, Miss Rogers was in the midst of it, up to her collar in suds.

The story of St. Teresa's would be incomplete without a description of the "bridge." The kitchen was an addition on the west side of the house, the side away from the highway, facing the farm. The "bridge" was the room over the kitchen. It commanded a sweeping view of the property as it was then. If there was some heavy work to be done, moving or lifting demanding the presence of one of the students, word would be passed to the look-out on the "bridge," and the Teresian on duty there would keep one eye on her work and the other on the landscape, to flag down the first passing laborer from the Seminary.

It seems there was a great deal of manual labor to do in those days. On holidays and during the summer, it was the usual thing for the students to work five hours a day. Manual Labor always began with a prayer to St. Joseph. For those engaged on a job at St. Teresa's Lodge or in the vicinity there were special inducements confected in the Teresians' kitchen.

St. Teresa's is among the thousand and one farmhouses where George Washington supposedly stopped. It could have been after the battle of White Plains when he went north, crossed the Hudson by the King's Ferry at Verplanck, and marched on to the Highlands. He would have passed along the original Pines Bridge Road, a vestige of which remains at the end of our farm.

Whether or not the house has this illustrious association, it is truly very old, just the place to break your neck, or a leg, with its rooms at different levels reached by a step up or a step down, its dark corridors and the uneven flooring. It is just the setting for a murder mystery. It has always been a fire trap, the Number One Problem for the student Fire Chief.

Fire drills in those days were focused on St. Teresa's, partly because of the real danger, partly because of the tradition which maintained that fire fighters should repair to the kitchen after their hazardous task to refresh themselves with coffee and doughnuts and tell one another how they did it. Some of them were even accused, falsely no doubt, of answering the alarm by making a bee line for the kitchen.

One of the early Fire Chiefs made the supreme mistake of planting his ladder in the midst of a bed of peonies. Sister Mary Gardener promptly popped out the door, lit into the Chief, and tossed him and his equipment out of her flower patch. The Chief later was demonstrating an emergency fire escape in the attic of St. Teresa's. It was a simple manila rope, hitched to the water pipes and dropped out the attic window. "In case of fire, you simply let the rope out the window and climb down," explained Brother William, the little Fire Chief. The listener was the same timid soul that had routed him and his ladders from the peonies.

"Who—you mean me?" she asked.

"That's right. Simply let yourself down the rope . . ."

"Let's see you do it," she demanded.

The Chief thereupon wound several turns of the rope around a radiator and let himself down. The Teresian thanked him for the interesting demonstration and assured him that in case of danger she would surely find a more dignified alley of escape.

Mary Joseph always enjoyed the drills. Once, when the fire fighters were scurrying here and there with ladders and ropes, passing buckets and shouting orders right and left, she appeared at a tiny window in the attic and cried out to the little Chief below: "Save me! Fireman! Save me!" That ended that drill. The Chief's face was very red in the kitchen afterwards as he dunked his doughnuts and listened to the banter of his subalterns.

Of all the rooms in old St. Teresa's, the Chapel carries the most memories. It was a holy place, a sanctuary hallowed by prayer and generous sacrifice, and it had witnessed many tears and smiles too. It seemed to take so little to start a laugh. Father Van den Besselaar, a Dutch priest of the Mill Hill Missions, gave Benediction one day for the Teresians. The vestment he wore was new and stiff. Arriving at the foot of the altar, he genuflected and disappeared inside the vestment. When he came up again, he was outside of it.

The funeral Mass of Sister Mary Xavier is unforgettable. It was in February, 1917. She was Mary Louise Wholean, the first Maryknoller to die. The family had come down from Massachusetts. The little community was still in its infancy. Father Walsh had given an impressive talk on her life, stressing her devotion to work in spite of terrible suffering. Returning to the sacristy I was surprised to find Father Walsh sobbing quite without restraint. It lasted only a few moments. It was a surprise to me, because I had thought him to be too well disciplined for such a display of emotion; but it was good to realize that within this disciplined exterior there was a heart that had to be reckoned with.

Mary Louise Wholean, or Sister Mary Xavier, as she was known at the time of her death, did most of the preliminary work on *The Field Afar* in those early days. Paging the magazine was a monthly task that required painstaking attention. Father Walsh was on hand whenever it was possible, but he depended on the Secretaries more and more as the growing Seminary drew on his time and attention.

It was largely due to the energy of these workers, Father Walsh often said, that *The Field Afar* readers had their little monthly visitor on time, and to them also they owed the appearance of occasional messengers like Dinny Dun, Hokey-Pokey, the Red Hand, and the Touch Family. To the Teresians the printer would look for the prompt appearance of copy, corrected proof, and the rest. The Ossining post office was swamped with the work of Teresian hands. Our office supply company would have lost considerable profit if the Teresians had been withdrawn from Maryknoll.

The Seminary counted on them for several household needs, and their stitch in time saved many a dime for needy students and for the not less needy faculty. "Loyal they are to a woman," Father Walsh wrote, "and this means that they are strong in their loyalty to Maryknoll and all for which it stands.

"It is hard to calculate mathematically the influence of individuals and groups in such a work as ours," he said, "but we believe that we should not be very far out of the way to say that humanly speaking one-third of Maryknoll's success can be traced to the daily labors, manual, clerical and intellectual, of the

Teresians; and this does not take into account the more important cooperation of prayers, Communions, and the consecration of their labor to the advancement of the world-wide cause. . . ."

Perhaps I am running ahead of my story again, but while still writing about the early Sisters, it is good to mention that they consistently played second fiddle to the rapidly growing men's community, always accepting our cast-off dwellings as we outgrew them. They put up with all manner of hardships, until such time as they could get into their own permanent home. When they did get into it, they filled it up very quickly and found themselves needing more room. Decades later the problem still remained to provide a convent for the lineal successors of the first Secretaries, the Sisters who devote their labors to the Seminary and administrative work of the Fathers and to *The Field Afar*. It was they who did so much to put the "Mary" in Maryknoll. In the pioneer days, they seconded Father Walsh in adding the many little touches to the mail that our friends loved, like this one:

> "Breathes there the man with soul so dead
> Who never to himself hath said:
> It's time I paid for all I've read,
> I'll send a check this morning.
>
> Thank you! — F.A."

4

The Two Founders

"He whom a dream hath possessed treads the impalpable marches,
From the dust of the day's long road he leaps to a laughing star,
And the ruins of worlds that fall he views from eternal arches,
And rides God's battlefield in a flashing and golden car. . . ."
— Shaemas O'Sheel

Father Price was always up and in chapel long before the rest of us. "Are these the best vestments, Brother?" he asked one morning when I arrived to serve Mass. "Are you sure this is the best set?" It was a feast day of our Blessed Mother, and Father Price always asked for the best vestments on our Lady's feasts. When he was vested and ready, he went off to a side altar and there said Mass in private.

It seemed strange to us that he should want the very best vestments, and then say Mass where no one could see him. I soon learned, however, that while, as we thought, Father Price said Mass where no one saw him, he himself felt otherwise. From his attention at Mass it was clear that he knew he was in a Presence where even the richest vestments in the world would seem unworthy. To see him say Mass was a lesson in faith.

He had been up early. He was the last one to leave the chapel the night before. If we went down to turn out the lights, we would find him still on his knees, not in his praying bench but down on the floor beside his chair. We all knew that during the night he would arise some time after midnight, and go to the chapel for an hour or longer. This was his usual practice.

After Mass his thanksgiving went on and on, after the rest of us were at breakfast. Finally, he would come for a bite and a cup of coffee, and then, if he was not going out on a begging errand that day, he would go off to a little shrine of Our Lady which he had made in the woods across the road, and there spend hours on his knees.

Father Walsh was as punctual as a trainman, always on time. He usually gave the introduction to our meditation and on big feasts, like this feast day of Our Lady, he gave the entire meditation, sharing with us the fruits of his own thoughts and long years of priestly life. He said our community Mass. He was always exact in the way he stood, the way he genuflected, held his hands, and so on, because he knew he was being observed by boys who would soon be standing at the altar themselves.

After Mass he knelt at his bench in the back of the chapel, and when the breakfast bell sounded, he went with us to the dining room. If there was reading at meals, he was quick to catch a mispronounced word and he would stop the reader and have him correct the mistake. If there was something humorous in the reading, he enjoyed it as much as any of us.

Not long after breakfast, he would be at the door, with his biretta on, brief case under his arm, ready to start for the office. His path was not always the direct route. He would make a detour by the barn, or the farm, or to a spot where we were doing some road building. He covered every corner of the place regularly, and there was hardly a trip during which his eagle eye did not detect something that needed attention. This he followed up with a little note to the priest or Brother or student concerned, with word to consult him.

Down at his desk in St. Teresa's Lodge he took up the day's mail, dictated letters, worked on *The Field Afar*. This filled his whole morning. Usually, he would not appear for the ten-minute noon visit before dinner. He told us that while he tried to keep the same schedule as ourselves, he made this one exception in his own case, since work at the office, or visitors sometimes, made it impossible for him to be on time for the noon visit in chapel.

Our spiritual reading before supper was given sometimes by Father Walsh, sometimes by Father Price. We learned a great deal from what they told us, and learned much more just from observing them. They had much in common, were so much alike in some respects, and yet at the same time, they were so different. Father Walsh was the man of action, the leader and organizer, always out in front directing things, yet insisting withal that everything be done with prayer, placing every effort and its outcome in the hands of God. Father Price was the man of prayer, spending hours on his knees, going to Our Lord and Our Lady and Bernadette for everything, and then traveling all over the Eastern States to beg for the new seminary, and this was after long years of horse-and-buggy apostolate in North Carolina.

When Father Walsh came to our school in Lawrence back in 1906, and that was the first time I saw him, he was Director of the Propagation of the Faith Office in Boston. There were only two or three offices of its kind at that time in the whole United States. As he told us later, he had decided that the missions would have to be presented more attractively to secure the right support for them and to get American vocations. The *Annals of the Propagation of the Faith* were filled with interesting facts, but served in a dull fashion, printed poorly, and illustrated with photos that were inferior and badly reproduced. So he started a new mission magazine. He modeled it after the most successful secular weekly of the time, edited it himself, and called it *The Field Afar*.

He believed that the Propagation of the Faith should not be a mere club for collecting small coins, but rather a means of stirring up the people in every parish of the country to pray and work for the conversion of the entire world. Someone who knew him well said that it was natural for him to found a foreign mission society, because he looked on foreign missions not as something necessarily heroic, but as a perfectly ordinary activity of the Catholic Church. If the Kingdom of God was intended for the whole world, everyone ought to be told about it. That was his idea. He didn't see any reason for making a comparison between mission work and pastoral work at home to decide which was the more or less important; he considered it all the same work, but under different conditions.

Father Walsh used to say that modern inventions and up-to-date methods should be used whenever possible to speed up the development of the mission cause. He liked the quotation: "To those that love God all things work together for good." He had it printed on the cover of *The Field Afar*. To him, "all things" evidently included typewriters, improved printing technique, addressographs, and modern filing equipment. Once, on returning from Rome, he told us how shocked he was to learn that in the whole Congregation of Propaganda Fide there was, so far as he could discover, only one typewriter. He could not understand why anyone should be asked to write all those letters by hand. To keep his own magazine apace with the times, he dissected and analyzed every issue of the most widely read weeklies of those days, particularly, the old original *Life* and *The Literary Digest*.

Father Walsh's mother died when he was very young, but he had a distinct memory of her and in his talks to us he used to quote her. Industrious and very active, she would say: "It is better to wear out than to rust out." His father was over eighty when I met him years later, on a visit home with Father Walsh, who had whispered to me: "Just watch him now. He's as lively as a youngster. He will be up and down stairs, in again and out again, before you're here ten minutes." It was so, exactly. These and later associations made it clear to me whence came Father Walsh's own ceaseless activity, at which I so marveled during those early days.

He was thoughtful and attentive to detail and he expected you to be so, too. He could not stand a disorderly room or office. He was vexed by muddled thinking. "Why do so many men leave things up in the air? Have they no aim in what they do, no purpose in doing it?" He always used a tickler file to jog his memory and expected us to have some similar system. He kept a pad and pencil always within reach, as we learned so often to our sorrow.

I recall a talk which Father Walsh gave us one evening. He was saying something about the growth of Maryknoll, the goodness of God in keeping us going, and finding friends to support us. The chapel was alongside the conference room, and turning towards the chapel he said: "No one knows how many of our blessings are due to the prayers of that man." He meant Father Price who, we all knew, was in there on his knees before the Blessed Sacrament. He made sure that we should appreciate all we owed to the holy life of Father Price. On different occasions he told us how the partnership started.

It was in September, 1910 during the Eucharistic Congress in Montreal. Caesar Augustus is the celebrated example of fame by coincidence, since he happened to have ordered a census which coincided with the Birth of Our Lord. Hence, he usually figures in the story of the First Christmas. The Windsor Hotel in Montreal will live forever in the memory of Maryknoll, not for its cuisine or for its tradition of refinement, but because Father Price and Father Walsh met in the hotel lobby, to discuss for the first time an American foreign mission seminary.

Father Walsh had been seven years at the Propagation of the Faith Office in Boston. Father Price was a missioner in North Carolina. They had heard something of each other; there had even been some correspondence, but they had never before sat down to plan what later became Maryknoll.

Father Walsh went to Montreal for the Eucharistic Congress and was guest of the Mayor of Maisonneuve, staying at the Mayor's house. This was a suburb of the city at that time, but since then has been absorbed as a part of Greater Montreal. The Mayor and Father Walsh were just getting into the car to go to the outdoor Mass at Fletcher Field, when the telephone rang. The Mayor's wife went to answer it, and the two men could hear her struggling with a strange name which sounded very much like "Price." Father Walsh said to himself: "That's Father Price of North Carolina and he wants to see me about starting a foreign mission seminary."

Father Walsh went to the phone. Father Price, with his usual impulsiveness, wanted to see him at once. They arranged to go on to Fletcher Field and meet in the Hotel Windsor after the Mass. Bishop Monaghan of Wilmington, Delaware, who was near by when the two had their heads together in the hotel lobby, said that they were oblivious of the hustle and bustle of all that went on around them, so absorbed were they in each other and in the vision of what they hoped for the future.

Father Price was a home missioner in North Carolina, searching out his scattered flock and bringing the word of God to those who found it easier to sit comfortably in darkness. He was much better known than Father Walsh, whose circle of friends was confined mostly to New England. Father Price had attended St. Charles College and St. Mary's Seminary, Baltimore, and was well known to the alumni of both places. Besides this, he had his own periodical, *Truth,* which had been started to help his convert work in the South and was being read all over the country.

Once Maryknoll was started, Father Price insisted again and again that his own name be left out and that no photos of him be published. This policy, formed and demanded by himself, may have caused some people to get an incorrect idea of the importance of his part in the work.

It is not unlikely that it would have been much more difficult to get Maryknoll started, if it had not been for the personal friendship of Father Price with Cardinal Gibbons. Little Freddie Price had been Father Gibbons' altar boy in North Carolina. Their close friendship continued right up to the Cardinal's death. It was so close, that each always called the other by his first name. This was not usual, at least with Father Price.

When it came time to support the new work, Father Price took to the road, visited his friends all over the country, and was invited to speak about the new seminary. This helped wonderfully to solve Father Walsh's money worries.

A Boston priest tells this incident. One day on a visit to the old Chancery on Granby Street, Father Price met a former classmate and friend of seminary days, Father Tim Mahoney, who at that time was pastor of St. William's, Dorchester. Father Mahoney looked at Father Price and pointing to the latter's suit, frayed and greenish, said: "Freddie! Why don't you get yourself a decent suit and dress up?" "Sorry," replied Father Price, "haven't the cash." Father Tim dug seventy-five dollars out of his pocket and handed it to him: "There now: get yourself a new outfit." Father Price rolled up the bills and slipped them quietly into his pocket. Then smiling at Father Mahoney with a twinkle in his eyes, he said: "James Anthony is going to be tickled when I hand him this." A month later Father Price could still be seen going around in the same old suit.

Cardinal O'Connell of Boston and Father Price had been in school together at St. Charles College. Their friendship continued all through the years, and in his memoirs, the Cardinal speaks of Father Price and tells the story of his escape from death after the shipwreck off the North Carolina coast. The Cardinal's esteem was genuine; he seemed to have a real affection for him. He used to speak of Father Price's deep spirituality and his zeal.

When Father Price gave us spiritual conferences, during the first two or three years, he would place his own chair, not on the platform usually used by the teachers, but down on the floor beside us. Later the numbers grew, and he had to use the platform. Then he announced: "Gentlemen, I am the only one here who has the right to be a hypocrite." He meant that as the Spiritual Director he had to take that place, but we were not to presume that he practiced everything he preached, although we all knew he did.

I can't recall any of his daily spiritual conferences in which he did not talk about humility. Sometimes, I felt that perhaps he was by nature a very proud man and had to battle against this pride all his life. He pounded it into us. Sometimes, he would stop us and ask: "Brother, are you convinced that you are a cesspool of iniquity?" The right answer was "Yes." Joseph Hunt was his star pupil, a worthy disciple, and the next model follower was Brother Aloysius, who had come to us from his home in Cuba. Father Price enjoyed the surprise one day when, after being carefully instructed and prompted by Philip Taggart, Brother Aloysius failed to answer this question with the usual "Yes," replying instead: "No, Father, I am the Temple of the Holy Ghost!"

Father Price lived close to God. He wanted us to do likewise. "Talk with God," he would say. "Talk with Him—often. He is right within you. He knows you better than you know yourself . . . How little your troubles will seem when you remember that He is right there with you . . .

"Before you do anything, stop a second and say: 'Lord, I am doing this for You. I am doing it because You would have me do it. It is for Your greater honor and glory . . .'

"Don't rush," he would say. "Don't do anything hurriedly or precipitately. Take your time, and make sure you are doing it because it is God's will. This will help to keep you living in God's presence . . .

"Remember: your first and most important job is to save your own soul. Other things may be important, but God wants this first of all."

Sometimes we felt it would be difficult to do everything he wanted. For example, he would say: "Keep recollected. Avoid crowded places . . . Avoid the hustle and bustle of city life . . . Avoid certain individuals that distract you . . ." But we had no excuse for not following other points, like these: "Keep away from certain types of reading that confuse the mind. Don't be careless about the control of your eyes and ears and tongue . . . You will be more certain to do God's will if you relegate yourself to the background . . ."

Father Price became a familiar figure in the village and countryside about Maryknoll. He went about the farm and along the highway, always with a noticeable stoop and always with his rosary in hand. He had a slouch hat of uncertain age, perhaps coming down from Confederate days, and an old cloak which had belonged to the brother of Bernadette Soubirous.

Many of his little habits sprang from his very childlike and beautiful devotion to Our Lady and to Bernadette. He wrote a life of Bernadette, the first to be published in English. At times, he wore blue denim overalls under his cassock and he wore white socks, because blue and white are the colors of Our Blessed Mother. He frequently rubbed his eyes, perhaps with Lourdes water, and very often, it seemed, he rubbed them first with a ring he wore, Bernadette's ring, as he called it. Why did he rub them? Perhaps to preserve them, or perhaps with a prayer for custody of the eyes.

On Mary's feast days, as I have mentioned, he insisted on having the best vestments. Whenever it was possible, he said a votive Mass in honor of Our Blessed Mother. Making his thanksgiving alone, he would leave his kneeling bench and kneel on the floor.

He recommended us to read St. Louis de Montfort's book on True Devotion to Our Lady. If he judged us sufficiently serious and faithful, he would permit us to make the act of complete consecration to Mary, handing over to her the full title of all we are and have, including all our merits. He would explain that no one need be anxious about this heroic act: Our Lady would never let herself be outdone in generosity, and she would never let us suffer any harm by reason of our love for her.

Just before he left for China, he asked me if I would care to have anything in his room as a souvenir. With trepidation I asked for the cloak of Bernadette's brother. He gave it to me.

He showed his affection for Bernadette in many ways. He gave her name to everything he owned. For example, he would ask for his "Bernadette hat," or his "Bernadette cloak." Every year, as long as he was Spiritual Director, he would begin months before the feast of Our Lady of Lourdes to tell about Bernadette and the apparitions. One Sunday evening, when Maryknoll was still at Hawthorne, he went to the house of the Secretaries to give a conference. He spoke about Bernadette and Lourdes. He began at four-thirty and ended at nine o'clock. He liked to be called "Father Bernadette."

He spent an hour before the Blessed Sacrament nightly, usually after midnight. Frequently, I entered his room and found him on his knees before a little shrine of Our Lady which we had made for him in a corner. He would be deep in prayer, and it was hard to get his attention.

Devotion to Mary was something the two founders had strongly in common. The first home of Maryknoll was in Hawthorne. The little house there had a porch, and one day, sitting on this porch, Father James Anthony was pondering a name that would link the new mission work with the Queen of the Apostles.

There were other institutions and societies named after her and they included some topographical link: Mary Mount, Mary Wood, Mary Vale. He had been to a resort called, "The Knolls." He liked that. They would build their seminary on a knoll and call it Mary's Knoll.

Shortly after that he wrote: "Maryknoll is not our post office. It is rather the title of a dream which we hope will, before long, be realized. . . ."

Father Walsh made sure that we were instilled with a devoted boy's love for Our Lady. When he was on a visit to Japan, a French missioner gave him an old bell that had hung in a pagan temple. He asked Father Walsh to use it at the new seminary, putting it some-place outside, near a statue of Our Lady where the students would gather in the evening to sing hymns to Mary. This bell became the Departure Bell. It hangs today in an oriental arch near Our Lady of Maryknoll in the Seminary quadrangle, and any May evening you may hear the seminarians as they gather to sing Our Lady's litany.

Once when Father James Anthony was speaking at the First Mass of one of our newly ordained priests, he said: "This young man from your parish comes back now another Mary. His word, like Mary's 'Be it done,' will also bring down Jesus Christ from Heaven. His consecrated hands, like hers, will hold the Babe of Bethlehem; his eyes will rest upon God in the snow-white manger of this new Bethlehem, this house of Bread . . ."

Father Price and Father Walsh had also this in common, that they were frugal and economic. Father Walsh had a horror of waste. He reminded us again and again that we were living on the offerings of the poor, supported by the widow's mite. Anything like waste or luxury in us was criminal. Father Price was the same, but perhaps with a little more color.

Father Price on trips to New York would take along his lunch in a knapsack which he threw over his shoulder and then, between engagements in the city, he would retire to Central Park for his midday repast. One day he had Brother Thomas with him, so they went to a restaurant. Brother Thomas ordered apple pie. When Father Price saw the bill—ten cents—he exclaimed in the presence of waiters and all: "My! All that money! Down in Newton Grove I could get a whole pie for the same price!" Coming back he would walk up the hill from the end of the trolley line, and when he reached the seminary, he would go straight to the chapel and spend a half hour or an hour there before taking anything to eat.

Finally, both founders had a sense of humor. Both were good entertainers. When Father Walsh sat down at the piano, it seemed that he changed it into a full orchestra. Mostly, however, he reserved his musical talent for the chapel. Father Walsh had an endless supply of good stories originating in Boston, and he liked to tell them. He took pleasure especially in telling those about the immortal Father Willie Orr, the famous North of Ireland pastor in Cambridge, who, incidentally, celebrated the Mass when my mother and father were married.

Father Price had many interesting anecdotes about his missionary days in North Carolina. These he sprinkled with darky stories that always brought a chuckle. He loved the one about the old southern colonel. He was a planter, the principal citizen in his town, but most of his time was spent in cussing, and drinking mint juleps. There was a revival meeting in town. A group of the more pious citizens waited on the old colonel and asked him to honor them all by opening the meeting with a prayer. "Ah knows nothin' about prayin'," he said. "Ah ain't prayed for an awful long time." They finally prevailed upon him and he got busy preparing a prayer for the occasion. The night the revival opened, he bolstered his courage and polished his eloquence with a good dose of gin. He threw himself into the meeting with powerful vigor, and after a long list of things he asked from the Lord, he made a final dramatic plea: "And Lord," he said, "curtail the power of the devil! Curtail the power of the old devil!" In the silence that followed immediately after this finale, a voice rang out from the depths of the tent, in unmistakable colored accent: "Dat's right, Boss! Cut his tail off! Cut his tail off!" It was the old colonel's valet who had followed him to the meeting, was with him during his prayer, and couldn't help this final burst of approval.

Father Michael Irwin, a big breezy man, six feet tall and weighing about two hundred and forty pounds, had been with Father Price in North Carolina. One day he reached Maryknoll just as Father Price was about to begin a conference. Father Price yielded the rostrum to him, and for the next hour we laughed over various apostolic ups and downs in North Carolina as described by Father Irwin.

The two founders bequeathed their gaiety to their spiritual children and grandchildren. They said a missioner had to have it. During the war days in Manchuria, when we were locked up by the enemy, I did my best to keep spirits light by re-telling many of their stories. The younger wits in the internment camp were apt disciples; soon it was hard to keep up with them. I had a book of Ten Thousand Best Jokes and After-Dinner Stories, given me by a priest friend during a stop-over at Detroit. This I scanned faithfully day after day, to bring the cream of the crop to the dining room. One of the pious rascals interned with me discovered my source of supply and noted the pencil marks which I had checked against the good ones. I came to supper one night with ten of the best ready to tell, only to discover that my storehouse had been plundered and the ten best had been rationed among the company, and before I could get my breath and catch up with them they told the stories one after the other amid bursts of laughter and many sly winks.

Another time they got ahead of me. It was the Feast of Our Lady, December 8th, 1942. It was the first anniversary of our going to jail and it called for a night of fun. We were only fifteen all told and we had to take turns sitting in as audience. I was to be Major Bowes and introduce the amateur talent. At supper, before the show started at all, the plotters again started story-telling, digging up some really good ones. Not to be outdone I told some of my best and when supper ended I suddenly woke up to the fact that I had already released the prize stories which I had been reserving for the night's entertainment.

Like the great Saint Teresa of Avila, whom both Father Price and Father Walsh revered and studied and loved, the founders of Mary-knoll believed that at times this old life could be hard enough, and would be unbearable if we didn't have some fun and nonsense now and then, with a good laugh.

5

Throwback to Boston

". . A little sad, don't you think, that
we are moving — oh, so slowly with the
word of peace, while the champions of
violence topple kings from their thrones
and go on 'foreign missions' by the
thousands to spread their bloody tidings?"
— James Anthony Walsh

I know a priest who used to fall asleep mornings when he tried to read a meditation book. So he switched to the *Daily Worker*. As a meditation book, this didn't soothe his intellect, but it did stimulate his will, and what he read got him so worked up that he made up his mind to do something, and he did it. He has been very successfully doing good, just where the authors of his meditation sheet had plotted evil.

Father Walsh found the religious magazines of his day insipid, and unpalatable. They were what he called "sticky." The truths of our religion and facts about the Church's work were presented in an unworthy style, far inferior to the sprightly style of the secular publications. He said that the Catholics of America had to be persuaded and won to the idea of missions. He told us how *The Field Afar* was started.

"One afternoon in the fall of 1906—October 4th was the day— four of us gathered in the Chaplain's room at the Daly Industrial School in Neponset, Massachusetts. I had known the Chaplain, Father John I. Lane, since seminary days. Father James F. Stanton, pastor of Hyde Park, was there, and the third was Father Joseph Bruneau of St. Mary's Seminary, Baltimore. I was the fourth and

46

at that time was Director of the Propagation of the Faith in Boston.

"We met to discuss a new mission publication, something to supplement the *Annals of the Propagation of the Faith* in Boston. We wanted to prepare the American Catholic mind for the call to supply apostolic laborers for the mission fields in heathen lands. We didn't declare this motive formally at that first meeting but we were fully alive to the need and we hoped in God's time to see it met.

"We discussed the format, the number of pages and we also settled on the price. We adopted the title, *The Field Afar,* and the following January the first issue appeared.

"It wasn't difficult to finance. Each of us four priests managed to find a hundred dollars. Desk room for a clerk was provided in the little office of the Propagation of the Faith, and the clerk addressed the wrappers, made a record of new subscribers and acknowledged the dollar bills or money orders that drifted into our little shack on Union Park Street under the shadow of the Cathedral . ."

This was in 1906, three years after Father Walsh took over the office of the Propagation of the Faith. In his talks to us he never spent much time on reminiscences about himself. Hence, it was from his associates and contemporaries who visited Maryknoll in later years that we learned just about all we know of Father Walsh up to the time he and Father Price started Maryknoll.

These men who had studied with him in St. John's Seminary, at Brighton, were already important members of the clergy and hierarchy, ordained about twenty-five years when I first met them or saw them at Maryknoll. Archbishop Dowling was a frequent visitor. Father Stanton we saw often. Father Charles Aiken, Father Francis Havey, and Father Peter O'Callaghan told us of those seminary days. Bishop Guertin and Bishop Anderson were also his classmates. Monsignor Duggan, editor of the *Catholic Transcript* of Hartford, always liked to talk about the days at Brighton.

Once when I was visiting the Cathedral rectory in Hartford, Monsignor Duggan thought he could have some fun with me. In his serious and dry, almost glum way, behind which his close associates knew there was always a twinkle, he began to bemoan the growth of Maryknoll, complained that it had lost that freshness and family spirit so characteristic of the early days, the spirit of his classmate

Jimmy Walsh. I was supposed to get indignant and object. Instead, I agreed with him and told him that we, too, were worrying about it. This spoiled his fun. Having learned something about him on his trips to Maryknoll, I knew that the best way to take the wind out of him was to agree with what he said. Bishop Nilan and Bishop McAuliffe, Monsignor Flynn and the others at table that day enjoyed this mild upset of the Rector's customary game. So he dropped his laments and told about something James Anthony had said or had done at the seminary. He seemed always to have some new incident to relate about their student days together.

On a visit to Boston some time ago, I stopped at the Church of the Immaculate Conception on Harrison Avenue, near the Massachusetts Memorial Hospital. Many people remember this church in connection with the famous Jesuit, Father Fulton. Stories about him are almost as numerous and good as those about Father Willie Orr. They tell of a lady who hurried into the sacristy one morning before Mass. "Father," she asked, "do you think I could still go to Communion? I was getting breakfast for himself and I took just the wee taste of milk, not more than half a teaspoon." "Sure, Ma'am," he replied, "and you might as well have swallowed the whole cow."

It was in this Church of the Immaculate Conception that James Anthony served Mass as a boy. He said there was a German Jesuit there, Father Weise, who got him interested in the Holy Childhood Association. His first foreign mission work started under Father Weise and it consisted of ringing doorbells in the neighborhood, to get offerings for Chinese and Indian and African orphans.

He entered the seminary at Brighton in 1886, when he was nineteen years old. The seminary at that time was directed by the Abbé Hogan, a man with a long interesting career. He had gone from Ireland to France when he was fifteen, was ordained, taught theology in the seminary of Saint Sulpice in Paris, and was a friend of great men like Lacordaire, Montalembert, and Ozanam. During the socialist uprising in Paris, in 1871, he almost lost his life, but was saved just in the nick of time, thanks to the intervention of the British Ambassador.

Father Hogan, usually called the Abbé Hogan, was a bright man, far ahead of his time, so far ahead, in fact, that some of his ideas in *Clerical Studies,* a very excellent book, were considered ultra-modern and dangerous. His only other book, *Daily Thoughts,* is still a favorite and should be republished. Father James Anthony for many years would give a copy of this book to his newly ordained priests at Maryknoll. We may presume that the Abbé Hogan's influence had a great deal to do with the development of fine churchmen like Father James Stanton, Archbishop Dowling, Father Charles Aiken, Father Havey, and other contemporaries of Father Walsh.

The Abbé Hogan told his students about Theophane Venard who had studied with him in the seminary at Paris. This young priest went off as a missioner to Indo-China, and was martyred in Tonkin at the age of thirty-one. Father Walsh listened to all this as a seminarian and later on he wrote a life of Theophane Venard, called *A Modern Martyr,* based on letters written by Venard from Indo-China to his sister, Melanie, in France.

Another man who influenced the life of James Anthony Walsh was Father Gabriel André, a professor at the Brighton seminary, who later returned to France and became Rector of the seminary at Avignon. At St. Mary's, Baltimore, he had taught Father Price as well. He had a deep interest in the missions and passed on his interest to James Anthony. Together, they prayed and made sacrifices for the missions, and together, they got out a weekly column in the old *Sacred Heart Review,* which Father John C. O'Brien published in East Cambridge and which was known at that time all over the country. Even in those early efforts James Anthony showed some of the charm, the humor, and the pathos that made his later writing such a boon to the mission cause. In the library at Maryknoll we have bound volumes of the *Sacred Heart Review,* extending over several years.

On May 20, 1892, James Anthony Walsh was raised to the priesthood and two weeks later received his first appointment, assistant in the parish of St. Patrick, Roxbury. Among the various duties assigned him there was the care of the altar boys, and from among these altar boys he encouraged several vocations. Four of these boys became Jesuits, one a Paulist, and two became secular priests. For the boys who could not go on for the priesthood, he organized the Sanctuary Boys' Alumni to keep them close to the Church and the parish life.

Meanwhile, the Society for the Propagation of the Faith was advancing in this country bit by bit. It had been started in France in 1822 with the purpose of helping Catholic foreign missions. The Church in America in the nineteenth century received much help from this Society. The Sulpician Fathers at St. Mary's, Baltimore, and at St. John's, Brighton, pushed the idea. They trained their students to help the missions. An office of the society was started in Boston by Archbishop Williams in 1898, and Father Joseph Tracy was appointed director. He worked hard at his task, and four years later, in 1902, when he retired on account of poor health, his office was sending twenty-five thousand dollars annually to the missions.

The Church in America, between 1822 and 1912, had received six million dollars from the Propagation of the Faith while during this same period it had contributed less than half that amount to the missions. This began to change as the Propagation of the Faith developed and grew stronger in the United States.

Returning from a trip to Europe in 1902, during which he visited the grave of his old Rector, the Abbé Hogan, and various places related to the life of Theophane Venard, Father Walsh gave lectures at St. Patrick's parish and illustrated them with stereopticon slides, all pictures that he had taken on the trip. While regaling his audience with picturesque scenes of his travels, he thrilled them with his descriptions of the three foreign mission seminaries he had visited— at Paris, Mill Hill (London), and Milan. He told them about Theophane Venard and the other martyrs whose relics he had seen. All of this was merely to help them become better Catholics at home. Beyond this, apparently, he had no thought at the time.

One Friday in March, 1903, Father Walsh read in the Boston *Pilot* that Father Tracy had resigned as Director of the Propagation of the Faith. Almost immediately, he said, the thought came to him that he would be the next Director. He put the thought out of his mind and yet he wondered why he had felt this way about it. The following morning, Saturday, he was in the rectory garden saying his office when he saw a bearded man go to the front door. He said to himself: "That's the Central Director of the Propagation of the Faith and he has come to ask me to take over the work."

That was precisely the case. Father Walsh asked for a day to think it over and then told the Director, Father Freri, that he would take it. The next Monday morning he was at his desk in the little office near the Cathedral. He said to himself: "I am going to stay at this work in some form or other for the rest of my life."

He realized that his first duty was to get out to visit pastors and assistants. He understood the normal attitude of the parochial clergy very well. He had been one of them and had heard them express their views. Thirty years later he said of them: "There were priests, good earnest men, who felt that a dollar sent abroad would weaken just so much the Church at home, and that it was nothing short of foolishness to encourage vocations to a foreign field." Some of these men lived to see the day when they, better instructed on the Church's world-wide mission, gladly yielded their pulpits to the director of the Propagation of the Faith and to missioners.

Father Walsh was out every Sunday talking in some church, and during the week he visited the schools. That was when I first saw him at St. Mary's in Lawrence. The system of collecting money was, as it is today, principally through memberships. The ordinary members gave sixty cents a year; the special members gave six dollars. The work was carried on by promoters under the supervision of the Director. Each member received a copy of the *Annals of the Propagation of the Faith,* poorly printed and badly illustrated, carrying mostly a collection of begging letters from missioners. These letters, often enough, were so lugubrious that they would restrain rather than stimulate the reader. The Director's job was to secure as many promoters as possible. To do this he had to make friends with the pastors, and in those days the majority of pastors could see little sense in helping the "haythen Chinee," while, as they said, there were so many to convert at home.

It was Father Walsh's job to show that while fairly large sums of money were going overseas to our missions, the Church at home was progressing quite normally, in fact, perhaps better than before. Then, again, the demands of the missioners were small compared with expenses at home. Entire dioceses, with seminary, native novitiate, works of charity, schools, etc. would operate on an amount of money no greater than the budget of one large city parish in this country.

Father Walsh realized that since he could not bring the clergy to the missions, he must bring the missions to them. For this, he needed to know many things about mission societies, their manner of operating, and the experiences of the missioners. He was in constant correspondence with numerous missioners, bishops, and heads of missionary societies.

After that, his appeals had a sort of hardheaded reasonableness about them. They were not just a vague romancing about faraway places, lepers, and abandoned babies. He quoted figures to show what we in America had received from other countries. He showed that we owed a debt of gratitude for what we had received. He argued convincingly that giving would increase the faith and piety of the giver, and, finally, when all was said and done and collected, the missioner's share would still be but the fragments. This was the motto of the Propagation of the Faith: "Gather up the fragments that remain, lest they be lost." (John VI, 12)

At that time France was giving to the missions five times as much as the United States, and the Protestant Episcopal Church was giving seven times as much as we were. This kept Father Walsh from any undue optimism and incited him to greater and greater effort. Our people heretofore had not responded, not because they were not generous but because they did not appreciate the problems.

Analyzing the situation, Father Walsh soon found the reason for the difference. Protestant Episcopalians had missionaries in the field, friends and relatives. So had the French Catholics. Hence, they couldn't be unaware of what was going on and what the needs were.

He felt that a seminary for foreign missions should be founded. Just when and how and by whom he did not presume to suggest. One thing he did see, and this very clearly. It was this: if he kept hammering away at the idea, sooner or later someone would start a seminary. That was the objective; get it started. He maintained in the face of much criticism, here and abroad, that American boys and girls would gladly sacrifice themselves for the work of Christ anywhere, just as young men and women of other nations were doing.

It was a long time, even many long years after these boys and girls were actually in the mission field, before some of the die-hards would admit they had been wrong. One of the strongest supporters of our American youth for this work, even from the start, was Cardinal O'Connell of Boston.

A spirit was beginning to move over the land that caused Americans to raise their eyes from their local problems and their own immediate tasks to take a look at the world. We were a very provincial people at the turn of the century. It is difficult for us to realize this fact now, after two world wars, after our efforts to help Europe recover from her second catastrophe. In the midst of new inventions that have improved communications to a point previously not imagined—it is difficult to place ourselves in the frame of mind of John Brown of Main Street as he pontificated on local politics at the turn of the century.

Thank God for the change! A good part of it is due to men of vision like Father Walsh, who kept hammering away to encourage the wider view. In 1909, he wrote in the *Sacred Heart Review*: "Are our boys less worthy, less courageous, and less heroic in sacrificing the amenities and conveniences of civilized life, to leave father and mother, and a dear home, to follow Christ and His Apostles, and the many thousands of staunch confessors and martyrs? Our faith is just as precious as that of the first Christians; it is the same in source, in strength, in divinity . ."

All his thoughts about the missions and his plans to stimulate greater sacrifices among American Catholics had led Father Walsh right up against a central fact which involved a principle, and this he had propounded in Washington at a meeting of the Missionary Union in 1904:

"While conscious of the need of priests in most parts of our country, I believe that to send some of our young men and young women to more remote districts would stimulate the vocations for home needs, and especially for the more remote missions of the United States. .

"The true priest lives his short life for the salvation of his fellow creatures. Every sincere Christian longs for the day when the Kingdom of His Saviour shall rule all men's hearts. What we priests and laymen can do by effort and prayer to win the world to Christ, this we should do, so that the altars may be more numerous on earth than the stars in the heavens; that multitudes in every land may be nourished with the Bread of Life—the Body of Christ; that this earth may be deluged in the Precious Blood of the Lamb, a ruby earth glistening like a radiant jewel under the sunlight of the glorious Cross of Him who died on it, not for you or me alone, but for every child of man."

In writing this talk Father Walsh was conscious of a certain supernatural light. He told Monsignor Duggan later that while delivering it, he felt his ideas getting clearer and the whole motive of his life becoming very clear cut. He felt that God was very near him and saying: "Here is your life's work. Go on: I will be with you."

Meanwhile God's time was approaching. What better occasion could there be than the first Eucharistic Congress in the New World, and what better place than Montreal, the city out of which had passed so many missioners to take up their lives of hardship along paths that sometimes led to a violent death among the savage Indian tribes of Canada and of our own country.

France has suffered in soul and in body. At present there is a confusion of mind among the French people, and there is a certain pessimism that is only a step from radicalism, but no one can separate France from her glorious history of mission activity. No other land has produced more or better pioneers, men who could live alone in the farthest places and plant there the religion of Jesus Christ.

In what was once called New France, this new American work was born. It was there in New France that these two Americans met, one a home missioner in the South, slow in speech and ordinarily slow in action but burning up with the idea and its urgency; the other an editor and mission-aid director. As we look back now, we can say that the hour struck unmistakably when Father Price called Father Walsh on that memorable day of the Mass at Fletcher Field.

All this started perhaps on that day when Father Walsh sat down for the first time at his desk in the little office on Union Park

Street, near the Cathedral, and said: "I am going to stay at this work in some form or other for the rest of my life." He never forgot his days in that office, and ever after up to the time of his death he supported the Propagation of the Faith with his pen and with his spoken word.

6

The Dusty Road

"Some feet halt where some feet tread,
In tireless march, a thorny way;
Some struggle on where some have fled.
Some seek when others shun the fray . . ."
— Rev. Abram J. Ryan

A highway marker has been set up at Wilmington, North Carolina, to point to the birthplace of Father Price. The New Hanover Historical Commission decided to honor this son of Wilmington. Though the members are not of our faith, they took the initiative under their Chairman, Mr. Louis T. Moore, and had the State authorities show this recognition to one of the Maryknoll founders.

A highway marker is an appropriate monument for Father Price. He spent much of his time on the highways. He tramped the roads around Maryknoll. Whenever we went out with him, to the country or the city, we had to be ready to do a good bit of walking. In the South he was always on the highways; and some of his experiences as he traveled up and down and across North Carolina he told us himself, but many more we learned from Father Michael Irwin, his partner in the home missions.

One of his former parishioners came up from North Carolina to attend a Departure Ceremony at Maryknoll. This was thirty years after Father Price's death, forty years after he left the South, but she still remembered him. He had received her into the Church and had presided at the ceremony when she was married.

"I recall," she said, "that he was a hard man on horses. He didn't give them much rest, no, sir, he didn't give those horses much rest.

He was always going, going. Yes, and I remember, too, he did like a good hambone." She hit the *bone* of hambone with a strong southern accent. "Yes, he did like a good ham*bone.*"

Going back to boyhood days, Father Price used to tell us that one of the happiest days of his life, perhaps the happiest for his mother, was the day of his father's conversion. On Christmas Day 1866, when he himself was only six years old, his father was received into the Church.

His father was a newspaper man, editor and owner of the Wilmington *Daily Journal.* Both his mother and father were southerners. Both were converts. When his mother came into the Church, her family disowned her, but she was taken in by the family of Doctor Frederick Gallagher, with whom she had boarded while going to school in Washington. It was after his father and after Doctor Gallagher that Father Price had been named Thomas Frederick.

He said that when he started school he had to be on his toes always because his two elder sisters, Margaret and Mary, were the teachers. Later they both joined the Sisters of Mercy. He was eight years old when Father James Gibbons was appointed Vicar Apostolic of North Carolina and chose for his cathedral the church of St. Thomas in Wilmington. That is where Father Price went to school. Thomas Frederick was just beginning to serve Mass, and so he became the new bishop's server.

Eight years later, when he was sixteen, the pastor, Father Gross, went to see his mother and told her that her boy wanted to be a priest. He suggested that she let him go to St. Charles College at Ellicott City with the hope later on of getting into St. Mary's Seminary in Baltimore. Father Price said that his mother hesitated at the idea because the journey was to be made by sea, and his eldest brother had been drowned. She left it all in God's hands.

What happened on that trip was one of the biggest events of his life. He never forgot it. He never told us about it, but he must have described it in all its details to one of his classmates at St. Charles, because one of them, Cardinal O'Connell, gives the complete story in his own memoirs.

He said good-bye to his mother, Father Gross and all at home and went aboard the boat, the *Rebecca Clyde.* The sky was threatening. The skipper delayed, debating whether or not he should turn back.

The wind increased. When the ship was off Cape Hatteras, the storm broke all around them. The Captain gave orders to abandon ship. Thomas Frederick was in his berth praying to our Blessed Mother. When he went on deck, the life preservers had all been taken. He and three other passengers groped along the wave-swept deck and lashed themselves to the mast. The boat foundered, turned over, and a great wave swept them into the sea. As the waves closed over him, he breathed a prayer and a promise to Our Lady.

Our Lady heard him. When he was picked up on the shore near Portsmouth, they thought he was dead. It had been a close call. A long sickness and convalescence delayed his studies. This experience was a major event in his life; of that there is no doubt. It led him to devote his whole life and all his energy to our Immaculate Mother. In the light of what happened that day and night off the coast of North Carolina, it is easy to understand the tenderness and affection he showed in later years for Bernadette and for all that took place at Lourdes.

He was convinced that the Blessed Mother had saved him. That was obvious, and he knew that she had saved him for a purpose. What an ingrate he would be if he failed to devote his life to this tender Mother and to the cause of her Divine Son! Thereafter, his life had much of the mystical nature, difficult to understand unless you knew all that went before.

His mother died when he was at home for his last vacation before ordination. This was a hard sacrifice for both of them, for both had been looking forward to the happy day that would mark the end of the long years of training away from home. His mother was a strong religious soul. Those who knew both of them said that her virtues were reflected in her son, especially her patient persistence and her unwavering devotion to an ideal.

On June 20, 1886, he was ordained in his own parish church at Wilmington, by Bishop Northrop. His first parish, after a few months in Wilmington, was Asheville, and he discovered that this included the whole western section of the State. He encountered much bigotry. Ignorance and all sorts of wild stories about the

Church resulted in a strong antipathy for any "Romish" priest. The people of the backwoods feared the priest almost as much as they feared the devil. Father Price suffered constantly on account of this.

Once when he was on the road, he was overtaken by a storm. He ran for shelter on a veranda of the nearest house. The owner came out with a gun and drove him off. Another time, he stepped into the general store to buy a few things for his lunch. The storekeeper refused to sell him anything. One farmer let him sleep in his kitchen, but then stayed up all night to keep an eye on him.

He understood these people, and such experiences never made him bitter. He used to say that you had to consider their state of mind, and what they had been taught. They looked upon him as something bad and perhaps they would go to heaven for having chased him with a gun. He was always kind and tried to be tolerant. Little by little some of them began to see that he was different, that he wasn't the sort of creature they had been told about from childhood.

The next year he took over another mission, New Bern. There were not many Catholics in this parish, but they were very good. He still had much to suffer. The people were poor. Often he had to spend the night in their barn or their woodshed. In the winter that could be a cold experience. Sometimes if he wanted to pass the night in their barn, he had to promise to leave and get out of sight before morning, so the neighbors wouldn't see him.

One day as a student in my early years at Maryknoll, Father Walsh buttonholed me and said: "Raymond, you know, you lack unction!" I couldn't imagine what he meant. What in the world is unction, I asked myself? Where do you suppose I could get some? As I look back now and think of Father Price, I know what Father Walsh meant by unction. Father Price had it.

His very appearance was a sermon. Just to see him say Mass would make you realize that he was a man of God. His sermons were inspiring. He seemed to breathe the spirit of a constantly attentive servant of God. A description of Father Price is the best definition I know of unction.

The reason for his unction was evident. It was the same that made him so respected by all of us seminarians at Maryknoll. No matter how busy he was, no matter how important the work he was doing at the time, he always made time for his meditation, for his pious reading, for the Stations of the Cross, for many Rosaries daily. These were his spiritual food. No wonder that he was always able to preach with unction! His words were the overflowing of his own communing with God, not something merely professorial, but something he had to say. Added to all this were his mortifications, one of which was wearing a steel belt next to his skin. Later, he had to abandon some of these penances, but all his life some sort of mortification was a daily practice.

Later he was given the parish of Goldsboro and Newton Grove. At Halifax, in the parish of New Bern, he had built a church and dedicated it to the Immaculate Conception. At Goldsboro, he built another and called it St. Mary's. Once a month he took the train to Mt. Olive and then went by carriage for twenty-one miles to Newton Grove. Sunday Mass there started at eleven o'clock. This allowed for those at a distance to get there, and for everyone to get to Confession before Mass. The afternoon was taken up with instructions and devotions. The people liked sermons; a sermon was one of the few diversions they had in their quiet monotonous life.

In later years when Father Irwin visited Maryknoll, he gave us a description of these Sunday afternoons. He told us as well about their missions for non-Catholics. Sometimes they would hire a hall. They would begin by having the colored boy, the priest's attendant, go about ringing the bell for a half hour. When they had a crowd in the hall, Father Price would mount the platform and then start something like this: "Now, Gentlemen, remove your hats, please. Now throw your chaws out the window." Then they would sing a hymn. This wasn't easy. He would play the first line and sing it, and then have them sing it after him. In this way, line by line, the hymn was learned, more or less.

After the singing came the sermon. This lasted an hour and sometimes longer. The people didn't mind. They weren't going any place. Father Irwin had an act that was always a success. He would start talking about the Sacraments. Then in the midst of his preliminary remarks, his colored boy would shout: "Dat's right, Folks! Dat's right! Father Irwin knows all about dem, cos he's done had 'em all." It was true! he had been married to a lady on her deathbed, and later went to the seminary. He had also been anointed during a grave illness.

After a Sunday filled with activity, morning and afternoon, Father Price usually spent the next few days visiting the homes to continue the instructions there. Frequently, he would go to the fields and talk to the men while they were at work. Then there were the visits to the sick and the aged. The work was trying and demanded an iron constitution, but he had the strength for it. A fair number of converts came from his efforts.

The enormity of the task and the ignorance he had to face, along with the prejudice that resulted from the ignorance, made him realize that something bigger had to be done. The effort he was making had to be multiplied over and over again, if the people of his beloved North Carolina were going to be brought into the Church. He began to think about something more systematic. The idea of specially trained lay catechists might be the solution. He went to the summit of Mount Mitchell, the highest point in the state, and prayed all night over his problem. He said Mass there on the mountain top the following morning, and then down to his work more determined than ever.

He made a ten-day retreat at St. Mary's Seminary in June, 1894, and told the Paulist missioner, Father Elliott, his problems. Father Elliott had some good ideas for him, but told him not to expect priests from the North. "Get your vocations right here," he told him, "get them from North Carolina where they will know the people and understand their problems."

He was eager to do something right away. He brought his plan to Bishop Haid. The Bishop thought that, financially at least, the plan was not practical, but he gave his permission. Father Price was released from his parish work and, after another retreat at Junalaska, a rustic spot near Mount Mitchell, he went out into the highways and the byways, preaching, passing out pamphlets, braving all sorts of dangers to explain the Church. He spoke in hired halls and on the street corners. Some of his audiences were friendly, some were unfriendly. In one place the crowd was particularly hostile. The only Catholic in the place took down his gun, cleaned it and carefully oiled it, and then stood by watchfully, hoping against hope, fearing that he would most certainly have to come to the rescue of his spiritual father.

One day, they greeted him with a barrage of old vegetables. Looking down at the cabbages and carrots and potatoes lying about him, he said with a smile: "Now if someone would only give me a nice piece of meat to go along with all these good victuals, I could cook myself a fine stew." This disarmed the people, and he continued his sermon unmolested.

Some of the non-Catholics felt that his sermons to them were an unwarranted presumption. They said this must be the beginning of the long expected invasion by the Pope of Rome. Father Price kept on, nonetheless, but he realized that something more practical and more comprehensive had to be started.

He saw the need of some kind of periodical to spread around among the people. When Bishop Haid asked him if he had the money to start the paper, he said: "I have twenty-five dollars, enough for the first issue of five hundred copies." It was called *Truth,* and the first copy appeared in April, 1897.

There were all kinds of reactions: ridicule, calumny, abuse. Some burned their copies, some read them, and some postmasters failed to deliver them. How the publication quickly reached a circulation of twelve thousand is one of those mysteries that happen in the lives of holy men. He had no leisure for the kind of writing necessary in a paper of this kind. He wrote at odd moments, at any place, and somehow managed to get the copy ready for the printer. There is a difference in the South today. But somebody had to blaze the trail.

Father Price thought of starting an orphanage, hoping that this might lead to what he saw was so necessary: a seminary to train priests for North Carolina and all the South. He purchased a six hundred acre plot west of Raleigh, with a dilapidated wooden mansion thrown in. Soon he had six Sisters of Mercy living there, while he was gathering in the orphan boys. He called it "Nazareth." His sister, Catherine, was superior of the community. He forgot one important item—food. The Sisters managed to get some for the first few days by begging in Raleigh. Holy people have a way of forgetting the daily needs, and, incidentally, the daily bills. His sister Catherine's experiences must have been something like those of Don Bosco's assistant.

Soon he had forty orphan boys there, so he started a new magazine, *The Orphan Boy,* to get funds for the place. Both of his magazines were published at "Nazareth." The boys helped on the farm. Later they had a trade school there. His friends, Catholic and non-Catholic, were on the increase. The little institution was winning considerable good will for Father Price.

Father Michael Irwin, his assistant, told us about those days. We were always glad to see Father Irwin at Maryknoll. He said that once he and Father Price were blessing a horse they had bought for their trips through the country. Both priests were vested with surplice and stole, and Father Price had the little bucket of holy water. The horse suddenly got excited and took to his heels, and the ceremony ended with Father Price dashing across the field after the horse, dousing him with holy water.

Father Irwin introduced Father Price to Father Walsh, when the two met for the first time at the conference of the Catholic Missionary Union in Washington, in 1904. It was, I suppose, a truly historic meeting, though neither one realized it at the time; and perhaps neither one dreamt that they would get together again in 1910, to start a foreign mission seminary. Father Price had read a paper on "The Progress of Localized Missions." Father Walsh, too, had read a paper, pleading for greater interest in foreign missions. This paper led to a discussion in which Father Price took an active part.

Father Walsh had said: "While conscious of the need of priests in many parts of our own country, I believe that to send some of our young men and women to more remote districts would stimulate vocations for home needs, and especially for the more remote missions of the United States." This was the very conclusion that drove Father Price, six years later, to give up his North Carolina apostolate, to join Father Walsh in starting a society that would, as he thought, do more, indirectly, for home missions than he could ever do while directly engaged in this work.

After his orphanage was well started, he began another work, a central residence for priests engaged in mission work in North Carolina which was at the same time a training house for boys who wished to give themselves to the same work. He called it "Regina Apostolorum." It continued over several years with various ups and downs.

He, and the little group he gathered about him, led a strict monastic life. They worked hard, and put up with all kinds of hardships. During this period, he had his heartaches. Opposition from the wicked, misunderstandings with the good, lack of coöperation where and when he needed it most, would have worn down and discouraged an ordinary man. He kept on with never failing trust in God and a confident reliance on the support of Our Blessed Mother. A disastrous fire destroyed his orphanage. Most of the boys escaped safely, but one died from injuries in a fall, and another was crippled for life. He lost everything, but he set himself to work at once and built the orphanage anew, this time making it completely fireproof.

During these years of the Mission Training House, "Regina Apostolorum," he had extra helpers in the summer, when seminarians came from the North to do catechetical work for him. Some came from St. Mary's Seminary and some came from St. Joseph's Seminary at Dunwoodie, near Yonkers. Among these were boys who later became well known throughout the States: John Mitty (Archbishop of San Francisco), John Wickham (Superior of the New York Apostolate), John McCahill, Michael Larkin and Thomas Larkin, pastors in the New York archdiocese, James Irwin, from Brooklyn, Timothy Holland and Arthur Kennedy, from Ogdensburg, and many others.

One of the priests would usually go with these boys on visits around the country. They would call on the farmers, hold meetings for non-Catholics, instruct prospective converts, make an attempt at taking the census. Our own Maryknoll seminarians have continued this work in recent years, going during the summer to several States of the South.

With all his enthusiasm still aflame and still anxious to be up and doing in his work of saving souls, Father Price, after almost twenty-five years in the priesthood and worn down by hard work and anxieties, found himself forced to admit that the apostolate of his State seemed to be a failure. He could not see at that time what great progress would be made in the next twenty-five years. Nor did he realize then that bishops and priests of the future would look back and thank him for the pioneer work he had done. At any rate, he decided, he would sacrifice himself for his native State, by going to the foreign mission work. He wrote out his plans for a society.

How should we estimate his work in North Carolina? Cardinal Gibbons has given us some idea: "He [Father Price] has accomplished a gigantic work. It is well I know the difficulties of the missions of North Carolina. Father Price's idea of establishing a community of secular clergy to preach the faith to benighted souls shall some day be realized."

And still who can say truly that he failed? Today, his memory is held in benediction by those who have followed him. The orphanage at Nazareth, the newly dedicated Father Price Memorial Chapel, *The Orphan Boy,* and *Maryknoll* all testify that Father Price made no mistake in trusting in God and relying on Our Lady.

Father Irwin, who knew him best, said: "I could tell of his poverty, his contempt of the world, his meekness, his cheerfulness, his innocence, his charity, his purity, his perseverance, his dreadful and secret austerities, his assiduity in prayer, his regularity in life, his zeal for the house of God, his intense and childlike love of the Blessed Virgin, his tender conscience, his chivalrous attitude toward all womankind, his sweetness with little children, his patience under trials, his tears of pity and sympathy, the delightfulness of his society, the charm that always clung to his humble and unpretentious exterior. I could recall the wonderful glow I once noted in his face after Mass—I could mention many things, but one would be more astounding than the other."

In the summer of 1908, Father Price made a retreat at Belmont Abbey and at that time made a resolution which he kept till the end of his life. He said that he would write a letter to our Blessed Mother every day. He did so, keeping the letters in a sort of diary. It was perhaps this practice that gradually led him into his spiritual relationship with Bernadette, the little servant of Mary. This, in turn, inspired those visits to Lourdes which he made on a subsequent trip to Europe, in company with Father Walsh.

When I was visiting Lourdes in the spring of 1949, I looked for the Soubirous home. I found the sister-in-law of Bernadette there, the one whose husband had given Father Price the cloak, the same cloak that he left to me when he went to China. I asked her about Father Price. She remembered him well. He had been a frequent visitor to their home up on the hill, not far from the old fort. She told me how Father Price would visit the home of Bernadette, the one in which I now was, how he would spend hours in the room of Bernadette, praying and communing with his friend. He would be quite upset, she said, when the loud talk of the sometimes not too reverent travelers and tourists would interrupt his devotions.

She also told me something that brought a smile. One day Father Price was in their garden talking with her husband and herself, when suddenly the cannon at the old fort went off with a tremendous report. It was the patronal feast of the town. Father Price must have thought it was something else, because he was already a good distance out of the yard before they caught up with him and called him back.

On August 25, 1908, Father Price wrote a letter to Our Lady, according to his daily custom. It shows that he was thinking much of the missions overseas. He needed the help of Mary Queen of Apostles, for he was to go through a period of misunderstandings, discouragement, and divisions. A later letter mentions a feeling of hopelessness about the success of his work. Another speaks of the betrayal by one in whom he had confidence. Again he wrote: "The reading of St. Alphonsus consoled me very much. The divisions in his community were so much like mine. Yet how great was his constancy! So I renewed my confidence in God and you, My Mother, and it seems to me that I should stick to my guns, confiding solely in your love."

He felt that the Church in America was too self-centered, that only a more Catholic attitude would stimulate the vocations required for the colossal task of converting the country. He wrote in his diary: "One thing has come to me with force, Mother. I must get men, and the foreign-mission development is the true and full end of my work."

In the May, 1909, issue of *Truth* he wrote about the need of a Foreign Mission Seminary: "Such a Seminary ought to be established around the Catholic University, and it ought to have preparatory schools in all our large Catholic centers—in New York, in Boston, in Philadelphia, in Chicago, in St. Louis, in San Francisco. With these preparatory schools all over the country as feeders, there would spring up an ideal of sacrifice for our Faith; there would be an outlet for the generosity of souls that would soon have the most far-reaching effects not only on ourselves, but on the foreign-mission work of the world . . ."

When Father Walsh in Boston read this, he wrote to him: "The foreign-mission seminary idea has also been very close to my heart. Speed the day when it may arrive! I believe the time is well ripe."

Father Price promised to write a long editorial on all this, and it appeared some months later: "It has always been a subject of regret that so little has been known or studied about foreign missions among our people. Even among priests and educated Catholics, there is very little real knowledge of this subject. With the exception of the *Annals of the Propagation of the Faith,* and some other papers founded for the local purpose of collecting money, and some missionary biographies, our literature on the subject is meager. The object of the Catholic Church is to convert the world—to 'teach all nations' —but before all nations can be taught they should be studied, and every effort should be bent to warm every Catholic heart to the work. In every parish, in every school and academy and university, the work should go on unremittingly—in study, in prayer, and in work. 'Thy Kingdom Come!' should be a continuous cry welling up from every human heart. There should be mission textbooks for every school, and more scientific works for the learned. No avenue should be left untouched. At the present time, however, we fear that even priests would be embarrassed if they were asked for an account of foreign-mission work, or of what works might be consulted to glean a knowledge of Catholic activities in the foreign-mission field.

"At the present time," he continued, "the Church in the United States is sending out almost no missioners to foreign countries. In a few years this is likely to be changed. We look for the Catholics of the United States to become the great mission force in the world, and therein lies the salvation of the Church in the United States. . . ."

Six months later he wrote in his Diary: "My heart fairly glows with love and happiness tonight, when I think that I may lead a band of men to China or Japan or Africa, and shed my blood for Our Lord. It is coming, Mother; it is coming!"

In the light of all that has happened since these lines were written, over forty years ago, they seem truly prophetic. It was coming, and it did come. The "Dusty Road" was long; it led him from Wilmington to Asheville, and on to New Bern, Goldsboro, Newton Grove, Raleigh, Rome, Lourdes, Maryknoll, and China.

7

The Holy Father's Blessing

"Why, it is all settled!"
— Pope Pius X to Fathers Price and Walsh

All the bells in Rome ring out on June 29th. It is a Roman holiday. Young and old leave school and work to celebrate Saints Peter and Paul Day. They go in throngs to St. Peter's at the Vatican, to the Mamertine Prison, to any place that links the days of two thousand years ago with today.

On subsequent visits to Rome, Father Walsh used to relive all that happened on June 29th, 1911. All the bells in Rome were ringing that day, too, when he and Father Price were told to return to America and start the seminary that would send out American boys to distant missions. The two of them joined the throngs going to St. Peter's, and thus they celebrated the first Foundation Day which we have celebrated every year since then on June 29th.

I, too, have recalled that day on my visits to Rome. Father Walsh told us about it often, and we read about it in the Chronicle, or Diary, kept by himself and Father Price. We felt we knew it all almost as intimately as they did. When I have gone to the Piazza di Spagna, entered by the big doorway into the Palace of Propaganda Fide, taken the elevator to the very top of the building, waited at the door of the Cardinal's apartment, and then looked down through the succession of brilliantly lighted waiting rooms, I could easily picture Father Walsh and Father Price in the very same place so many years before.

"We took our turn going up in the elevator," Father Walsh said. "It was run by water and would carry only one person at a time.

Up on the top floor of the old building, we waited at the door for
the Cardinal's attendant to let us in. All about the building one
could see big bees worked into the decorations. These, I was told,
were the Barberini bees, taken from the coat of arms of the Barberini
family. Pope Urban who built the place three hundred years ago
was a Barberini. The door opened, and we were let into the long
series of waiting rooms at the end of which we would find the Cardinal." This was to be the climax of their mission that started a
month before, on May 30th, when Father Walsh and Father Price
sailed from Boston on the *SS Franconia*.

After their meeting at Montreal in June, 1910, they had corre-
sponded steadily; forming their plans, they had sought the advice of
Archbishop O'Connell, Archbishop Farley, the Apostolic Delegate—
Archbishop Falconio, and Cardinal Gibbons. It was Cardinal Gibbons who took the positive steps in getting everything started. He
sent a letter to the Archbishops and Bishops of the country, telling
them all about the project, and leaving it to them to make a decision
at their next meeting in the spring of 1911.

After this letter went out, Father Price got a message from a
former classmate, Bishop Muldoon of Rockford, Illinois: "I knew
you would get into trouble sooner or later, and from now on you
will be, but it is God's trouble. Please remember me to Father
Walsh. May God Bless the work!"

At their meeting in April the American Archbishops and Bishops
unanimously endorsed the plan and expressed their approval in this
resolution: "We heartily approve the establishment of an American
Seminary for Foreign Missions, as outlined in the letter sent by His
Eminence Cardinal Gibbons. . . . We warmly recommend to the
Holy Father the two priests mentioned as organizers of this seminary, and we instruct them to proceed to Rome without delay, for
the purpose of securing all necessary authorization and direction
from the Sacred Congregation of Propaganda Fide for the proposed
work."

Father Walsh and Father Price agreed to meet in Boston on May
29th, the day before the sailing. The next day Father Walsh was already aboard the *Franconia*, still waiting and watching for Father

Price, wondering if he could possibly reach Boston in time for the boat. Just as the gangplank was being raised, Father Price appeared and hurried aboard. He smiled at Father Walsh, handed him his pocketbook and said: "Here: you'd better be the treasurer." Father Walsh had purchased the tickets including those for the return trip. Father Price evidently had made little provision for the journey, whether in clothes or money. His pocketbook contained two checks and some dollar bills, totaling one hundred twenty-five dollars.

They arrived at Liverpool on June 6th and immediately went to the Mill Hill college at Freshfield. Father Walsh made notes wherever he went. These he recorded in his Diary, which in turn made up the Chronicle. Year after year, this Chronicle was read to new students at Maryknoll. We always enjoyed it.

At Freshfield he noted that the policy was to take only boys who had to make a real sacrifice to give themselves to foreign mission work. He observed that "gutter boys" usually make poor subjects. Most of the boys at Freshfield were tradesmen's sons. It cost the College two hundred dollars to keep a boy for a year. The boys, or their families were asked to give seventy-five or fifty dollars. Most of them paid only twenty-five dollars. No boy was received absolutely free.

There were various notes about the boys' clothing, vacations, and the day's routine. They rose at five o'clock, except the boys under sixteen, who rose just in time for Mass at six. The rest of the day was very much like our own, except for two entries which always intrigued us: "10:45 A.M.—Soup and Recreation.—4:14 P.M.—Merenda, consisting of currant bread and tea."

Another paragraph spoke of the various points to be considered by the faculty in deciding whether or not a boy was called to this life. They would be observed for their conduct in chapel. Extravagant piety was a dangerous sign. What did all the professors think about him? Was he impertinent? Did he show selfishness and thoughtlessness in small matters? How did he do his Manual Labor? Was he careful in his sweeping, taking care of rooms, etc.?

More points followed on discipline. Private friendships were utterly condemned. The rule was: *"Numquam solus—Raro duo—Ad-*

minus tres." (Never alone—rarely in twos—at least three.) In regard
to the Spiritual Life there is an observation, brief and without comment: "Don't leave boys long on their knees."

Two days later the two priests went to the major seminary of the
Mill Hill Fathers at London, and the Chronicle records more of
their observations there. They were visiting these places with the
idea of planning their own seminary, which they hoped to start on
their return to America.

At Mill Hill they noted that a professor presided at each student
table in the dining room, but the Fathers were present only at lunch.
The tables were plain wood and very clean. The Brothers ate with
the students. Ale was served at dinner. The Fathers took turns
"week about," presiding at breakfast and dinner. There were no
chairs in the dining room. Presumably, there were benches. The
reader gave forth from a high pulpit. They were reading Elizabeth
Boyle O'Reilly's *Heroic Spain.* The windows in the dining room
were high so as to prevent drafts and distractions.

The Chronicle noted that the Rosary was said by the seminarians
in groups, walking up and down. At the end, going to their places
in chapel, they sang the *Ave Maris Stella.* Morning and night prayers
were in chapel, and all the professors were present. At the close of
Night Prayers they sang, three times: "O Sacred Heart of Jesus, I
implore, that I may ever love Thee more and more." Then a blessing
was given by the Superior General.

On June 12th they went from Mill Hill to Paris and arrived at
the Seminary of the Paris Foreign Missions. They met the Rector,
Père Fleury, and were taken in tow by one of the students, a son of
Sir Charles Gavan Duffy. Father Walsh's Chronicle contains copious
notes made during their stay in the Paris seminary. He was thinking,
of course, how some of these details would fit in the American mission seminary.

In the seminary refectory the reading at meals was in a high
sustained tone, without any inflection or modulation whatsoever. The
Night Prayers in chapel were impressive. They ended with the *Salve
Regina,* chanted after the manner of the Monks of Solesmes, by alter-
nate sides of the choir. The meditation points were given out at
Night Prayers. The first point was read in the same high sustained

tone as in the refectory. The second and third points were introduced in a much lower voice. There was a system of bells for calling the students when they were wanted. They were called according to their room numbers, and since there was no way of ringing a zero, room numbers like ten or twenty, three hundred or three hundred fifty, were eliminated.

Various charges were assigned to the students: care of the chapel, haircutting, charge of the infirmary, purchasing books, bringing meals to needy families, reading in the refectory, lighting and putting out the gas. Two of the charges were voluntary, introduced by Theophane Venard when he was a student there. These were cleaning the toilets and water taps. Father Walsh had a note here: "Responsibility is necessary for formation of character."

Every Wednesday the students had a walk, usually for about six miles. Nothing was allowed to interfere with this walk. They went in groups and they had a choice of 1) A direct, short walk, 2) A visit to churches along the way, or 3) a rapid long walk. In the winter they started out at eight o'clock.

Father Walsh filled several pages of his diary with notes made during his two days in Paris. Then they left and went to Milan. At the Milan Foreign Missions they asked many of the same questions they had asked in London and Paris, and after a few days continued on to Rome.

Fathers Price and Walsh had letters of introduction to Cardinal Gotti from Cardinal Gibbons and the Apostolic Delegate, Archbishop Falconio. They had a letter to Cardinal Merry del Val from Archbishop O'Connell.

They arrived in Rome Sunday evening, June 18th. They had a hard time finding a place to stay. There was no room at the American College or at the Canadian College. They spent the first night at the Minerva Hotel and late the next day, finally, got accommodations at the English Church, San Silvestro in Capite. During those first days they were greatly helped by a Dutch priest, Doctor Schut, a Mill Hill Father, who taught at the English College in Rome for many years, and was still teaching there twenty years later, when Father Walsh returned to Rome to be consecrated Bishop by the Cardinal Prefect of Propaganda Fide.

After some preliminary calls they finally made their first visit to Cardinal Gotti. He was out when they called at five P.M., so they went for a walk in the Pincian gardens, just above the Piazza di Spagna. When they came back at six, the elevator brought them to the top floor. They were let in through the heavy door of the Prefect's apartment, and they found the Cardinal waiting for them at the end of a line of waiting rooms. He gave them each an easy chair and he himself half leaned against and half sat on a big safe in the corner of his studio.

Father Schut interpreted for them and told the Cardinal the purpose of the visit. The Cardinal didn't bother to open the letters of introduction they had brought along. When Doctor Schut explained their presence, the Cardinal said that he knew about it; Msgr. Laurenti, his Secretary, had told him all the day before.

Then the Cardinal started and did most of the talking for the rest of the visit. Doctor Schut interpreted. Father Price held his beads and said the Rosary. Father Walsh answered questions about the dependence of the mission seminary on the Bishops of the United States. The Cardinal told them to draw up a complete plan of the project which he could present at the next assembly of the Congregation. He seemed pleased with a bound volume of *The Field Afar* which they gave him.

The next day, June 21st, they went to see Cardinal Merry del Val. They reached the Vatican at eleven o'clock and waited until twelve. He was very gracious with them. Apparently, he knew nothing of what they had in mind. He read the letter from Archbishop O'Connell and was interested in all they had to say about the future of America in foreign mission work. He asked about Archbishop O'Connell, and said that he had heard he was in Germany or somewhere, looking up somebody or something, but perhaps would not get to Rome.

Later that day Father Price and Father Walsh went to the Church of St. Ignatius. It was the feast of St. Aloysius, and little boys dressed as pages were taking Rosaries and other objects of piety held by visiting pilgrims to touch them to the reliquary of the saint. Then the two priests from America went back to their rooms to work on the plan that Cardinal Gotti had requested.

In their various visits about Rome the two priests had several opportunities to discuss the background of the foreign mission idea in the United States. At the turn of the century there was in our country very little interest in the missions of the Church; in fact, there was very little knowledge about them. Consequently, hardly anything was being done for them.

The previous century was a period of missionary activity in the United States. America was considered a land of missions. Priests leaving their homes in Europe, coming, for example, from Ireland or from Germany, were considered to be going on the foreign missions.

This situation changed rapidly after 1900. Native-born American priests became more numerous. They became more conscious of the needs of others. The first stage of the brick-and-mortar period was passed. Parish plants, with rectory, convent and school, were being completed in large sections of the country. There was a definite interest in home missions. The Propagation of the Faith was growing and being introduced into more and more dioceses. Some important churchmen in America were saying that it was time for us to start turning our attention to the foreign missions.

On June 23rd, all within their first week in Rome, Father Walsh had another audience with Cardinal Gotti. He brought along the plan requested by the Cardinal, which he and Father Price and Doctor Schut had drawn up to give a detailed idea of what they proposed as a foreign mission seminary in the United States. This schema also answered the questions the Cardinal had brought up at the first meeting. Father Walsh noted in his diary:

"The Cardinal read over two or three points, said 'Very good,' and then laid the paper on a sofa. He said they would take up the matter at their meeting the following Tuesday. He said he was anxious to put the matter through, but he couldn't do it alone. He was very much interested in finding out just what the American Bishops thought of it and what they thought of the eventual connection between the Seminary and the Congregation of Propaganda Fide, and also what they thought of the proper location for the Seminary.

"He was most affable. In arranging for our next interview, he mentioned Thursday, at eleven A.M., Feast of Saints Peter and Paul. We feared he would be occupied, but he smiled and said that many did not work on that day, or rather they were absent, but he himself never had vacations. There would be few to see him, and we could talk at leisure, as today."

The following Monday they called on Monsignor Bisletti. He said that they would have an audience with the Holy Father the following Friday or Saturday, and he told them what they should do and what questions they should be ready to answer. "Monsignor Bisletti is bright and he doesn't waste words," Father Walsh wrote.

"At 8:10 P.M. the same day we were en route again, once more in borrowed black capes, this time to see Cardinal Martinelli. The 'cabby' pulled up at a large building that might have been anything. Two or three weary-looking people lounging around the entrance nodded when we asked if Cardinal Martinelli lived there. 'Third story,' was the reply. And when we climbed to it we found the name Martinelli, over a door bell.

"We were admitted without delay. The interior was fairly pretentious, at least there was considerable red about, and a string of rooms as at Cardinal Gotti's.

"Cardinal Martinelli was most simple and kindly. He spoke with an Irish brogue. He asked several questions about the proposed work. Like all the others, he referred to location.

"He told us that for the present we could hardly expect anything more than permission to begin the work, and this ought to be forthcoming at the latest in a few months . ."

On Wednesday, the 28th, Father Walsh called on Monsignor Bonzano. Father Price was to have gone with him, but he could not be found. "He had flown," says Father Walsh. "He had the art of disappearing."

Monsignor Bonzano was the Rector of Propaganda College. He had been a missioner in Shensi Province, in China. "He was simple, unaffected, pious and interesting . . . He suggests that we have several fields in different climates so as to meet the different conditions of health in our priests. He does not believe in teaching any native language at the seminary. 'It's a waste of time,' he said. 'Once they are on the missions they will learn it quickly.' He admitted, however, that if you have a native Chinese from the very district you intend to evangelize, then some results might be accomplished.

"He remarked that preparatory schools generally lose two-thirds of those that enter.

" 'And please, Father, please—do not take stupid men! Don't take stupid men. And give your boys the full seminary course with all the studies and continue them for the regular length. Bright men are needed on the missions. They are needed to form native seminaries and for other important jobs. . . .' "

Like all rectors of seminaries and other experienced educators, he knew the mistake of trying to perform the impossible by making a scholar of one who lacked either the will to work or the ability to learn. The poor Curé of Ars has often been put on the witness stand to support the faulty logic of such people in similar cases who either have not read the life of the Curé of Ars or have failed to recognize his saintly character from childhood or have failed to see the persistent divine intervention in his regard.

Father Walsh and Father Price were due for their final call on Cardinal Gotti, on Thursday morning, June 29th.

"We were with Cardinal Gotti about a half hour. He was most gracious. The Propaganda Council is most favorably disposed towards our petition and gives us permission to begin the work, authorizing us to purchase land and a house, and to appeal for students. Father Price and I should conduct the society jointly under the direction of the Bishop in whose diocese we locate. We should keep the Propaganda Council informed of our progress.

"The Cardinal signed his photo for us, telling how it had been stolen, that is, taken from a group into which he had been brought after a ceremony at St. Peter's. He gave us his blessing. . . ."

The two priests went to St. Peter's for Vespers, but Father Walsh first hurried to the telegraph office to send a cable to Boston. It was simple and brief: "Washington Press, Boston. PRINT F A." Before leaving for Rome he had prepared in advance the July issue of *The Field Afar,* instructing his printers not to go to press until they received his cable.

This issue carried a special notice that, thereafter, the magazine would be the organ of the Catholic Foreign Mission Society of America, and that it was hoped Rome would put its seal of approval on the resolution taken by the American hierarchy. The readers were asked to join in prayer that the organizers of the new Seminary might be guided in the many details incidental to so important a work.

Father Walsh and Father Price spent the afternoon at St. Peter's and the next day they were received by Pope Pius X. Once again they were dressed in black capes borrowed for the occasion. The Swiss Guards let them pass through the Bronze Door. The various sentries scanned their passes and then sent them on and on, up to the antechamber outside the Pope's study.

In a few minutes the door opened, a Bishop passed on his way, and Monsignor Bisletti took Fathers Price and Walsh and Doctor Schut into the Holy Father's office. Before they could finish the customary reverences, he motioned them to their chairs.

"The Holy Father remarked that there was a great number of pagans in America," Father Walsh wrote. "And then he admitted that work for the heathen abroad would react on America.

"I gave him our schema, four pages, which he read through with keen attention. Evidently, up to the end he was under the impression that nothing had been settled, but when he came to the action of the Council of Propaganda, he said: '*Ma, è finito!*' (Why, it is all settled!) He then turned to us and wished us God's blessing on the work and on all connected with it. He took time to write six closely worded lines on the photo we had brought.

"When we were going out, he shook a 'day-day' with both hands."

Father Price wrote in his daily letter to Our Lady: "Such a dear, fatherly, good-humored Pope! I couldn't help falling in love with him . . . He understands and sympathizes . . . When he was told about *Truth,* he turned to me and said: 'Thomas, I bless you and your relations and benefactors and all connected with your work. Several times he looked at me and smiled, and it went all over me . . .'"

When Father Walsh and Father Price were at St. Peter's on the afternoon of the 29th, they noticed a strange decoration suspended in the air just over the main entrance to the big basilica. It was a framework like a huge enclosed basket, wreathed round with the leaves of laurel and boxwood and cloth of gold. It was a form of net and signified the net of Peter the Fisherman. It recalled the words of the Master to Peter: *Duc in altum!* These words remained ever dear to Father Walsh and to Father Price. "Launch out into the deep! Let down the nets for a catch!"

They had already launched out, and would soon be ready to let down the nets for a catch.

8

Hawthorne

"We have come to Hawthorne, Mother."
— Father Price's Letters to Our Lady

Westchester County's parkways converge at the Hawthorne Circle, five miles north of White Plains. As you go round and round the Circle, you have your choice of several exits. You may go south to New York City, northeast to Mount Kisco and beyond, north to Albany, the upper parts of the State and New England, and there are other roads leading to intermediate points of the compass.

If you are lucky and get off the Circle by the right exit, you will find yourself after a minute or two in the village of Hawthorne. The village is laid out in terraces, not unlike the hanging gardens of Babylon, set on the side of a beautiful green hill which continues to rise high beyond the rows of houses.

Midway up the slope, fringed with trees and shrubbery, is a road that would correspond to the main alley of Nebuchodonosor's azalea patch. Here, it is called Manhattan Avenue, and on the highest point of Manhattan Avenue you will find the Chapel and Priory of the Holy Rosary. There is a flagpole in the garden, just beyond the hedge, and at the foot of the flagpole there is a heavy granite monument with a bronze tablet on top. The tablet bears an inscription which says that Maryknoll, cradled here at Hawthorne, is everlastingly grateful to the Dominican Fathers for the hospitality given in the first days, grateful to the Sisters of the Rosary Hill Cancer Home for all their kindness, grateful to the Archdiocese of New York for its welcome.

When I reached Maryknoll in 1913, almost a year had passed since the transfer from Hawthorne to Ossining. On free days, however, our walks often took us back to where Father Walsh and Father Price got together with the first few students and Brothers. The three or four houses rented in the village and used as a seminary, a home for the Secretaries, and an office for *The Field Afar,* are still there, now occupied by parishioners of the Dominican Fathers.

A few years before he died, in 1932 to be exact, when I was Rector at the Maryknoll Seminary, Father Walsh went to Hawthorne for the Thirtieth Anniversary of the parish. At that time he summed up for us the story of the early days in Hawthorne.

The French Dominican Fathers were expelled from France in 1880, when the Government seized all their monasteries. They took refuge in Switzerland for three years, later in Holland, and finally, in 1894, they came to America. Archbishop Corrigan brought them to New York, and they acquired property at Sherman Park, which is now known as Thornwood and Hawthorne. They bought the Tecumseh Hotel, changed it into a monastery and called it the Convent of the Most Holy Rosary and St. Michael. More commonly it was called Rosary Hill Convent.

By 1900, conditions in France had changed, so the Rosary Hill Convent was closed and most of the Fathers and students were called back to France. Some of the priests stayed behind, because they had begun pastoral work among the people of Pleasantville, Kensico, and Valhalla. The buildings on Rosary Hill were sold to Mother Alphonsa Hawthorne Lathrop, youngest daughter of Nathaniel Hawthorne, who wanted them as a home for incurable cancer patients.

Father Alexander Mercier was left behind to look after the parish. He rented a house in what is now Thornwood, at the corner of Sherman and Circular Avenues, and lived there about a year. Later he built the Holy Rosary Rectory; the Chapel was added later. The house rented by Father Alexander at Thornwood became the first Maryknoll Seminary in 1912, and that is where the pioneers lived for nine months up to the time they came to Ossining.

Father Walsh said that when they were crossing the Atlantic late in the summer of 1910, after receiving the Holy Father's approval to start the seminary, they knew only that they were homeward-bound;

they were not just then concerned about a future domicile. The only idea they had on the subject had been expressed by the American hierarchy: they wished to be within fifty miles of the metropolis of New York.

This, of course, would not be the geographical center of the United States, but it would be very convenient for a society that was to be national in its foundation and world wide in its outlook, for New York is a national and international point on which lines from the ends of the earth converge.

Cardinal O'Connell was ready to welcome the new mission seminary into his diocese, where he felt it belonged. Father Price was his old friend and classmate. Father Walsh, born and brought up in Boston, was Boston Director of the Propagation of the Faith. In February of that year, 1910, the Cardinal wrote a long letter of praise to Father Walsh, commending *The Field Afar*. Why should these two men look farther afield? When the seminary was started away from home, he was disappointed. I suppose anyone in his position would have been disappointed.

Father Walsh, looking far ahead, saw that it would be a mistake if the new mission movement were not started as something clearly national; to link it too closely to one particular diocese, or even to one section of the country, would hurt its eventual growth. It was a heartache for him to have to turn away from the friendly associations of Boston, but he was looking forward to a future America when enthusiasm for the missions would not be confined to New England or the Eastern States.

Twenty years later, when Cardinal O'Connell turned over his farm at Bedford, Massachusetts, to be used as a novitiate for our Maryknoll students, the Cardinal was on hand for the dedication exercises. On that day he spoke in the little chapel which he had just blessed, and in the presence of Father Walsh and the student body, he said that he was surely mistaken in 1910 when he wanted to have the seminary started in Boston. He said that he could see in the light of subsequent development that it would have been the wrong start to keep the seminary away from a national center. The students were impressed by the Cardinal's frank confession; everyone makes mistakes, but it takes a good man to admit them.

"In which diocese we should find a roof tree in 1910," wrote Father Walsh, "we did not know, but a few days after landing we were in Washington to report to the Apostolic Delegate, and while visiting the Catholic University our first problem was solved. The late Cardinal, then Archbishop Farley, was there for a ceremony and, aware of his sympathetic interest, we asked if he would like to have us establish ourselves within the limits of the New York Archdiocese. The reply was immediate—opened arms, a smile, and the warm word *'Welcome!'*

"As we turned north from Washington, we began to ask ourselves where to settle in that large Archdiocese where both of us were strangers. We must find some place without delay for ourselves and for *The Field Afar,* which already had a subscription list of several thousand and was housed temporarily at a printing press in Boston.

"There was just one place that suggested the possibility of at least a temporary home, and that was Hawthorne.

"Two years previously I had visited Hawthorne at the request of the late Monsignor Cothonay, Prior of the French Dominican Fathers. Father Cothonay called me, because he wanted to urge me to start a foreign mission seminary and he offered to supply professors, if needed. The idea pleased me greatly but at the time it could not be considered, unless remotely.

"As soon as Father Cothonay learned that we were to locate in the Archdiocese of New York, he lost no time in extending hospitality to the homeless organizers, and to Hawthorne we went with bag and baggage on October 20, 1911. For each of us our host found a cozy 'cell' on the south side of the old frame house, and places near himself in the little basement refectory.

"The house today has undergone changes and additions, and with all due respect to my hosts of other days, it looks brighter and neater than it did then; but there was something in the atmosphere of our Hawthorne retreat that caught and held me, and I believe it radiated from the personality of Father Cothonay. His was not a vivacious temperament and he had a habit of heaving long sighs, but I knew him to be genuinely sympathetic, happy to have us with him, well informed, and full of the mission spirit.

"The countryside, too, in autumn foliage was good to look at, the hills gave restful views; and the consciousness of an actual start—poor as we could be in material possessions, but rich in prospect—had set our souls free and brought us peace of heart after hectic years.

"I often look back on those early days in the Dominican house at Hawthorne as an extraordinarily happy period of my life," Father Walsh said. "They were in fact too pleasant to last, but they continued well into December. In the meantime, Father Cothonay was transferred to Europe, and later to Tongking, and although the kind hospitality of the Dominican Fathers continued under his successors, we were adding recruits and the time had come for us to move, which we did in January, 1912, renting a small cottage about a mile to the north, in Thornwood. It was while here that we settled on the word *Maryknoll*.

"Meanwhile, *The Field Afar* had been transferred to another cottage that was occupied by a small group of faithful women who, living near the Dominican rectory, attended daily Mass in the little chapel of the Holy Rosary. They were the nucleus of our present Maryknoll Sisters. Three of them arrived on the Feast of the Epiphany, 1912, and the next morning started out for Mass across the fields trying to follow the general directions that had been given them. They went to the only building in the vicinity that looked like a chapel, since it was surmounted by a cupola. After trying the doors and getting no response to their knocks, they looked through the windows and discovered that it was the engine house of the volunteer fire department. The Holy Rosary Priory at that time had only a small chapel in the house; the separate chapel wing was added later. The ladies had moved into what the townsfolk called 'The Haunted House.' Their cook saw ghosts roaming around night after night.

"To Hawthorne also came two men who wished to be Brothers, one from Austria and one from Brooklyn. Both have now gone to God. They were the pioneer members of our Auxiliary Brothers of St. Michael.

"The 'infant' stayed at Hawthorne until September 18th—almost a year—when an ancient hack, hired for the occasion, conveyed three of the first group of students and their Superiors to the hill-top known today as 'Maryknoll' at Ossining-on-Hudson. All three of these first students became priests and went to China. . . ."

All three likewise became Bishops, Bishop James E. Walsh and Bishop Francis X. Ford in China, Bishop William O'Shea in Korea.

The diary of those months at Hawthorne became a feature for public reading at Maryknoll and, year after year, newly arrived students listened to the recital of that winter of cold furnaces and broken water pipes.

There is a page dated January 15, 1912, which reads: "The *red letter day* for the Catholic Foreign Mission Society of America, Hawthorne, N. Y. On the afternoon of this date, Father James Anthony Walsh, one of the organizers, and Father John Ignatius Lane, a helper and volunteer, both from Boston, took possession of the Klingler house in Hawthorne for the first time. For some time previous, Father Price, the other organizer, Father Walsh and Father Lane had been guests of the French Dominican Fathers at Hawthorne.

"It was an auspicious day, for it was the feast of the *first* known Martyrs of China, who were beatified. It was the feast of Blessed Francis de Cappillas and his Companions, who were martyred in China in 1628, two years after the establishment of the Manchu dynasty. May these holy martyrs intercede for us, who are going to try to advance God's glory in foreign lands—perhaps in the very land whose soil they blessed by their blood.

"At seven P.M. Fathers Walsh and Lane sat down to the first meal prepared in the house . . . Father Price was away on business . . .

"Father Walsh acted as assistant kitchen help. He opened cans of tomatoes, etc., set the table, cut bread, and so on. The Menu: tea, bread, potatoes, meat, peaches—preserved and canned. The Lord blessed our appetites and we were happy. Snow was on the ground, and the wind was coming up to a decent blow, but the house was comfortable.

"January 16th:—Very cold this morning. Water frozen, and the boiler nearly empty, so that the fire had to be drawn . . . The plumber was here all morning and succeeded in stopping leaks, starting the fire, but left some work undone, e.g. the water does not run from the bath room faucets . . .

"The Ladies at Maryknoll and the Fathers of the Seminary are going to combine to send their orders for meat and vegetables, in order to get free expressage. A certain amount must be ordered before that privilege is granted, and we must be economical.

"January 17th:—More trouble with the plumbing. No water. Washed again at the pump in the kitchen. The plumber comes and after considerable time finds that the cistern is dry, that there is a leak in the steam pipes, that we will be obliged to get water from the spring in the yard. We write to the landlord and arrange for the perfecting of the plant.

"Father Price has the attic room, his preference, nearer Heaven, perhaps. Today sent our first order of meats and vegetables to the Ladies of Maryknoll, to be sent with theirs to New York. Took our first exercise at the pump. Good exercise.

"January 18th:—No water. The plumber promised to come. Did not. Speaking of the young Ladies of Maryknoll—the Misses Dwyer, Wholean and Sullivan—it should be said that they are volunteers, who have a desire to do something for God, and who offered their services to Father Walsh. They came to Hawthorne on Epiphany, 1912, and are working away with the best of intentions and with all their strength. Father Cothonay called the young ladies the 'Three Wise Women from the East.'

"It is very quiet here, only the blow of an engine at the Sherman Park Station just below our house breaks the silence, as the train goes on its way to and from New York.

"January 19th:—It is a great treat to see water flowing from the faucets and to know that there is a chance to keep clean.

"February 23rd:—In the mail today came a letter from His Eminence Cardinal Farley in which he said that he had read *The Field Afar* with edification, interest, and inspiration, that he wished to be put down as a Founder of a burse (five thousand dollars). This was in his own handwriting. . . . Word has come from Father Price. He sent his first valentine from the field, a gift of fifty dollars from Mother Katherine Drexel. Pleased to hear from him.

"February 24th:—A beautiful day; morning very fine. The mail brought a check for five hundred dollars from Bishop Ryan of Alton, Ill., also five dollars for his subscription to *The Field Afar*. The afternoon mail brought one hundred dollars from Mrs. Fraser of Roxbury, for the furnishing of two rooms in the Seminary,—dedicated to the Sacred Heart and St. John the Evangelist.

"Fathers Walsh and Lane, and a visitor to the Mary Knoll Cottage, had a carriage ride to Briarcliff. The visitor is Miss Rogers, a brave worker for the cause and who, if she could, would give up teaching school in Boston and join the small band at Hawthorne. The purpose was to get the air for Father Lane and visit a prospective home near the Salesian Fathers. Briarcliff is a beautiful place but rather out of the way for a Seminary. The other place is a very attractive piece of land, good in every way visible. . . . A telegram comes from Father Price at Philadelphia to ship to him, at once, twenty thousand offering cards. A modest request!

"February 29th:—This is leap year. Signs are not wanting that our new maid is getting discouraged. She is nervous and restless. . . ."

The Diary goes on and on, the record of successive days of worry about cooks and housekeepers, leaky pipes, cold furnaces, gifts in the mail, reports from Father Price who was on the road, the activities of the Secretaries, and the search for a permanent site.

There is a record, made December 1, 1911, when Father Walsh was on a visit to Boston. A Mr. Joseph Cassidy, sophomore at Holy Cross College, called on him with the idea of joining the new Seminary. "Seemingly an excellent subject," Father Walsh noted. Mr. Cassidy was unable to join us until after his ordination. Father Cassidy's time at Maryknoll was spent in the footsteps of Father Price, going about the country begging, and later in the missions of Korea.

On March 28, 1912, there is this note: "We had two visitors, boys from Cathedral College, New York, who may be our first pupils. One is Francis Xavier Ford, of Irish fame, a very nice appearing young fellow and a good sensible boy. The second was Alphonse Vogel, whose father came from Austria, a quiet boy who seems to be thinking . . . There was another application from a philosopher of Brooklyn."

"April 19th:—Rumors of war in our kitchen. Afraid someone must go.—All the country has been in mourning since Monday because of the wreck of the *Titanic,* which was making her maiden voyage from England. She was the latest in shipbuilding, the largest and most luxurious of all steamers. The survivors arrived last night, and the news was confirmed of the loss of over seventeen hundred souls, mostly men, as the rule was: 'Women first.'

"April 23rd:—A Mr. Walsh of Cumberland, Md., wrote to Father Walsh about his boy, a graduate of Mt. St. Mary's College, who desires to join this group. The father is willing. The boy worked for a year and now desires to come to us.

"May 4th:—A Mr. O'Shea of New Jersey, a clerk of rank in the Brooklyn Navy Yard, came to see Father Walsh about applying for admission. Father O'Rourke, S.J., recommended him. He seems to be a very sensible young man of twenty-seven. Desires to go where he can do the most good and feels that he can do good with us. Father Walsh sends him to Father Hughes of Cathedral School, to be examined as to his standing. He has been studying privately and coached by the curate of his parish at night after the day's work was over . . ."

The Diary that year has many references to the Pocantico Hills property. Fathers Walsh and Price had put down several thousand dollars on a desirable piece of property near the estate of John D. Rockefeller. The real estate man, to gain a larger sum for his property, then attempted to ignore the original deal and sell to Rockefeller who apparently wanted no such neighbors as a foreign mission seminary. It was not bigotry, very likely, but rather the desire to have that section of the Westchester hills all for himself. A long-drawn-out dispute went on in the courts. It was finally settled in favor of Fathers Walsh and Price after they had already found and purchased the more desirable site at Ossining.

All during this Hawthorne period I was at home in Lawrence. I had graduated from St. John's, Danvers, in 1911 and then worked with my father in the mills at Lawrence for two years. My mind was made up and I had been in correspondence with Father Walsh.

Month after month I watched for each new issue of *The Field Afar* and I remember how I read and re-read every line about the doings at Hawthorne. Father Walsh always drew a good picture:

"Hawthorne, we are told, means in the language of flowers, *Hope*.

Such it has meant to us, as we watched at the cradle of our 'babe' and looked forward to the future.

"It has been our Bethlehem which we entered in the bleak December of 1911. Our Nazareth will doubtless be elsewhere but Bethlehem will never be forgotten.

"Our experience in getting a future site has been one succession of set-backs or devil-blocks, whichever one prefers to call them.

" 'Good signs,' everybody said, and we believe so ourselves, but we whisper the hope that Mr. Oldboy will soon get tired of following us up on this particular matter and give us a chance to get in under cover of our own roof, for a change.

"We shall be tempted some day to give you a chapter on 'Cooks that passed us by.' We will tell you, too, about the army-tent annex to our little home here, a tent which no descendant of a Flatbush mosquito has ever dared to enter, even to meet an old friend of his father. September 18, 1912, was our last day at Hawthorne, the first at Ossining.

"It was a raw evening when we left Hawthorne, under cover of the darkness, so as to spare the feelings of the villagers. We had six miles to drive, and into a carriage built for four, seven of us crowded, just as some of our ancestors used to do, that they might give decent burial to their departed friends. We, however, were attending a resurrection, not a funeral, and as we clung to some oil lamps that were to give us the first heat and light in our new home, our hearts were glad.

"We had something to eat. The cook—we have forgotten her number, but may she read these lines!—the cook *was* a cook, and she saved our lives during a trying period.

"One morning, a few weeks later, we filed into the dining room, said grace, sat in silence and had to eat words in place of bread. She had folded her tent at five A.M. and quietly stolen away.

"She was a good girl, with a perpetual smile, which she was simply afraid to lose in the making of a complaint. And we imagine that she walked away smiling, took her train smiling, and is smiling still. God bless her and keep her smiling!

"Our Secretaries were still at Hawthorne and we sent out to them a signal of distress which brought the 'flour of their flock' and their mistress of foods to our relief. It was hard on the Secretaries, but they have learned how to suffer. Besides, they could cook if they tried, and we would not try if we could, lest we be accused later of an attempt to kill.

"So we are beginning to feel free to rig up our flying machine and soar, occasionally, to all kinds of heights. Occasionally,—for it will be a long time before we are settled, although some of our friends imagine that we are already in a new and perfectly equipped seminary building.

" '*Poco a poco!*' This is what our Professor of Philosophy says, or rather it is what we say to him when he asks for something that he can't have. 'Little by little!' So shall it be, and that is why we are always glad to get the little.

"As we finished the above paragraph, we experienced a shock, but learned that it was only a blast of dynamite that had just been set off in the cellar under our office. We expect to meet the charge later, but it struck us a warning that we had devoted enough space this time to Maryknoll."

9

The Venard

*"To be born a gentleman is an accident;
to die one is an achievement."*
— Bede Jarrett, O.P.
(Father Walsh's Bulletin Board)

Less than a month after arriving at Maryknoll, I went to Scranton with Father Walsh. I was going to be the first student at the new Venard Apostolic College. I spent one full school year at Scranton, which ended in June, 1914.

We went by train. At the Grand Central Station Father Walsh took me to the restaurant for lunch. There were artichokes on the order. They were new to me. He showed me how to eat them, and prefaced his instructions by saying that as a missioner I should have to travel much and it would be well to know how to handle these unusual dishes. He added, "An artichoke can be a man's best friend, especially when you haven't anything else to eat." I told him that I had never seen them before, and I told myself that it wouldn't make a bit of difference if I never saw them again.

The truth of his words came home to me years later, when I discovered that a missioner does have to make the best of unusual dishes. I lived on hard-boiled eggs and watermelons for two days after the war, during a trip from an internment camp in Manchuria to the French mission at Mukden. I felt I could supplement Father Walsh's first lesson on unusual dishes: "A watermelon can be a man's best friend, especially when you haven't anything else to eat."

We took the train at the Lackawanna Station. As we approached the coal regions of Pennsylvania, I was impressed by the moun-

tains of culm and slag that dominated the view and spoiled the otherwise attractive hills and valleys. I marveled that the cars could be
kept so clean amidst so much heavy dust and the flying cinders of
the locomotive.

There was a placard in the car that you couldn't help noticing,
and on it was a rhyme that just impressed itself on your memory
even if you didn't try to remember it. The advertisement showed an
attractive young lady with waves of auburn hair. She was dressed all
in white, in the fashion of the times, with a high fitting collar and
sleeves to the wrists. She had a hat, also white, that sat on the top of
her head like a small cloud, and she had a corsage of violets. She
was sitting in a railroad carriage looking out over the coal fields, and
alongside were the lines:

> *Says Phoebe Snow*
> *About to go*
> *Upon a trip to Buffalo:*
> *"My gown stays white*
> *From morn till night*
> *Upon the Road of Anthracite."*

The cars were pleasant and clean, but I think Phoebe had better
luck than we did. It was a warm September day and when I mopped
around the back of my neck, my handkerchief gradually became
coal black. Our trip ended at the very attractive station in Scranton.

At the turn of the century Scranton was one of the eastern dioceses that seemed to be producing more vocations than were needed
at home. Priests were being released for other dioceses. Hence,
Scranton was picked as a likely site for the first preparatory school.
Bishop Hoban had said that he would be only too willing to have
this school in Scranton. It would be very simple at the start, just a
hired house, and the students would attend class at St. Thomas
College, which at that time was conducted by the Christian Brothers.
This institution has since become Scranton University, staffed and
directed by the Jesuit Fathers.

Bishop Hoban's house was our first objective. The Bishop was
most kind and gave us a grand welcome. In answer to his question:

"And who is this young man?" I took a bow, while Father Walsh introduced me as his first student, intimating that up to that moment I had no place to sleep. The Bishop said: "He can be your secretary. You'll have the guest suite."

We talked with the Bishop for about a half hour, and then Father Walsh rose to leave. I noticed a look of disappointment as we left the house, just a light cloud passing before the sun. As we went down the steps we heard a voice: "Father Walsh!" We turned back. It was the Bishop calling. He had a check in his hand. "Something to help you get started," he said. Father Walsh's eagle eye caught the figure, 500. As we started again down the steps, Father Walsh nudged me in the ribs, and said: "The country's saved."

I feel quite sure that Father Walsh had gone to Scranton without funds, confident that Bishop Hoban would come to the rescue, which he did. We set out forthwith on a shopping spree, most of which was spent in the Five-&-Ten Cent Store. There we bought our "silver" and our "linen."

We visited St. Cecilia's Academy, just across the street from the Bishop's House. Then we took a look at what was to be our new home at 640 Clay Avenue. We wound up the day with supper.

As I sank into the comfortable bed assigned to the Bishop's secretary, for we were in the rooms kept for the Bishop's guests, I could not help feeling the strangeness of it all. Many experiences had been packed into those three weeks since I took the train for Ossining.

The next morning I was awakened when Father Walsh put his head in the door and announced: "Your bawth is ready, Sir." He always came out just at the unexpected moment with a little flash of humor that made him such an attractive superior and companion.

We got an early start for 640 Clay Avenue. Later on, we used to say it was the worst house on the last street in Scranton. Natives of the town might correctly dispute both points of the allegation. At any rate, that's the way it seemed to me. It had been vacant a long time. There was some vague story about someone ending his life there. Of course, that could have been concocted by the first students. Things were beginning to arrive, and I was supposed to get busy and straighten them out.

Late that afternoon, Father Walsh and I went back to the Lackawanna station to meet student Number Two, John Murrett. He had reached Maryknoll a week after myself. Five others were due to come directly to Scranton, after we got things in some order. John Murrett made the trip from Ossining under the watchful eye of Miss Rogers. Somewhere along the way, she had taken him into a drug store for an ice cream soda. Her reputation, already high, rose higher and higher.

That day we sat down to a typical Boston Fourth of July lunch:— canned salmon, peas, and lettuce. Father Walsh went back to the Bishop's house. Miss Rogers stayed at St. Cecilia's Academy. John Murrett and myself spent the night on and off a couple of army cots we found there. Father Walsh had taken me aside to explain that John Murrett was a bit nervous and might not sleep well under those unusual circumstances. John sawed wood all through the night, peacefully and rhythmically. I was the one to see spooks and hear strange noises.

The experience was difficult, though at the time we didn't stop to think about it, chiefly because Father Walsh would surprise us every now and then with some ludicrous reference to our "college build- ing," "the campus," the "chef," and other bits of wit to make us laugh. Later on that month, when *The Field Afar* arrived, we read about ourselves and the first days at what we called then *The Ve- nard Apostolic School:*

"Signals of distress had been thrown out in various directions, and Friday morning a procession of butchers and bakers, grocers, express men, 'gas-pipers,' and ice-men responded, all as anxious to serve us now as they will be to render bills later. We were glad to see them and they were pleased to meet us. Time will tell the story of our mutual continued devotion.

"The first meal was, shall we say *served*—Friday, September 5th, at one-thirty. It came an hour behind the scheduled time, but it was worth waiting for. A pulverized salmon, caught with a can-opener, some green bullets, sliced peaches, and light-complexioned coffee gave nobody an excuse to say that he was starved or suggested his posing as a martyr. The spoons, large and small, were too shy to appear, but butter-individuals were used effectively to scoop up the little green balls, and each man's trusty fork stirred his coffee, salmonizing it as it did so.

"It was a fitting banquet and those who sat down to it will treasure the memory of that opening feast. There were five of us, including three students, who represented, in the order of arrival, *Lawrence, Mass., Buffalo, N. Y.,* and *Scranton, Pa.* As we were at the camping stage, the newly arrived chief cook, Mother of our Teresians at Maryknoll, was allowed to join the group and compelled to partake of the food prepared under her direction.

"Speaking of cooks, a delicate subject with us, we had at first five lines out, all baited, and we waited breathless, with our legs dangling for the first good bite. But, by Saturday, the bait was off three hooks and a cook was yet to be caught.

"A pleasant surprise was furnished us that evening, when two Ladies Bountiful of Scranton came to us bearing gifts, palatable things that made some youthful eyes glisten. These friends in need were about to leave, when a second similar convoy arrived, and we were in danger of being spoiled.

"God bless these Catholics of Scranton! From the Bishop down, they have extended a hospitality without stint and all are evidently glad that their diocese has been chosen for the site of the first apostolic school connected with the Catholic Foreign Mission Seminary of America. Nor must we fail to recall here, the Sisters of the Immaculate Heart of Mary who made us feel the warmth of a welcome as hearty as could be given.

"Sunday, September 7th, was not entirely a day of rest. Midnight of Saturday found some of the little community more awake than asleep, on various kinds of improvised beds, and at two A.M., we received a burly sergeant of the police who had been summoned for an interview with a burglar in our house.

"Now any burglar who would take away our twelve kitchen chairs, or the tin spoons we had just bought at ten cents a dozen, would be beneath our notice, and the sergeant agreed with us that an injustice must have been done to the burglar confraternity of Scranton."

Five students were due to arrive. To John Murrett and myself was given the job of getting the house in order and going to the station to meet them. Joseph Hunt was the first to put in an appearance. He came from Brookline, Mass. He had on a hat that looked like a mushroom. He carried an umbrella in the mid-Victorian manner, and he had a green baize bag filled with books and sandwiches and fishing tackle.

James Quinn came from Central Falls, Rhode Island. He had been working as a conductor on the trolley cars. He was quick in his movements, natty in appearance.

William McNamee was from Washington, D. C. Not robust enough for the foreign missions, he did not stay with us long.

Martin Walsh, a slow-moving lad from Jersey City, soon became a model student. He had been manager, or assistant manager of a theater, and was more mature in his manner than the rest of us.

There was another lad, a tall heavy-set fellow from the Bronx. He arrived one night at midnight, about a week after all the others were here. He made a rather noisy entrance when I let him in, asked if this were the Venard College, gave his opinion of it all, wanted to know where the campus was. I told him that the back alley was the only campus I had seen. "Father Walsh mentioned an athletic field," he said. I sometimes felt that Father Walsh may have stretched a point and referred possibly to a playground in the neighborhood above us, which we never succeeded in entering.

"Do I have to sleep in that thing?" the new arrival asked, as he took hold of the light iron cot and pushed it from one end of the room to the other. We were standing directly over Father Walsh's room, and so I tried to terminate the inspection tour there and then. I told him that was the idea, and that he had better hop right into it and let the rest go till morning. He was evidently more interested in baseball than in seminary life.

Three of that first group were eventually ordained. Father Hunt and Father Murrett went to the missions of Japan.

Mrs. Kelly was our cook. She holds a lasting place in our Hall of Fame. As she strode across the kitchen waving the dish cloth, she would tell us about her husband, gone to better lands I know. "He was a grand man. He drove a spike in every railroad tie from Boston to Slocum Hollow." This was an old name for Scranton.

John Murrett was helping Mrs. Kelly one day when some new-comers saw him going from the kitchen to the dining room. "This must be a swell place," one of them said. "They have a Japanese cook." John was short and dark and could easily impersonate a Japanese. In later years the Japanese detectives had a hard time finding him on a trip between Dairen and Korea. By the time they had been informed there was an American aboard, John had already changed into a Japanese kimono and sandals, had on his heavy black tortoise shell glasses and was squatted on the deck reading a book along with scores of other "Japanese."

These few days during the first week at Scranton gave us a chance to see Father Walsh at his best. He was a master of detail. In no time, he had us organized and fully briefed. Everyone was given an assignment. I was named senior student and had complete instructions regarding my duties.

I recall vividly the night of the burglar alarm, referred to above in Father Walsh's notes. Joe Hunt had been prowling around about midnight. To see what was going on I lit the gas; we had no electricity. We talked for a time and then went back to bed. Not many minutes later I thought I heard someone jump out a window and run down the alleyway between the houses. Perhaps a thief had got in, I thought, but there was so little to lose I let it go at that.

I awoke later when a deep voice sounded near by: "Is this the house?" From my window I looked down on what I thought was the biggest policeman I had ever seen in all my life. He had a flash light in one hand and a revolver in the other and was looking in a window of our first floor. When I asked what was the trouble, he said: "This chap says there's burglars in there." John Murrett was on the veranda of the house next door, looking very timid. "Come down and let us in," said the Law.

"That's a bright prospect," I said to myself. "With an armed militia on the outside and desperadoes on the inside, I must go down into the bull pen to let in the toreadors." I was getting my metaphors mixed in the muddled atmosphere of midnight. I struck a light, put on something, and then slid down the stairs as stealthily as I could, all the time hugging the wall. My heart was between my teeth when I turned on the gas in the hall. Nothing happened. I let in Mr. Policeman and he told me to lead him through the house. If a burglar had popped up, the officer would have had to shoot over my ears to get him.

We entered Martin Walsh's room. The policeman turned his spotlight on the bed. Martin rolled over and opened one eye. "We're going to look around a bit," the officer said. "Sure," said Martin, "go ahead." And he rolled over and went back to sleep. I don't know what the officer thought of us; we seemed to be used to burglar alarms.

By this time I had figured it out. John Murrett had seen Joe Hunt's flashlight as he wandered about. He heard us talking. Then he jumped out the second-story window. The wonder is that he didn't break an ankle. He rushed down to the Caseys at the hotel and told them to call the police.

When it was all over, the officer asked Father Walsh if he should make a report. "Please, don't," Father Walsh begged.

Every day we went to class at St. Thomas College, fifteen minutes away. Some of us wore hard derby hats, quite the style at the time. Father Walsh didn't like them and had us change to a flat soft hat, quite out of style. These flat hats became the pet target of the family when I went home each year for vacation.

We made many fine friends among the priests, Brothers, and students of the College. Father Boyle and Father McHugh, both secular priests, taught us the classics. They were excellent professors. Father Boyle discovered that Joe Hunt and myself had already had Virgil. This made it embarrassing for me but not for Joe. He didn't mind it a bit when the professor would ask him to run through the next day's assignment, and he would read at sight forty or fifty lines of the Aeneid.

One night in the study hall Joe was engrossed in his book. "What are you reading?" Ed Gleason asked him. "Don't stop me," Joe pleaded. "It's a boat race. The *Chimera* and the *Scylla* are pulling ahead, but I'm betting on Mnestheus to win!" Perhaps you remember the boat race in the Fifth Book of the Aeneid. Gleason couldn't understand how anyone could really enjoy Latin verse.

The Brothers were kind to us at St. Thomas College. Brother Abdas, the Director, Brother Ephrem, Brother Gerardian, with whom I am still in correspondence, Brother Ferdinand, and many others will live always in our memory. The Scranton boys and the Scranton people in general were most friendly. I shall never forget all the kindness shown us that year.

Time after time we would find provisions left at our door. Ice cream and cake and other "hardships" were sent our way. It would be difficult to name all the friends. The Misses Hoban, sisters of the Bishop, Mrs. Cunningham, Miss Chase, Mrs. Wills, and Miss Nellie Brown stand out in my memory. The Caseys made a habit of sending a turkey with all the fixings every year at Thanksgiving and Christmas. Later on the Stones of Olyphant and, likewise, the Connertons were outstanding for their helpfulness.

We had two Directors that first year, Father John Lane and Father McCabe, of Mill Hill. Father Lane held on until about mid-year, and then had to return to Maryknoll. His rheumatism made it impossible for him to continue. We hated to see him go. He was a strict disciplinarian, but he had a way with boys. His weekly talks hit the mark. He had a system of reminders to keep us on our toes. He called them "knocks." Once he called me to his room and asked very solicitously whether or not I was getting enough sleep. I assured him I was. He kept pressing me. I told him again that I was getting the required hours every night. "Why then," he asked, "are you always yawning during my talks?" I could have told him the story about the Bishop who complained to the Mother Superior about a nun who stood up and walked out of the room while he was giving a conference. "Oh, don't mind, Your Excellency," she explained. "Sister Anasthesia always walks in her sleep."

Now and then, there were little experiences that were hard to bear. One of the students clearly had no intention of continuing on to the seminary. He cared nothing for study and he annoyed the others when they were preparing their classes. Besides that, he used to make a nuisance of himself on our trips to and from the College. He thought it was fun to take the ash barrels standing in front of a house and let them roll down the hill. The climax came one day when he rolled away the barrels of a family who had been very kind to us. Shortly after that, I announced that things had gone too far and, as senior student, I would have to bring it to the attention of the powers that be. This was a most distasteful job. The American boy abhors nothing so much as reporting on others. I simply told him ahead of time what I was going to do, and then went and laid the whole thing before Father Lane.

The trouble-maker, bigger and stronger than myself, was going to pulverize me and, no doubt, he would have done a fair job at it; but Martin Walsh, good old Martin, came to my defense. Father Lane was an ace in the way he tried to soothe my injured sensibilities because of the unpleasant job I had. He was all kindness to the boy athlete, who later realized that his place was elsewhere than in our college.

Father Price had charge of us for part of that first year in Scranton. He had the students puzzled for a time with his exercises of piety, continuous rosaries, his sort of mystic manner of celebrating Mass. We felt that he was far beyond heights we could ever hope to reach.

One night he called me to his room. "Brother Raymond," he asked, "what makes the chain on that light swing back and forth every so often?"

"We are directly over the mines here, Father," I replied, "and whenever they blow off a charge of dynamite down below, the vibration shakes the house."

"Do you think we are in danger?" he asked. I reassured him as best I could, but he was still alarmed, especially after I told him how some of the houses in the Scranton area had a way of disappearing, which, I suppose, was not the best way of reassuring him.

We ended that first year of the Venard in June, when we returned to Maryknoll for Daniel McShane's ordination to the subdiaconate which was to take place in our own chapel on June 22nd.

Father Walsh recorded in his notes that we reached Maryknoll on a perfect June night, welcomed by faculty and students and even by the life-savers in the kitchen who greeted us with a smile, although we meant more work for them. Father Walsh added: "And not one of the travelers refused to eat."

The Primitive Observance

"Now there were giants upon the earth in those days."

— Book of Genesis

It was customary each night at the end of night prayers to sing an invocation, and this immediately preceded the blessing by the priest in charge. It was a practice brought back by Father Walsh from his visits to the seminaries in Europe. In those days it was simply: "O Sweetest Heart of Jesus, I implore, that I may love Thee more and more."

It came Martin Walsh's turn one night to intone the invocation. To pick a note out of the air and strike a pitch that will suit the register of varied voices is no small feat even for an experienced singer. Martin Walsh was not an experienced singer. Most of his audience were in the same category. Father Price, though not exactly tone deaf, was certainly not a Caruso. He was presiding on this night.

When the dread moment arrived, Martin took a deep breath and intoned an "O." It was just a plain "O," on no particular key, no particular note. It was indescribable, perhaps something like the farewell honk of a sea lion just before it submerges. Father Price began to shake. The tears rolled down his cheeks. It looked almost like hysterics. He couldn't give the blessing. We, who had an exalted view of Father Price's holiness, took courage in finding a saint so decidedly "out of control."

Six of us came back from Scranton to Maryknoll at the end of June, 1914. Joseph Hunt and John Murrett were in the group.

Jimmy Quinn was with us, too. He left later and during World War I he went to France. He was killed in action. A shell burst beside him, and when the dust and smoke subsided there was nothing to be found of Jimmy but his rosary beads. There was another lad, William McNamee, and finally, there was Martin Walsh. In later years Martin worked in a bank in Jersey. The day after our arrival, Thomas O'Melia and Joseph McGinn arrived from Philadelphia, becoming Venard students No. 7 and No. 8, respectively. They were to spend the summer at Maryknoll.

We had come early to be on hand for Daniel McShane's ordination to the subdiaconate. This was to be the first ordination in the little chapel at Maryknoll, and Bishop Cusack, Auxiliary to Cardinal Farley, came up for the event. Bishop Cusack was always a good friend. Later on, as Bishop of Albany, he took title for our newly ordained priests when we had no title of our own.

Many important things seem to have happened that year. Cardinal Farley arranged with Bishop Hoban of Scranton to have some of the Sisters of the Immaculate Heart of Mary come to Maryknoll, to train our Teresians in preparation for the novitiate.

That same year we lost some priests who had helped Father Walsh and Father Price to get things started. Father John I. Lane had been ill and was called back to Boston. Father McCabe, who had been teaching and directing our manual labor, went back to Mill Hill. Father Van den Bessalaer, also a Mill Hill missioner, went back to Holland.

Father Van den Bessalaer was famous at Maryknoll for his recipes, especially his directions for cooking chicken in Uganda style. He called it, "How to Cook Schicken à la Uganda." He said you didn't have to dress the "schicken," no need to take out the insides. Just roll it in thick mud and bake it. Afterwards take off the mud, and the feathers would come too. The entrails meanwhile would be congealed into a ball and would come out easily when you cut the "schicken." It would be ready to eat.

He had a tremendous beard. One day he shaved it off, and then we discovered he had a tremendous nose. When he appeared without warning at the altar ready for Mass, the community almost shook itself to pieces with suppressed laughter. He looked like old John

Silver or Israel Hands. His face was covered with gashes; someone said he took off the beard with a jack-knife.

When war broke out in August, 1914, we had at Maryknoll, small as the community was, representatives from Austria, Germany, Russia, France, Italy, Holland, Ireland, and, of course, the United States. Father Walsh decreed that there would be no discussion regarding politics or international problems. The order habitually was well observed, but now and then a minor incident flared up. Our own States, at least the Eastern ones, were fairly well represented.

I remember one day when a lad from Jersey was reading at dinner. It was something about St. John the Apostle and mentioned his being placed in a cauldron of boiling oil. Our student from Jersey read: "burling earl." Father Walsh tapped his bell. "What was that, Brother? What was in the cauldron?" The student repeated it: "burling earl." "How do you spell it?" Father Walsh asked. "B-o-i-l-i-n-g, burling." "Just a minute, please," Father Walsh interrupted. "How do you pronounce e-a-r-l?" "Oil," was the reply. Father Walsh hit the bell, "Ding-Ding!" two rings, meaning "Keep going." It would take time to cure that one.

There were several other events during that summer of 1914. We put up our first silo. It came pre-fabricated from Kalamazoo. We were anxious to see what a pre-fabricated silo looked like, and discovered that we had to do a lot of fabricating with it ourselves, before we had it in place and ready for the corn. Another innovation was the laundry equipment installed in the cellar of the old seminary. We thought it was the last word in tubs and washers. Housewives nowadays wouldn't look at it, but it kept our clothes clean and somehow the clothes seemed to last longer then.

We were twenty-five students all together. Thirteen belonged to the Major Seminary, and twelve to the Venard. There were four Brothers and ten Teresians. That year the Teresians went off to Scranton to make their retreat. They were going to become Sisters.

Our retreat at the Seminary was given by Father Joseph Bruneau, of St. Mary's, Baltimore. I remember asking him what would be the best spiritual reading for a prospective missioner. He told me to read the New Testament. "Read it constantly," he said. "Read it over and over, and get familiar with the life of Our Lord."

Another event that same summer was tragic. Billy, the horse, died one day while coming up the hill. He had been a fine trotter and a strong puller in his day, but like the last straw that broke the camel's back, it was just one climb too many. He lay down on the road, heaved a big sigh and died. We buried Billy that day.

Anything connected with the animals was an event for us. Father Walsh remarked once that the other cows were making life miserable for one in particular. "The rest are all picking on that one. You would think they were almost human," he said.

We watched breathlessly while our first artesian well was being dug. It was a matter of dollars and cents, and we wanted to strike water as quickly as possible. After a certain depth was reached, the fee was two dollars and a half for every foot. The drilling had to go down more than two hundred feet, and, even then, it was not a great success. The well gave only eleven gallons a minute.

That summer we bought a horse for eighteen dollars. Father Walsh pushed the deal and drove a hard bargain. When Father Cashin, the Chaplain at Sing Sing, heard about it, he said to Father Walsh, "That man must have had an awful thirst when he sold his horse for eighteen dollars."

We went to Sing Sing, now and then, to see a ball game. Relations between our two institutions were good, though we paid Sing Sing more visits than the inmates there paid us. The train from Grand Central Station to Ossining often carried relatives and friends of the prisoners going up for the day. Sometimes, the trains carried prisoners. They rode with the guards. When you went to the ticket window in the Grand Central and said: "Ossining—one way," you had a feeling that the clerk was giving you a queer look.

Bernard Meyer arrived from Iowa the following year. Born and brought up a farmer's boy, he took over our farm. He eliminated the hogs, at least the breed we had at the time, and emphasized chickens. Father Walsh started calling him "Brother Hennery." The students from the city rebelled and protested when they saw his selective methods of thinning out the undesirable chicks. If he saw one of the little furry creatures limping or showing signs of anemia, he would pick it up in his big Iowan hand, snip the bird's neck with a pincer movement of his thumb and finger, and toss it out the window.

Under Barney Meyer's management the place began to look more and more bucolic. We acquired a flock of sheep. The hogs were coming back into their own. Chickens were thriving, attesting the survival of the fittest. Most of this was due to "Brother Hennery"; he knew his business.

Sometimes he would be at the barn working to the last minute and then rush to the seminary to take an examination or go to chapel. He would simply throw his cassock on over his overalls or work clothes. Always, there was an intriguing odor of the barn on his shoes, and this neutralized the atmosphere of the chapel or classroom so long as he was there. As soon as possible he was out and off again to the barn, making a quick exit, which we generally greeted with genuine approval and a relaxed sigh.

That year we had a big harvest of apples. We sent a shipment of them, three wagon loads, I think, to the orphan asylum in Peekskill.

Father Walsh began what he called "The Doctor's Column" in *The Field Afar,* filled usually with notes by Doctor Paluel Flagg. Doctor Flagg came up from the city once a week year after year, to give us lectures on medicine. He got other doctors interested in medical mission work. Later he moved to Yonkers. He brought up a large family and passed on to them his own fine religious spirit. His eldest daughter became a Maryknoll Sister and went to the Far East.

We acquired a skeleton to be used in connection with Doctor Flagg's medicine classes. The house being small, we had no permanent laboratory, and so we used to keep the skeleton in a closet of the guest room. One night a guest, just arrived, pulled aside the curtains of the closet and met the skeleton staring out at him with empty eye sockets and a hideous grin. Our guest let out a whoop and rushed through the door. We had to go after him and bring him back, and then we escorted the skeleton to another room, where it wouldn't interfere with our visitors.

As time went on, the skeleton was constantly getting into scrapes. You might come back to your room and find the skeleton sitting in your chair, with glasses on, reading a book, or you might find him tucked away in your bed. Unfortunately, we failed then to realize the reverence we owed to what had once been the dwelling of a human soul.

It was a big family, and all sorts of things happened. A new arrival came in late one night, intending no doubt to give himself to a life of work and sacrifice for the foreign missions. Most of us had retired. He was gone again in the morning, up and on his way before breakfast. In his room we found the reason: the sheets were battle scarred with the marks of a night-long encounter with bed bugs. Our "B.B. Squad," as we called it, must have overlooked that room. It was one of the unhappy consequences we had to accept along with an old house and second-hand furniture.

Little by little the old farmhouse was getting to be more like a seminary. Its face was lifted in various stages. It sprouted new wings to the right and to the left. One of these wings was our new Chapel, finished in the fall of 1914. The sanctuary was simple, but beautiful and correct. It was planned by Father Walsh. He was careful to develop good taste and liturgical exactness among his students. We were blessed with some beautiful statues, which Father Walsh had secured at the Sibbel studios, and which we have to this day in our Seminary chapel. They are statues of Our Blessed Mother, Saint Joseph, Saint Paul and Saint Francis Xavier.

Bishop Hayes came up from New York on November 21st and conducted our investiture ceremony in the new Chapel. That is the day on which new students begin to wear the cassock. Monsignor John Dunn was here for the occasion, and with him Father Dineen from New York. Father Collins, the pastor in Ossining, also came. Father Walsh decided to kill two birds with one stone, or rather, to kill a whole flock of them. He had an intolerable antipathy for guinea hens. They were too noisy. This gave him an excellent excuse to slaughter the whole tribe with one fell stroke of the axe. We and our guests that day picked over the bones of the last of the guinea hens.

Perhaps the outstanding event of that year was the ordination of Daniel McShane. It was at St. Patrick's Cathedral, on November 10th. The ceremony was to begin at eight A.M., and so we had to get up at an ungodly hour to catch the train for New York. Cardinal Farley ordained our first student priest. Only a handful of people attended the ceremony. Monsignor Dunn, ever faithful, was there. Monsignor William Hughes, head of Cathedral College, gathered his students for the occasion. Dr. Mitty, later Archbishop of San Francisco, and Dr. Ryan, both from the Diocesan Seminary at Dunwoodie, were there to help with the ceremonies. Others present were Father Donovan, of St. John the Evangelist, New York, and Father McShane from Indiana, a brother of our first priest.

Daniel McShane's parents had come from Indiana. There were some friends of the students at the Cathedral, also, and the usual morning church-goers. But all together, they made only a small group. After the Ordination, Father Walsh and our new priest had breakfast with Cardinal Farley.

We all started back for Ossining. When we got off the train we filled the little Toonerville trolley; the car was small and practically everyone at Maryknoll had gone to New York for the ordination. Mr. James Cranston was both motorman and conductor that day. Later, when the cars were discontinued, he joined the Ossining Police Force, and we used to meet him cruising around on his motorcycle.

That same month, on the 28th, James Edward Walsh was ordained subdeacon in the Chapel of St. Joseph's Seminary at Dunwoodie. He was the first subdeacon ordained by Bishop Patrick Hayes, later Cardinal, who had just become the Auxiliary to Cardinal Farley.

With so many cows, chickens, horses, and pigs on our place, our interest in farming awakened, and we began to write here and there for farm catalogues to buy seeds and tools. Word got around that we had an up-and-coming farm, and Father Walsh's name was put on the list of good prospects for farm supplies. Thereafter, he was flooded with catalogues and circulars telling how to make the most money out of your farm with the greatest speed and the least possible work.

One day he got a letter from the owner of a famous grain mill in Detroit, addressed to him as a very dear friend and telling him that he was being let in right on the ground floor of a very good thing:

"I have selected you for my personal representative in your territory and I am very anxious that you should act, if you will, please. I figure that for the winter months, anyway, you will have spare time on your hands, which my plan will convert into money-making hours.

"I have men just like yourself who sell my Golden Era Corn and Grist Mills during their spare time of the winter months and receive from me in commissions from $50 to $175 per month.

"Now, my friend, you can earn this money and probably more. All you have to do is accept my proposition and cinch the Agency—now that you have the opportunity.

Your friend, etc."

Father Walsh remarked that he didn't have the spare time, and so could not "cinch the Agency." But, he added, if our land slips, burse cards, mite boxes, and other appeals should fail, it is pleasant to know that we have this opportunity ahead to earn enough to keep our ducks afloat.

In 1915, Father William Kane of the Archdiocese of Portland, Oregon, was released by Archbishop Christie for several months to go through the Diocese of Scranton to speak about Maryknoll. He made many friends for Maryknoll on this lecture tour.

"A deep bass voice from the wilderness of the West," said Father Walsh, "has been sending sound waves over the diocese in an ever-widening circle and Scranton is rapidly awakening to the idea that a young organization, still poor and struggling, but with good promise, is trying to settle among its worthy people.

"Father Kane has, of course, met some obstacles, but this was to be expected. One of his adverse experiences, while it was annoying, amused him as it did us, because it was so refreshingly cool, even for the winter season. Agents of a certain well-known magazine did Father Kane the honor of attending one of his lectures. A little later they made a canvass of the district, armed with copies of their own magazine, containing a printed speech delivered by Father Kane months before. It was a really thoughtful act, though not altogether considerate, and undoubtedly not sanctioned by the society represented. In any event, some subscribers were lost to *The Field Afar,* but we are happy in the assurance that a good paper is going to them."

That year we acquired our first automobile, a decrepit Ford which came from a kind-hearted soul in New Jersey. It was a bit asthmatic, especially coming up our hill, but it served us well and gave speedier deliveries where formerly we had depended solely on horse flesh. Father Walsh christened it the "Tin Lizzie." He said that our roads were very fond of the little unpretentious machine that leaked oil and water on them occasionally, and from its wagon-box was liable to drop any kind of present from a bottle of ink to a banana.

At almost the same time we acquired a huge Mercedes-Benz, one of the first machines with an electric shift. It was a beautiful thing, but always a headache with something or other out of order, and to buy fuel for it made it almost as expensive as a locomotive.

We also received a yoke of oxen and a stump-puller. In a few days the oxen uprooted more than a hundred deeply bedded stumps, each leaving a hole big enough to bury a horse. The roots came out clear and clean from the ground, and Father Walsh remarked that a dentist would surely envy the process. But a dentist can toss away a tooth with a turn of the wrist, while it took a pickaxe, two mules, and a man to haul away those tree roots.

We still needed a horse, with all our gasoline acquisitions, and we asked for one in *The Field Afar*. A young lady wrote that she would be glad to give us a mule. This brought joy to Father Walsh, but Barney Meyer assumed the attitude of a horse-trader and showed no enthusiasm. He admitted, however, that a good mule might be better than a horse and he condescendingly decided to think the matter over between a class on the History of Religions and the French class. The latter over, he reported that if the mule still had youth and possessed gentle manners, he would agree to accept it. "But," he added, "better have your friends give us two." And they did.

When Father Price and Father Walsh were getting started at Hawthorne in 1911, Cardinal Farley advised them to have the mission society incorporated as a civil corporation, according to the laws of New York State, and to include some laymen as members of the corporation. They did this, and meetings were held annually.

In the spring of 1915 this corporation met, as usual, in the Cardinal's residence. Cardinal Farley presided. Bishop Hayes was present, and Monsignor Dunn acted as Secretary. The Honorable Victor J.

Dowling and Michael Maginnis, Esq., both lawyers and members of the corporation, attended the meeting. Father Walsh represented the Seminary. A summary of the report read at that meeting, which was accepted and approved by the corporation, gives a peek at what had been going on:

"Alterations on the Seminary have been completed. A new altar and a vestry have been installed. An electric laundry has been set in the basement. St. Michael's and St. Teresa's have been shingled and painted outside (and to some extent, inside).

"Two extra hen houses and a brooder have been added to the poultry yard, which had been enclosed with wire fencing. The barn and silo have been painted.

"The live-stock has been increased, and we now have enough milk and butter for ordinary consumption. We also have procured a yoke of oxen.

"Tile drains have been set in the land. An artesian well has been sunk. Fire protection is still inadequate but better than it was a year ago. We are well supplied with extinguishers in all departments, and the new watermain has been tapped for outside connection at two convenient points.

"The Venard Apostolic School at Scranton more than doubled in numbers. At present we have eleven students. We had planned to secure a permanent home for this school by the coming fall, but at present we cannot see our way to do so. We shall, in all probability bring the students to Maryknoll to remain for at least a year.

"We have seven complete burses, one of which is not yet operative. Twenty-seven other burses are being gradually accumulated, and towards these we have received $14,730.16."

Later that year, the more or less famous dispute with John D. Rockefeller over the property at Pocantico Hills came to an end, after dragging out for three years. Father Walsh said, "We came out with a credit balance of six thousand seven hundred fifty dollars, and the check we received bore the name of John D. Rockefeller. We would have photographed the check but we needed the interest and could not spare the time. Besides, we were afraid we should wake up and find it was only a dream. We appropriated enough of it at once to dig the sea-serpent's grave, our new sewer. The remainder we applied to water-pipes, ditches, and so on. We had hoped to take a slice off our mortgage, but there is a limit even to six thousand seven hundred fifty dollars."

The Sea Serpent's Grave was what Father Walsh called the long ditch we were digging in 1915, to connect our sewer with the village disposal system. He knew it would be hard to interest friends in contributing to this expense, since they would much rather give a chalice, an altar, or something more noble by which they would be remembered. He had received some gifts, however, with letters like this one:

"I did not fail to notice that 'dirty' hint referring to the cost of digging the sewer. Once I helped you with a mite, when you were buying land by the foot, and now you want to throw it away by the handful, or rather shovelful. I'll also aid you—but not much, I'm sorry to say. The little bit extra might secure a patch for poor Dinny Dun's torn traveling suit."

During their trip through England in 1911, Father Price and Father Walsh learned of the work done for the missions by Lady Herbert of Lea. Father Walsh hoped that some similar work of mission-aid might be undertaken by American Catholic women. He had organized the Maryknoll Auxiliary with that idea. Prominent in this group were Mrs. Ada Mary Van Brugh Livingston, Mrs. H. W. Taft, sister-in-law of the President, and Mrs. Jacob Doelger. They had periodical meetings, and on these occasions Father Walsh would speak to them or send one of us or a visiting missioner to speak to them. That was my job for a time after ordination.

At one of these meetings, Father Thomas Gavan Duffy had been asked to speak. He was just back from India and had a prominent red beard. One of the visiting ladies, long since passed to her reward, spotted the new arrival. There was a rustling of satins and taffeta as she hurried across the salon, trained her lorgnette on the red beard and gasped, "Oh my! How exciting!"

At least once a year the ladies of the Auxiliary would come to Maryknoll in a group. On these days Father Price habitually took off to the woods. About four in the afternoon you would see him come cautiously around the corner of the house, hail the first student or Brother in sight and ask in a whisper, "Are they gone?"

Bishop Biermans, a Mill Hill missioner from Uganda, was with us for a long visit during 1915. One day he was reading his Breviary in the yard when a dynamite blast went off in the Sea Serpent's Grave, and a piece of rock, escaping from the mat and hurtling over the roof, narrowly missed the Bishop's head. He picked it up and brought it to Father Walsh and asked, "Is this the way you treat your guests?"

Bishop Biermans dined at Oyster Bay with Colonel Teddy Roosevelt, whom he had entertained some years previous in Uganda. Another day, he met Billy Sunday on a trip to Paterson, New Jersey. The Bishop traveled through all the Eastern States on a begging tour for his missions, but war times were hard times, and he was not as successful as he had hoped to be.

The horses and cows, chickens and ducks, lambs and pigs, all members of the family, continued to occupy the community. One of the newly arrived piglets was rolled on by the old sow. Philip Taggart came to the rescue with his first aid. He brought the little pig to the Seminary kitchen, where Mrs. McGuire furnished bandages and wood for the splints. Phil carefully set the leg and then took the patient off to his corner of the dormitory. In the middle of the night the little pig rolled over on the splints and started squealing. Nearly everyone in the place jumped up. Phil quickly wrapped the pig in something and hurried down below. He found a warm spot in the cellar, but in the darkness and in his rush he failed to note too carefully just where he deposited the patient.

After breakfast he hurried back to visit the sick, and then to his dismay discovered that he had deposited the piglet on top of the boiler. Several hours of steady temperature had converted his charge from a little pig into a small portion of roast pork. Returning from his emergency trip to the boiler room in the middle of the night, Phil had met Father Vincent Dever who heard the commotion and thought that the boy's nerves were upset. He asked: "What's wrong?" Phil, intending to throw Father Dever off the trail of the midnight squeal, put on his most forlorn look, rubbed his abdomen and said, "I'm all right now, Father."

John Murray and I were down by the artesian well, one day, working on the pump. We were both covered with grease. John Murray had left Harvard before his senior year and then worked for ten years with the W. F. Roberts Engineering Company in Cambridge. He was also a first class musician with the trombone, and for a time he played in the Pop Concerts with the Boston Symphony.

The two of us were on our knees replacing the motor, when Father Walsh came along with a stranger. "Brothers," he said, "let me introduce our new History Professor, Doctor Phelan." So Father Thomas Phelan appeared on the scene. Pastor in Brewster, he was going to make the trip to Maryknoll twice each week by the "Old Put" Division of the New York Central. He was a colorful figure, right from the start, like someone out of a Dickens story.

On special occasions Father Phelan would give a speech and describe the various conveyances that were sent to meet him at Millwood where he got off the train. Trucks, ancient Fords, wagons, everything but the hay rack, went from Maryknoll to bring Father Phelan from the train to our history class. Once a single-seater racing gig was sent for him. Another time Father Walsh himself drove the "Tin Lizzie," and Father Phelan's heart missed several beats.

Before Father Phelan's arrival there was a teacher who later became a legend. He was an excitable genius of indeterminate parts and Latin antecedents, called Doctor Barile. He had an antipathy for Willie O'Shea. "You beast, O'Shea!" he would call out in class.

A tone of respectability was given the place when the Dominicans arrived. Father Hyacinth Foster had made his higher studies in Europe. Father William Owens came to us from Providence. Both were brilliant men and excellent teachers. They taught us Moral Theology, Scripture, and Philosophy. They maintained a high standard all the time.

These two Dominicans were with us for two years until the Master General came on a visit and announced that all the Hawthorne Dominicans, who belonged to the French Province, and were really in exile in the States, would have to decide either to return to France or to join the American Province. Our Dominicans elected to join the American Province. They were sent to Washington, however, and were replaced by Father Charles Callan and Father John Ambrose McHugh.

Fathers Callan and McHugh, who have taught at Maryknoll for

over thirty-five years, were on leave of absence when they first came
to these parts. They had been sick, were recuperating at Graylock
Rest in the Berkshires, and then were sent to Hawthorne to continue
their convalescence. At that time their Superiors thought that they
might not be able to continue active teaching very long. When
Father McHugh died, on Easter Sunday 1950, the *New York Times*
said: "All the Maryknoll priests throughout the world have been
trained by Father McHugh." It is very nearly true.

There was another French Dominican with us before that, Father
Cyril Coudeyrt. He taught us French. He used the "Lettres de Mon
Moulin," by Alphonse Daudet. These stories scandalized Father
Price, with their occasional irreverence and their comical but mildly
anticlerical situations. I am afraid this appealed to our youthful
bumptiousness. I recall one story about the Pope's Mule, another
about the Curé of Cucugnan. Daudet had one about a priest who
rushed through his Three Christmas Masses because he could smell
the turkey cooking in the kitchen of the chateau. The devil, disguised
as a server, urged him on and on, ringing the little bell faster and
faster. He skipped most of the Third Mass, rushed to the dining
hall, stuffed himself, died of apoplexy, and every Christmas since
then has returned to the old haunted chateau to say the Three Masses
of which he had cheated the Lord.

Another of our professors was Father Thomas Gavan Duffy. He
was the son of Sir Charles Gavan Duffy, who as a young man had to
leave Ireland for political reasons, went to Australia, rose rapidly,
and became Prime Minister. Later, he was knighted by Queen Victoria. He retired and with his family, settled at Nice, in France. Sir
Charles lived to be eighty-seven years old.

Father Walsh and Father Price, as I mentioned previously, had met
the son, Thomas Gavan Duffy, on their visit to the Paris Foreign
Mission Seminary in 1911, where he had acted as their guide and
guest master. Later he was ordained and went to India. He came to
us after he had spent some time in India.

His arrival caused a stir at Maryknoll because of his radiant red
beard. Father Walsh remarked: "There was a positive hush at his first
appearance. The beard took on various hues with the changing light
of the day, but the whiskers were always there . . ." His beard gave

him a striking resemblance to the death mask of Francis Thompson. On the train to New York one day, two Hudson River suffragettes were in the seat behind him. "I think it's horrid," one of them was saying. "Someone ought to get him a razor."

Father Gavan Duffy used to make our blood boil with his decidedly British view of things American. He taught us English and said that there wasn't much in the so-called American literature worth bothering about. Edgar Allan Poe had a few good things, not too bad, but as for the rest, oh well. He worshiped the compositions of Father Cyril Martindale who had been his teacher. He was always quoting him. One of the pieces had some lines about Philippides, and we promptly proceeded to murder Philippides in our private gatherings with various parodies on Philippides and Phillipidose and Philippidem.

Whenever the question of American habits came up, Father Gavan Duffy would give us all the camel eye, and make some pitying remark. Perhaps he was only teasing us. He said he was the only Irishman in the Paris Foreign Missions and they had resolved never to take another. He was an excellent teacher of French. While he was with us, he wrote *Yonder,* and returned to India shortly afterwards. He was a tip-top missioner, a genius in education.

Father Alexander, O.P., taught us History of Religions. The first class and each class thereafter began the same way: "Now we will take up de History of Religions-z-z-z." He always lingered on the final "s", with a buzzing sound like a bee trapped in a bottle. He wrote a book of Theology, but it was never published.

When Father Patrick Byrne came to us after his ordination in 1915, he taught us Apologetics. He continued teaching various subjects up to the time he left for Korea. He had made a brilliant course at St. Mary's Seminary, and was released by Cardinal Gibbons to come to Maryknoll. When Father Walsh asked, "What can he teach?" Father Bruneau replied, "Anything."

We had only one classroom at that time, and so we had to use the dining room as well. Later we used the reception room and eventually the priests' recreation room on the second floor.

From the start Father Walsh insisted on the full seminary curriculum. This was hard on the professors. We, too, found the schedule rather full. Daniel McShane and James Edward Walsh took their theology at St. Joseph's Seminary, Dunwoodie, commuting back and forth to Yonkers every day.

Besides the regular seminary studies, we had special features that were to give us a preparation for the missions. Our spiritual reading and our reading in the refectory had a missionary flavor and consisted of the lives of missioners, or letters from missioners then in the field. Every missioner who visited the place was held there by Father Walsh long enough to give us a talk. Father Verbrugge told us about the Philippines and the customs of the Igorots. Father Baumgartner told us about the Dyaks and the Wild Man of Borneo. We usually asked these men what was the most necessary virtue for a missioner. They mentioned several and emphasized one—patience. I never forgot this, though often enough I failed to practice it.

Thirty years later, when we were locked up in Manchuria during the war, we waited day by day for a visit from the Apostolic Delegate. We had a long list of woes to present to him: we were deprived of various liberties, no communications from home, no means of sending word to our families, we didn't have this to eat, we couldn't get that, we were not allowed this, that, and the other thing. Finally, after some months, the Delegate reached us after long delays and entanglements in police and military red tape. I opened up and told him woe after woe, complaint after complaint. He listened to it all and at the end heaved a deep sigh, looked at me and said, "Patience, Monseigneur."

My reaction was not exactly enthusiastic. I had not expected anything quite so elemental. It was simply a little laboratory work in the lesson I started to learn thirty years before in the seminary at Maryknoll. The Delegate, incidentally, failed to practice his own lesson that same day, when he ran up against some annoying Military Police at the railway station.

Public reading in our refectory was an ordeal for us, that is, an ordeal for the one doing the reading. Father Walsh was a stickler for exact English and correct diction. He might stop you to correct a pronunciation ten times at one meal. The result was that we took the book ahead of time and carefully prepared the pages we expected to cover. I looked up all words of questionable pronunciation and wrote them in a little book. I marked primary and secondary accents and the vowel values. I had a book full of these words.

Father Walsh started a crusade to annihilate the New England final "r." His hair stood on end if one of us read: "Our Lord went into Judaea(r)." We soon got the "idea(r)" and watched our step and our "r's". Then, too, he lay in wait to catch us saying "Gawd" for God. Some of us never completely fathomed his phonetics of some vowel combinations. He would ask us to take pity on the prepositions, not to hit them so hard, and he would say, "Of course, he sat *on* the bed; what else could he do? But why don't you say, he sat on the *bed?*" "Why do you have to say, the calf walked along *with* the cow? What would you do if you were a calf? Wouldn't it be better to say, the calf walked with the *cow,* and then we would know that it didn't walk with the man next door, or the fire engine."

In those early days he taught us, or tried to teach us, how to write. Here was one of his chief skills, one that he used well on behalf of the missions. He had a remarkable facility of expression. He abhorred verbiage, all unnecessary adverbs and adjectives. He was a master of precise writing. He had developed his powers of observation and had a way of making his reader see what he saw. All of this was mixed with a nice sense of humor and a keen sense of the incongruous which, I suppose, is the same thing.

Father Walsh used to tell us that when we got to the missions, we should be particularly alert during the first few years to write down whatever caught our interest. He said that once these strange sights and customs became familiar we would no longer be inclined to describe them for others, at least in a language that would hold their attention. That was a wise admonition. Missioners find it hard to discover something interesting to write about, after things that were new and strange in the beginning have become part of their daily life.

He spoke to us about writing letters, what to say, what not to say, when to say it, and how often. A favorite axiom of his was *Scripta Manent* (the written word remains), and he warned us never to write what we would have reason to regret later.

"Don't use big words," he would say. In letters, sermons, and in anything we wrote, he urged us to be simple. "If you use big words, only some of the better educated will understand you. If you are simple and use ordinary words, everyone will understand you."

Father Walsh had an artistic side to him that was genuine, but I think that its expression annoyed some of us who were not similarly inclined. He had a fine sense of the beautiful and a good understanding of literature and of music. All of this, plus his sense of order, gave us many a headache, but it helped to rub off some of the rough corners, rounded us out as much as we could be rounded out, and made something of us that we should not have been without him.

He could not stand seeing anything askew, like a crucifix or picture not perfectly centered or hanging straight. He was an enemy of the school that believed in "studied carelessness," or any kind of carelessness. He liked to refer to Saint John's account of the Resurrection and the appearance of the tomb when the disciples entered and saw "the napkin that had been on His head not lying with the linen cloths, but folded up in a separate place by itself." "Please note," Father Walsh would say to us, "that the napkin was *folded* and in its proper place."

He taught us plain chant. He taught it well. He had a way of making fun of the old school of the clergy and their way of hanging on to certain notes of the Preface, and dragging it out like a dirge. He would tell the story about the two old Irish fathers, both with sons in the seminary, who would meet occasionally and inquire about the progress of each other's son. One would say, "My boy is getting along; he's up to that part of the Mass now where the priest cries." He referred to the singing of the Preface and Pater Noster. Father Walsh warned us against the exaggerations of some of the parish High Masses and the "Amens" of Maggie Murphy, the choir girl, at the end of the Gloria.

He did his best to help his tone-deaf pupils to render the sung parts of the Mass as well as possible. Once he came upon a man who was utterly unable to sing either up or down the scale; everything he sang was on one sustained tone. Father Walsh tried over and over to help him catch the intervals. Finally, he shook his head: "Incredible!" he said, "that's incredible." Then he gave up, which was unusual.

Of all those who taught us in those early days, Father Walsh naturally made the greatest impression. He was with us a great deal in the first years. His influence was constantly felt, especially through his conferences. Father Price's spiritual direction, perhaps had a deeper effect, but Father Walsh's formation was general and seemed to cover every tiny detail.

He used to say, "Think of the man who comes after you." He gave us positions as house officers, sacristan, infirmarian, master of ceremonies, and so on. He would have us make notes constantly on the duties connected with our charge, and, on big events like ordinations or visits of important persons, he would have us check on what was amiss and make a record of it to be on our guard the next time. These notes were to go on cards and into the tickler file which we were supposed to keep up in connection with our office. He said we should also have a file with handy reference for doctors, craftsmen, friends, benefactors, and the like. He stressed the need of a waste basket to be kept at hand and used.

He also taught us the importance of saying, "Thank you!" He reminded us that it was a Christian virtue to be grateful and that we owed it to our parents, friends, and to our benefactors to thank them. He was so faithful himself to this rule that some of his friends used to say, "If you send Maryknoll a dime, they'll use half of it to thank you." If we ever did anything for him, he always thanked us. His thoughtfulness was the best way of teaching us the same. Notes of thanks in his own handwriting would fill a large file.

Father Price, of course, had a very important part in our life all during those years, although he never took over the teaching of any class subject. We had him frequently for spiritual reading. We went to him for spiritual direction, and he was with us here and there about the property during recreation or manual labor or when out on a walk.

For a time my job at manual labor was cutting hair. I used to cut Father Price's hair, and he would tell me jokingly to be careful about the curls in front. He had a few wisps that bridged the gap between the two temples. He would say, "Don't eliminate these last proofs of a once very luxuriant growth." Somehow I felt that, with all his holiness, he had an attachment to these last few strands.

Father Price never wanted his picture taken, but one day while I was cutting his hair a student managed to get an excellent snapshot of him showing his profile. It was one of the best of the few photographs we ever got of him. He was sitting on an upturned box and had a sheet about him as I applied the clipper. He found out about it somehow and he asked me to get the film and bring it to him, which I did—after we had made several copies. This photo was printed later in *The Field Afar*.

The ring which he wore caused a great deal of speculation. One day, Brother Martin, urged on no doubt by the students, asked Father Price just what was the ring and why he wore it. "Can you keep a secret, Brother Martin?" he asked. "Oh yes, certainly, Father," replied Brother feeling that he was about to receive a great revelation. Father Price smiled at him, "So can I, Brother."

In September 1915, we were thirty-five students all told—twelve in theology, seven in philosophy, and sixteen in the Venard college classes. Father Walsh had brought the Venard students back from Scranton in the spring. The lease on the Scranton house was due to run out in May, no suitable property had been found, and besides he did not see the way clear for the added outlay necessary to set up a new institution and provide a faculty. In April, therefore, the Venarders moved to Maryknoll and occupied the renovated carriage shed, vacated by the two horses.

In September, with seminarians returning to class, the space in St. Michael's was needed for the nineteen students in the seminary. The college youngsters had to move out, therefore, and go into the barn. They took over the hayloft; the horses were on the main floor. Each morning until December they rose at the sound of the bell, went over to the buckets at the end of the loft, looked down through the hay chute to bid the Top o' the Mornin' to Caspar and Starlight stamping in the stalls. The cows were mooing in the cellar below.

Impressive little mottoes, and quotations from the Scriptures, began to appear here and there, in the chapel, and on the walls. Father Walsh also kept his own bulletin board on which he posted striking phrases relating to life, work for souls, and various pertinent subjects. The use of the Greek letters Chi and Rho in a monogram encompassed by a circle gradually became our standard. This is found frequently in the catacombs of Rome. The X and the P, equivalent to our "ch" and "r," are the initial letters in the Greek word for Christ. The circle indicated the world, and the complete device expressed our purpose of bringing Our Lord to the people all over the world.

Other favorite quotations were carved into the wood of the altar. Some were illuminated on paper or cloth, framed, and hung on the walls. There was a striking motto attributed to Cardinal Vaughan: "It matters not who does the work, as long as the work be done." Returning in later years, I noticed that this frame was missing. It may have been because the boys in fits of genius had parodied the expression, and their own version may have reached the Superior's ears: "It matters not who does the work, so long as somebody else does it."

In the School of the Founders

*"There is a danger in giving too much
time to the works of God and too
little to the God of works."*
— Father Walsh's Bulletin Board

"Don't worry. Don't worry about anything. Nothing prevents you so much from remembering God's presence as worry: worry about your studies, worry about this and that and the other thing." This was the gist of Father Price's advice, when he saw us tightening up under the burden of studies and household duties.

"When you have many things to do," he would say, "and only a few minutes in which to do them, don't cram and rush: stop a minute. Size up the situation and then go ahead slowly." He returned frequently to this idea.

In 1914, Father Price celebrated his twenty-eight years as a priest. Practically all of this time he had spent in the missions of North Carolina. He was giving us the fruit of his experiences. Few men had worked harder, suffered more, planned and persevered more, had been set back and forced to start over again more times than he. He had acquired a great sense of values. If we only realized it then, and perhaps we did, we would be very wise to listen to him and do as he said. To do so would be wise in the sense that Father Walsh liked to quote: "Nine-tenths of wisdom is being wise in time."

We could see that Father Price and Father Walsh were both hard workers. But both of them insisted over and over again that a work is good only through the power of God. Father Walsh liked the saying of St. Vincent de Paul: "We shall never be fit to do the work of

God if we are not convinced that of ourselves we are better fitted to spoil everything . ." Father Price believed with Saint Thomas that he who walks daily in the presence of God and is always ready to give Him an account of his actions will certainly never be separated from Him by sin.

Father Price's retreats at Belmont and at Junalaska, but especially his long hours alone on the road, and in strange corners of his State, filled him with an accumulation of wise standards. His work among the people, his building days at the orphanage, at Regina Apostolorum, his activities to keep both going and to keep his flock clothed and fed, his crusade with *Truth*—all this gave him great experience in getting things done, and he wanted us to learn by his experience.

He sifted what he had been gathering for over a quarter of a century and he gave us the nuggets. "Live always in the presence of God," he said, "and you will live a good life. If you keep your mind on who you are and where you are and for Whom you are working, everything you do will have merit. If you could just imagine yourself living with some important person, I think you would be pretty careful to treat him right and certainly you would not want to hurt his feelings. Now, this is no matter of imagination: you are with God all the time. Actually, he is right within you. Why not talk to Him, then, talk to Him all the time.

"How little our worries and our difficulties seem when we know that God is right at hand! How terrible sin is, when we realize that He is looking on! How foolish it seems to be vain and puffed up when the Lord and Master of the whole universe is right beside us, He who makes the sun and moon and the stars move in their spheres, He who created the world and everything in the world and from moment to moment keeps us all alive.

"Don't forget it, He is always with you, always looking. Before you do anything, stop for an instant, and say: 'Lord, I'm doing this for you. I'm doing it for Your honor and glory. I'm doing it because I know You would have me do it.' "

Father Price talked slowly with a distinct Southern accent, which he sometimes exaggerated, particularly when telling a story, and this he did very well. His smile was delightful. Often it came slowly, but it was something to see and enjoy. He always followed up his stories with an infectious laugh, which was more of a chuckle than a laugh, soft and quiet like the sound of running water.

He walked rapidly, as a rule, and with a decided stoop. Though he talked of avoiding haste and rush, he himself gave the impression of being in a hurry to get somewhere—to Heaven, no doubt.

His practice of constant prayer sometimes gave him an air of distraction. You might meet him and be scarcely noticed. No one knows how many rosaries he said daily; his beads were always in his hands. I think he imagined that he was not noticed when he rubbed his eyes. This he usually did after rubbing a ring he had on his finger. After his death we found that the ring had a number of dates inscribed, probably days on which he received special favors from Our Lady. The ring was always a matter of mystery to us and provided a great field for speculation.

He had the eyes of a mystic, as indeed he was, dreamy, preoccupied, and searching. When he looked at you, he looked right into you.

With Father Price the teaching and practice of humility went hand in hand. He was our Spiritual Director during those first years. While he covered the whole range of virtues, humility took up most of the time. He never tried to make an impression; quite the contrary. He tried to lower himself in his own eyes and in the eyes of others.

In some people perhaps this self-effacement might lead to some extravagant and artificial attitudes. In him it was different; we knew that his attitude, whatever it was, was genuine. He himself had a story which illustrates this very thing, or its opposite. A gentleman asked for an interview with a certain banker, with the idea of getting a position. The banker asked him to have a seat. The visitor, ignoring the invitation, went on talking and enumerating his qualifications. After some minutes of evident annoyance, the banker said; "Have two seats."

As a speaker Father Price lacked polish. There were no studied gestures and no attempt at oratory. He plunged into his subject, and what he lacked in finesse he more than made up for in earnestness. He was really eloquent. At times when talking to us quietly in the conference room, just before supper, Father Price gave the impression of being distracted, of searching for something, or better still, of carrying on a process of thinking quite independent of the thought he was propounding at the time. Perhaps it was simply recollection in practice. I am inclined to think, however, that he did everything through Mary and that he was trying to catch her spirit and to say what he thought she might say under the circumstances.

There was no nonsense about his private spiritual direction. There was no beating about the bush. For a man who seemed to have plenty of time because he gave so much of it to his spiritual exercises, he would not let you waste a moment of it with vague and rambling thoughts about your spiritual difficulties and hopes. He insisted that you be prepared before going to his room, that you have the points to be discussed written out on paper ahead of time, and that you present them simply and as clearly as possible.

On visits such as these, he would sit low in his chair, his head practically touching the back of it, and then while gazing at you, or into you, or through you, he would give the answers to your questions. For two years I used to go back to my room and write down what he had just told me. These notes made up a wealth of solid, conservative and practical advice, on the usual matters that bother most seminarians and beginners.

He was a great admirer of the works of Rodriguez and recommended his *Practice of Spiritual Perfection* as the soundest and safest of all guides. He was influenced more by Jesuit spirituality, perhaps, than by other schools. He wanted to join the Jesuits, I believe, but was advised to give up the idea because of his age. He recommended other books, too, including Father Faber's writings, but Rodriguez was his stand-by.

He suggested that his clients recite the Little Office of the Immaculate Conception daily. He encouraged several to read Grignon de Montfort's book on *True Devotion to the Blessed Mother,* and sometimes permitted them to make the act of complete consecration.

Of course, Father Price's talks were not merely a repetition of "Do this" and "Don't do that." He had a never-ending supply of stories and experiences from real life, accumulated during his years at the Seminary, at Wilmington, Asheville, New Bern, Newton Grove, and all along the line. He had descriptions of Lourdes and Nevers and Rome. He knew the lives of the saints and he had always the right anecdote to illustrate a point.

Occasionally, he seemed to insist in an exaggerated manner on points of modesty. He told me the reason for this emphasis. He said that the people of the world were becoming more and more lax in this essential Christian virtue, and that it behooved those who were priests or religious to go a bit to the opposite extreme in order to stem the tide of growing remissness. He once visited a benefactress who had been helping him in one of his projects. The good woman appeared in a costume that was too décolleté for Father Price. He asked her to retire and come back with a more modest gown, which she did.

He had a dread of being incapacitated, though he was not unwilling to be ill if that should be God's will. His rheumatism gave him trouble. He felt that the water at Maryknoll was doing him no good. Together, we scoured the neighborhood in quest of softer water. I was the infirmarian at the time. Perhaps I was too much of a "valetudinarian." What we both needed right then was the authoritative statement of a good doctor, and that would have ended all our foolishness. It seems absurd now, when I think of the trouble we made for ourselves trying to get the right drinking water. In the end, the mere inconvenience and work of carrying water from a distance, ended our project and our quest.

Father Price was not slovenly but he had a real antipathy towards bathing, or rather, towards the over-emphasis on bathing which characterizes our modern American civilization. He said that all virile peoples began their downward march when they took to "hot water." Perhaps there is something in what he said. Ancient Rome and Pompeii, as travelers know, had a craze for hot baths. Psychologists may find the reason easily enough. At any rate, Father Price's habit of retiring completely dressed, except for his shoes, and his insistence on cleaning his own room, made it necessary for our clean-up squad to tackle his domain whenever he was absent for a few days.

With all his humility and diffidence, there was one practice that seemed to go contrary to his accustomed tendencies. This was the way he insisted on having the best vestments on feast days of Our

Blessed Mother. On these days he was brighter and happier than usual. From Communion time on, he would seem to take off for another world and spend the day with Mary and Bernadette. To celebrate on one of these days, he even smoked a cigarette.

I feel that Father Price must have been very proud by nature, inclined to temper and impatience, impulsive, and temperamental. He fought all these natural drives until he had complete mastery of himself. Occasional flashes of the old Adam would appear in a retort, just a bit sarcastic but very effective, in those rare instances when some student would forget himself and presume to impose on Father Price's simplicity or forget his authority.

Mystical, in many ways impractical, Father Price had a far greater share in Maryknoll beginnings than most early readers of *The Field Afar* realize. He forbade Father Walsh to mention him in the magazine. This was often embarrassing for Father Walsh, who would get letters inquiring for Father Price, asking if he were alive and where, and wondering why he was never mentioned. Not till he left for China did he relax this rule.

It was precisely during those early formative years that he exerted his greatest influence. In his trips about the country, visiting old friends of seminary days and making new friends, he stimulated many vocations and corralled many a precious dollar for the cause.

Father Walsh spoke to us often of the many graces that must certainly have come to us thanks to the holy life and prayers of Father Price, who had deliberately chosen the role of Bethany's Mary. Both of them understood the necessity of resisting a feverish activity, for this, they knew, is like a strong current sweeping souls down into the stagnant pools of self-esteem, religious tepidity, and eventual loss of interest.

Father Price's life was a warning for us against giving too much attention to activity; it was a mistake for us to think that we could conquer the world by our brilliant sermons and clever works. He would have us reflect that we could render far greater service to the Church and become ourselves far more pleasing to God, if we would only use a good part of this same time on prayer and meditation. Then, we would certainly do more with less labor, more with one work, than with a hundred and one, thanks to the merit of prayer and the spiritual power of a life that we were trying to live in a way pleasing always to God. To act otherwise would be merely beating a drum, doing little good, sometimes absolutely no good, and perhaps even harm.

In some ways, the world might judge Father Price's life a failure. Surely his early ventures in North Carolina were not crowned with success; later in Maryknoll's formation he seems to have taken a minor part. To those that know, this is far from true; even in his failures there was a certain success, not the least of which was the effect of his saintliness on all who knew him.

Father Price's talks to us had the atmosphere of North Carolina, but when Father Walsh told us of missionary ventures, they were usually drawn from the French countryside. He had visited the homes of martyrs in France and he was filled with the life and work of Theophane Venard, Henri Dorie, Just de Bretenières, and others. He compiled a little book on *Thoughts from Modern Martyrs*. We read his life of Theophane Venard. In those days Father Walsh had a devotion to Sister Therese of the Child Jesus. That was before she was declared Venerable, and ten years before she was canonized. He was in correspondence with Père Roulland, the "missionary brother" of St. Therese.

You could not meet Father Walsh, or even see him, without being impressed. Father Price was of medium height, but Father Walsh was just a little below the average. He had a quick, slightly nervous way of acting, and yet he always gave the impression of having things perfectly under control.

His face had three striking features: rather extraordinary, slanting eyebrows, a very prominent nose, and piercing eyes. He was always neat about his person. I shall never forget his hands, they were so expressive. His unconscious gestures gave an idea of the man's character, better than anything else perhaps except his words. As I think back now and recall Father Walsh speaking to us in the conference hall, I am strongly reminded of Willa Cather's reference to the Archbishop's hands, in her book *Death Comes for the Archbishop:* "Father Latour stood lost in thought, drawing the plume of tamarisk blossom absently through his delicate, rather nervous fingers. His hands had a curious authority, but not the calmness so often seen in the hands of priests; they seemed always to be investigating and making firm decisions."

Father Walsh was death on studied gestures. He poked fun at this type of oratory and at any exaggeration. I have good reason to remember this. Shortly after my ordination, in 1920, I was at the convention of the Catholic Students Mission Crusade, at Washington, and it was my duty to give a short introductory speech to a play presented by our students. I thought I had done quite well, but not Father Walsh. He said, "Why didn't you stand in one place? You were marching up and down like a lion in its cage. The people could not follow your words; they were too interested in wondering where you were going and what you were going to do next."

He was no orator, but he was a very effective talker, particularly when he was talking to us, his future missioners. Any man who can talk Sunday after Sunday, year after year, and still be interesting, is surely a clever speaker. Trying to analyze his ability, I feel that his success was due, first of all, to his absolute sincerity, and secondly, to the fact that we were all interested in the subjects he brought up. He put things in an attractive way. His gestures helped, too, because they were natural and logical. When saying something especially important he had a unique way of setting his shoulders. He had a way of squinting, of setting his chin down on his chest, of expressing his thoughts with various motions of his delicate hands and fingers. Of course, like all speakers, he had his good days and his bad, but his Sunday evening conferences seemed always good.

I imagine that he may have borrowed his method from Abbé Hogan, his old superior at St. John's, Brighton. He would first give us some outstanding news of the week, as it affected our work. Then he would mention important people, bishops especially, whom he had met during the week, what they said about the missions and our seminary, and he would say something about his plans for the future. He made us feel that we were being taken into his confidence, that we were really part of the work. Then he would spend five or ten minutes on some spiritual subject.

Almost always these were little homilies based on the day's Gospel or on some incident in the life of Christ. He had a talent for description and he would reconstruct biblical scenes—the Boy Christ in the

Temple, Our Lord at Jacob's Well, Our Lord and His Mother. We got the impression that these little talks were not laboriously planned and prepared, but rather they were the simple overflow of what was always in his own heart and soul.

"We Americans," he would say, "are often spoken of as gauging all things by the standard of money. We live in the land of the dollar. We talk dollars. We think dollars. This estimate of American idealism was so common that even our Catholic confreres in Europe could visualize no other form of mission coöperation from Americans except money, with some emphasis on a few prayers. We resent this estimate of ourselves, and already there is a change of heart towards Catholic Americans, whose representatives have shown themselves worthy of the best apostolic traditions.

"That we are, however, influenced to some degree by the importance which Americans generally place on money, most of us will readily admit, and we will likewise admit a danger to our spiritual development in emphasizing money needs rather than in first seeking the Kingdom of God.

"The Apostolate of Christ was expressed above all by prayer. To Him, while on earth, can be traced few converts, but His hours of prayer have produced results that have changed the face of the earth. First the Kingdom of God—and all things will be added. This earth, in whatever position we are laboring, is an extended Palestine, Christ is still walking over it, speaking through His priests, and now that the fields are ripe, if we turn to Him more frequently than to human aid, we should reap abundantly."

Father Walsh had a happy way of characterizing certain mannerisms which he wished to correct in us. His descriptions were terse and cogent, just a word to summarize some student's idiosyncrasy, but it was the correct word, right to the point. There was one who intrigued him by his resiliency, and sometimes annoyed him. "That man is like a cork in the water," he said, "You push him down here, and he comes up there." And he made an expressive gesture with his hands.

Many of his spiritual maxims he communicated to us through his bulletin board. This was a special board in the corridor, smaller than the usual board for routine notices, and marked "Father Superior's Bulletin." His secretary could be seen changing the little cards on this board, and sometimes pinning up a little hand-written message. These bulletins were saved and later a number of them were printed.

A little card that went up regularly was: "The Society will be what its members make it."

Many of his bulletins were borrowed from the Saints, or from other spiritual writers, like these:

"True service of God is cheerful, generous, and self-forgetful." (Archbishop Ullathorne)

"Learn to love solitude for there alone God speaks to your heart!" (Cardinal Mercier)

"Laugh and grow strong." (St. Ignatius)

"Kindness has converted more sinners than zeal, eloquence or learning." (Father Faber)

"Oh, what a multitude of souls is shut out of heaven and falling into hell through your fault!" (St. Francis Xavier)

"At each moment we ought to think of the happiness towards which we advance every moment." (St. Bernard)

There were other bulletins which we felt he had composed himself, and some of them perhaps in a moment of annoyance when he had suffered because of someone's thoughtlessness or selfishness.

"Big enterprises will fail if details are not watched."

"Leadership must be not only recruited but trained."

"Be generous—but not with the money or time of others."

"What is everybody's business is nobody's business."

"Self-denial consists in:
        doing what you don't like to do;
        not doing what you like to do;
        being gracious under either condition."

"The greatest trouble makers in every organization are usually those with the least brains."

"When everybody runs a place, it runs into the ground."

"The witty man laughs at you; the humorous man laughs with you."

"The Lord is not in noise."

"The real pessimist is the person who has lost interest."

"Kind words are the music of the world."

Trust in God's providence was a favorite theme with Father Walsh. He spoke from experience. Bothersome problems often solved themselves at the eleventh hour. Many times the treasury was just about empty; we were down to the last nickel, it seemed. Then help would come from an unexpected quarter.

"Never make an important decision in a hurry," he would say. "Think it over. Sleep on it at least for one night. Don't give a decision in something really critical, until you have had a chance to talk it over with Our Lord in Communion at Mass."

" 'Seek first the Kingdom of God,' " was his favorite maxim. "Let this be our motto. And 'to those who love God all things work together unto good;' let this be our consolation."

Father Walsh quoted a friend once who said to him: "Luxury and independence of spirit are too strong in the American youth to produce ideal apostles." Father Walsh said that he did not believe the man; he doubted whether the man believed this himself when he said it.

"We are mindful of the fact that independence of spirit is characteristic of the American youth," he explained, "but if these two influences can be counteracted by grace—and every Catholic knows that this is an everyday experience—we have reason to believe that the successful struggle will produce better apostles than if no struggle were necessary."

Father Price and Father Walsh made this clear: all our preaching and praying, our writing, lecturing, studying, tramping, and suffering—all would be just so much sounding brass and fruitless effort if we didn't begin with the idea of always trying to please God perfectly in everything we did and said and thought.

In his visits to the homes of martyrs in the French countryside, Father Walsh had most likely visualized the homes of American missioners in New England, New York, and the other states, and that is why he said one day:

"To many it is a new thought that ours is an age of saints and martyrs. The reader of current news may note everywhere the spirit of evil and the huge towers of commerce that dwarf the spires of our churches, proclaiming the people's greed of gold.

"Yet in the throngs that daily walk the busy streets in every center, large and small, the good touch elbows with the bad, and lovers of God are found where children of darkness are thought to be.

"On the missions, the martyrs of our day have brought to the Church of Christ visible blessings in which, consciously, we have all shared, and for which grateful acknowledgment is due.

"The future accomplishments of your work on the missions demand that you undergo a martyrdom—if not a physical one, at least a living one. Your work for souls will not be completely fruitful unless you develop within your heart the same sentiments that enabled the martyrs to endure all for Christ.

"I am always deeply moved when I read the letter which I received from a member of the Paris Foreign Mission Society. This holy missioner had labored long and hard in a sterile field, a section in which martyrdom was practically unknown. This is his letter:

" 'It is sixteen years since I left the seminary, with the fervor of a youth and a strong desire to give my life for Christ, and, if necessary, to shed my blood for Him. These sixteen years have passed in hard work, with very poor results. I have accomplished little, and have come to the conclusion that nothing can be done in this district until some man's blood has been spilled for Christ. And I tell you in all sincerity, as friend to friend, coldly, far from the fervor of young apostles, that, if tomorrow I were called upon to meet death for Christ and for souls, I should be the happiest of men!' "

"Pray that you may be a martyr," Father Walsh said to us, "and pray that no one may know of it!"

12

The Byways of Westchester

"Then came waddling the sturdy chivalry of the Hudson. There were the Van Wycks, and the Van Dycks, and the Ten Eycks; the Van Nesses, the Van Tassels, the Van Grolls; the Van Warts, the Van Winkles, the Van Dams . . . the Ryckmans, the Dyckmans, the Hogebooms, the Rosebooms, the Oothouts, the Quackenbosses . . . all brimful of wrath and cabbage. . . ."

— Washington Irving's *Knickerbocker*

The Albany Post Road lies between Maryknoll and the Hudson River. It is the land route to Croton Point where we went swimming. You could also go by rowboat, pushing out across the Tappan Zee from Ossining. It was four miles by land, and two if you went by the Zee. Just across the Croton River on the Post Road was the old Manor House of the Van Cortlandts.

Stephanus Van Cortlandt built the Manor House in 1681. It was a sort of fort for himself and his family, where they would be safe from the Indians. The Kitchewan Indians roamed the woods in those days. After them came the Dutch, and all this section up and down the Hudson and into Connecticut was the New Netherlands. Stephanus Van Cortlandt had acquired practically all the land of what is now northern Westchester, between Connecticut and the Hudson River and as far north as Putnam County.

We went camping at Croton Beach, which in those days was hardly known to the public. There was a little beach at the end of the Point, which later we had all to ourselves. It was close by a sand bar where the water would boil and churn whenever the tide came in, rolling on its way up the river. The Indians used to call this place Senasqua, while during the days of the New Netherlands it was called Teller's Point. Sometimes we would take a tent along and camp at the beach for a few days. Father Walsh said we should get used to that sort of life.

During the school year we had all-day hikes. At the prearranged place and time the Tin Lizzie would arrive with a pot of beans, coffee, rolls and doughnuts. Thus many spots in our neighborhood obtained a connection with the early days of Maryknoll.

Westchester is full of history. When André and Arnold failed in their plot against West Point, the British warship, *Vulture,* was anchored in the Hudson just above Croton Point. The Croton patriots dragged a four-pounder all the way from Verplanck to Croton and then out to the tip of the Point and blazed away at the *Vulture.* The boat sailed down the river, leaving Major André high and dry at Joshua Smith's treason house near Haverstraw. You can see Haverstraw right across the Tappan Zee from Maryknoll, along with Snedekers Landing and Doodletown. A few miles down the Post Road, at Tarrytown, there is a monument where the local boys apprehended Major André on his long walk back to the British lines.

Names that we met nearly every day revived for us the stories of the past. Spuyten Duyvil, Nepperhan, Beverwyck, Rensselaerwyck, and Stuyvesant began to mean more to us.

One day a visitor arrived from across the Atlantic. Along through Westchester on his way to Maryknoll, he had taken note of the signs by the roadside. He turned to Father Walsh, and asked, "Oh, I say, Father Walsh" (I think he pronounced it "Welch"). "I say, Father Walsh, tell me, what are Yonkers?" Father Walsh explained that Yonkers *are* not, but *is* a city. No doubt, he went on and gave the story about young Van der Donck who wished to become a landed patroon and bought from the Weckquaesgeck Indian tribe a tract of land north of Spuyten Duyvil. The people called him the "Jonkheer," that is, "the young lord." De Jonkheer's Landt evolved into the present Yonkers.

Washington Irving's stories meant more to us than ever before. We read about the people of Pavonia migrating from Communipaw to the island of Manna-hata, and how Oloffe, the Dreamer, proved himself a great land-speculator. We followed the direful feud between the rival bosses, Ten Breeches and Tough Breeches. We knew all about Wouter Van Twiller and William the Testy, the Pipe Plot, and the great Oyster War.

Sing Sing was the old name for Ossining, and we couldn't help wondering whether our hilltop figured in one of the battles described by Washington Irving. "On a rising knoll were gathered the valiant men of Sing Sing," he says, "assisting marvelously in the fight. But as to the Gardeniers of Hudson, they were absent on a marauding party, laying waste the neighboring water-melon patches."

Our founding fathers are colorfully described in Irving's account of the interview between Peter the Headstrong and General Van Poffenburgh. "First of all came the Van Brummels, who inhabit the pleasant borders of the Bronx: these were short fat men, wearing exceeding large trunk-breeches, and were renowned for feats of the trencher. They were the first inventors of suppawn, or mush and milk. Close in their rear marched the Van Vlotens of Kaatskill, horrible quaffers of new cider, and arrant braggarts in their liquor.

"After them came the Van Pelts of Groodt Esopus, dexterous horsemen, mounted upon goodly switch-tailed steeds of the Esopus breed. These were mighty hunters of mink and muskrats, whence came the word "Peltry." Then the Van Nests of Kinderhoeck, valiant robbers of bird's-nests, as their name denotes. To these, if report may be believed, are we indebted for the invention of slap-jacks, or buck-wheat cakes.

"Then the Van Higginbottoms, of Wapping's Creek. These came armed with ferrules and birchen rods, being a race of schoolmasters, who first discovered the marvelous sympathy between the seat of honor and the seat of intellect,—and that the shortest way to get knowledge into the head was to hammer it into the bottom. Then the Van Grolls, of Anthony's Nose, who carried their liquor in fair round little bottles, by reason they could not bouse it out of their canteens, having such rare long noses.

"Then came the Gardeniers of Hudson, and thereabouts, distinguished by many triumphant feats, such as robbing water-melon patches, smoking rabbits out of their holes, and the like, and by being great lovers of roasted pigs' tails. Then the Van Hoesens of Sing

Sing, great choristers and players upon the jewsharp. These marched two and two, singing the great song of St. Nicholas. Then the Couenhovens, of Sleepy Hollow. These gave birth to a jolly race of publicans, who first discovered the magic artifice of conjuring a quart of wine into a pint bottle.

"Then the Van Kortlandts, who lived on the wild banks of the Croton, and were great killers of wild ducks, being much spoken of for their skill in shooting with the long bow. Then the Van Bunschotens, of Nyack and Kakiat, who were the first that ever did kick with the left foot. They were gallant bushwhackers and hunters of raccoons by moonlight. Then the Van Winkles of Haerlem, potent suckers of eggs, and noted for running of horses, and running up of scores at taverns. They were the first that ever winked with both eyes at once.

"Lastly came the Knickerbockers, of the great town of Scaghtikoke, where the folk lay stones upon the houses in windy weather, lest they should be blown away. These derive their name, as some say, from Knicker, to shake, and Beker, a goblet, indicating thereby that they were sturdy toss-pots of yore; but, in truth, it was derived from Knicker, to nod, and Boeken, books: plainly meaning that they were great nodders or dozers over books. From them did descend the writer of this history. Such was the legion of sturdy bush-beaters that poured in at the grand gate of New Amsterdam."

Westchester has many links with the British period and the days of the Revolution. After the battle of White Plains, the Yankee troops were so elated and heated with liquor that they set fire to their own village buildings, including the town Court-house. The British tried to say this was by order of Washington himself, who had some barns and outhouses burned before moving to Northcastle.

Washington and his men were all through this area in those days. After the battle of White Plains, the British had Washington and his generals guessing. They seemed to be planning to move up the river. Washington ordered his forces to commanding positions along the possible route. He himself got ready to go to Peekskill and on to the highlands. There is a letter from himself to General Lee: "I think all your baggage and stores, except such as are necessary for immediate use, ought to be to the northward of the Croton River.

You will consider the post at Pine's Bridge as under your immediate care. . . ."

Maryknoll is on Pine's Bridge Road. A section of the old road runs through the end of the farm. Local legend has it that Washington stayed at the old farm house that later became our St. Teresa's Lodge. No document exists to prove the report. The house was probably standing at the time, and was one of the very few along Pine's Bridge Road.

Pine's Bridge is a short afternoon walk from Maryknoll. We needed an all-day hike to visit White Plains, the Kensico Reservoir, and the Valhalla Dam, and it usually meant an all-day outing to visit the new Croton Dam. This was built about 1900 by New York City, to conserve the waters in the chain of Croton Lakes as part of the city's supply system. Croton folk say that it is the second largest hand-hewn masonry job in the world, surpassed only by the Great Pyramids of Egypt.

While the dam was being built, the city's engineers invited artisans from Italy. Some of them returned to Italy later with their earnings, but many of them settled in the attractive little vales of Glendale, Croton and Ossining. So today, their children and grandchildren, the Giulianos and the Giordanos, the Agostinis, the Martinis, the Riscuccis, the Malluccis, and the Petruccis, are numerous among our neighbors, all worthy successors to the Roerbacks, the Garrebrantzes, the Vander Hoofs, the Vander Voorts, and the Vander Spiegles.

Father Walsh usually let us go camping for a full week just before classes started in September. This was to prepare us for mission trips in the East. Croton Beach was our favorite camping grounds, but we also went to Rye Beach. That was years before the development of Playland, but at approximately the same spot on Long Island Sound.

On one of our trips to Croton Point, I was in swimming with Jimmy Walsh and Brother Fred Maguire. Both were strong swimmers; I was not. I tried to keep up with them. A cramp in my leg soon put me out of commission. I called to them. Very calmly they told me to place a hand on the shoulder of each, which I did, and then, slowly and steadily, they ferried me back to safety. I have been pulled out of the water three times in similar situations that could have been fatal.

On the same camping trip I used a bit of the first-aid technique I had picked up while working in a drug store in Lawrence. Daniel McShane had a very bad earache one night at the camp. We had no medicines with us. I built a fire, heated some sand from the beach, poured it into a sock and had him rest his ear on this hot pillow. In no time he was alseep. My stock went up, and to the pioneers of those days I became "Doc."

Sometimes our expeditions took us farther afield. It was a long day's walk to West Point, one way, and this was attempted only occasionally. Two of our group made a journey into New England. Father Walsh wrote about it to his friends; "Those of our readers who live anywhere along the high road between this blessed Knoll and Boston, or from there to the wilds of Maine, may expect sometime this coming summer, to be visited by two of Maryknoll's aspirants—or to be passed by with nary a nod if the Chi Rho sign is not high on the door post.

"One of these lads, tall and lean as a German periscope, hails from Connecticut and will pay an afternoon call upon his family the third or fourth day out from Ossining. He will be seen afar off as he looms up on the horizon; but no fatted calf will long detain him under the parental roof. The other aspirant is of 'low visibility,' but can be detected at close range, standing 5 ft. 3 when not too much down at the heels, as he is likely to be before making *his* afternoon call upon relatives in Maine.

"The two will walk. The plan is to leave Maryknoll with neither 'scrip nor purse,' to sleep under haystacks when other hospitality is lacking, and in general to trust to an all-seeing Providence as the good Maryknoller habitually does.

"Will any readers who meet these travelers on their journey report latitude, longitude, and other observations to Headquarters-on-the-Hudson, for the edification of our more conventional and less venturesome souls?"

Our neighbors to the south were the Ryders. We acquired part of their farm, and the present seminary stands on the site that we used to gaze at wistfully from our fence close to Rosary House. Relations were good, though it took a barrel of diplomacy at times.

An enterprising lady in New York City had the bright idea of promoting dollar-a-trip bus excursions from the city. No questions were asked, no references demanded; her conditions were simple: one dollar. Naturally, these excursions brought sight-seers from some of the dubious strata of New York's united nations.

After satisfying themselves that milk did not originate in bottles and after laying waste our own orchards, the excursionists would descend upon the neighbors. One day we were in a terrible fix. Some big boys had gone to the neighbor's orchard. They were told to get out, and refused. The farmer's son came out with a gun. They took it away from him and even took his coat. Somehow word got to Mr. Cranston, the mobile officer for the preservation of peace, former pilot of the Toonerville Trolley.

When one of our priests reached the scene of battle, things were in a bad way. "Gee, Father!" said the innocent from the City. "He pulled a gun on us! Think o' that! He pulled a gun on us." Things were settled amicably by a board of arbitration, but we soon had to call a halt to these invasions from the Big Town.

Naturally, we were looked upon with some suspicion during those first years. We were Catholics in a predominantly non-Catholic neighborhood. Copies of the yellow *Menace* circulated around us. The original property had been bought through a real estate dealer in Briarcliff, and the purchaser was "a rich young lady from Massachusetts, named Mary Rogers." The chauffeur on that famous afternoon was a man named James Anthony Walsh who had lived in Boston for some years previous; at that time, he was staying at Hawthorne. This bit of a ruse was necessary at that time.

Mr. Thompkins owned the farm across the road. He had a stentorian voice that filled the neighborhood, and on a sultry spring or summer afternoon could be heard across the road addressing his horses with the most endearing epithets which caused Father Walsh to cough and color slightly and start talking unusually loud if there were visitors about, or Teresians, or even students. We helped to save his house and barn from fire one day. We became great friends. Father Price had a little Lourdes grotto in the Thompkins woods.

That's where he spent hours on his free days. One day he had to leave in a hurry, when the bull got loose and approached the domain of the grotto. The farmer told us afterwards that he wished Father Price would blow out his candles before leaving. He didn't want any more fires around his barns.

That property has now become the site of the Sisters' Motherhouse, and the old farmhouse high on the hill is the Regina Coeli Cloister where Maryknoll Sisters of the contemplative branch pray day and night for missioners all over the world, a language surely in sharp contrast with the farmer's philippics over his plough.

We tramped all over the countryside on our Wednesday afternoon. We were allowed to smoke one day a week—Wednesday afternoon. Some of the boys had three pipes ready and loaded, one in each pocket and one in the mouth. Because we were without too much spending money, we had to purchase our tobacco with caution, and the usual brand preferred by several was "Sailor John." You got a tremendous package, it looked like a half-pound, all for five cents.

In the course of this one afternoon we would smoke like the Van Blarcoms, the Schermerhorns, and the Stoutenburghs. The result was that at Night Prayers you might see two or three of the crowd turn a pale green and slip out of the chapel, hoping to be unnoticed. One Wednesday evening we had a visitor, a prospective student. He raised his eyebrows when he saw two students, one after the other, turn a sort of sickly gray in the face and, sweating at the forehead, hurry out of Chapel. A few minutes later when he saw some students rise and carry out another, chalk white with his eyes closed, while no one else seemed to pay attention or remark anything strange, he asked himself, what in the world sort of place is this?

During the course of our walks we talked constantly, or I should say, argued. There was no limit to what we knew, or thought we knew, or at least to what we had a right to argue about. One discussion which I recall in particular, and which went on for days after the walk ended, was on whether language or music is the best medium for interpreting a man's feelings.

Sleepy Hollow Cemetery was an easy afternoon's walk from the seminary. This place, famed in history and legend, had a special charm for us. The epitaphs on the tombstones tell stories of life in times gone by and recreate scenes of days now long past. The Old Dutch church, said to have been put up in the seventeenth century, recalls the Coüenhovens and their jolly race. We connected the place chiefly with Washington Iriving's Ichabod Crane.

We associate those days too with many kind deeds done by our friends in the Village of Ossining. The Kirbys and the Doyles, the Cashins and the Walshes and the Quinns, Reverend Doctor Mahoney and Father Collins, Mr. James Sands at Sing Sing, and many others too numerous to list were good neighbors and friends when we needed friends.

Yarns about what we did and what happened during our ramblings around Westchester would fill a separate volume. One day two of our students were crossing the Hudson in a canoe when a sudden squall upset their craft. They were clinging to the capsized canoe for some hours before they were spotted by a passing day liner, hauled aboard and carried on to Yonkers, where they were put ashore. From there they took the less romantic but safer land route back to Maryknoll.

Another day, a group of the boys had rowed from Ossining to the tip of Croton Point for an afternoon's swim. A thunderstorm broke on them there. They hauled the boat up on the beach, turned it over and put their clothes underneath to keep them safe from the rain. After the storm was over, they dressed and rowed happily back over the two-mile stretch in the cool clear air. The waves were still choppy, but they rode them safely and dryly.

A lad from the village with a high-powered sea sled spotted our boys on their return, and thought he would do a favor by towing them to port. He threw them a chain. They were delighted with the idea of relaxing with a free ride home. But it was a mistake. Rowing along, they had mounted each wave as it came, but the speed of the sea sled allowed no time for riding the waves; they were pulled right through them and were completely drenched by the time they reached the landing stage at the village.

By way of consoling themselves, they stopped at the Greek restaurant for an ice cream soda. When they got up to continue the climb up the hill, they noticed that their soaked trousers had changed the varnish on the chairs to a milky white.

Among the various jalopies that figured in the history of the early years was a Buick touring car. It had seen better days. A series of loose bearings produced a deep throbbing engine noise, like the rocks sliding in the old steam rollers. There were no brakes; you had to keep it in a safe low speed and shift to reverse when you approached too close to danger.

It wasn't safe to wander too far afield with this engine of destruction, but one day the aspirant drivers took it as far as Bear Mountain Bridge. No scenic railway, nothing in all Coney Island, could produce the thrills that came with riding this relic over the torturous curves of the Storm King Highway, up the side of cliffs, and round projecting noses of the mountain.

In those days there were two toll houses, one just above Camp Smith as you approached from Peekskill and another at the entrance to the bridge on the Bear Mountain side. You paid as you entered and left free. The toll was seventy-five cents. To save seventy-five cents, our driver decided to turn around on the bridge and go back. As soon as he made known his intention and pulled to one side to put it into effect, all the car doors opened and his passengers abandoned him in one leap. After all, a car without brakes, cutting figures on a bridge hundreds of feet above the wet waters of the Hudson, has few attractions for a life-loving youth. We used to say that we had more and better proofs for the existence of Guardian Angels than were given by those who wrote the theology books.

Sports figured in our days of recreation too. We had baseball, basketball, hockey, and "Gentlemen's Football." Once the hockey players from New England banded together to play students from other parts of the country. It was "New England versus the World."

In "Gentlemen's Football" we had enough students for two teams, and we called ourselves "Holy Cross" and "Boston College." This "Gentlemen's" league continued until one day the two captains met in a head-on collision. One of them lost two teeth, and that was the end of our modified football.

13

The Written Word

"A short time ago, say three years ago,
A modern apostle, quite feeble,
   Went home for a rest
   And by urgent request
Gave a glowing account of his people.

For myself, though I joy in my calling
When the time to make ends meet is falling,
   I take up my pen,
   Then hide it again,
For 'appealing' is awfully galling."

— Peter Rogan

The strains of a familiar air were coming through the open windows in the basement of our new stone building near St. Teresa's Lodge on Pines Bridge Road. Passers-by, descended from ancestors who kept the watch on the Rhine, would say that the melody was "O Tannenbaum." Our student from Cumberland said it was "Maryland, My Maryland." But the not over tuneful chorus in the basement was singing words that sounded like "Maryknoll, My Maryknoll."

We were getting out *The Field Afar,* wrapping the copies, bundling them into packs according to their approximate destination around the country, and dropping them into mail sacks. Father James Kelly was there, sleeves rolled up, face flushed, wrapping and singing, and contributing his bit to the general din. He was pastor of Hough's Neck, Massachusetts. He called it Horse's Neck. He was always welcome, and his biggest benefaction was his simple presence, which helped Father James Anthony to relax.

Getting out *The Field Afar* was a major event each month. We all had a feeling that it was our bread and butter. Father Walsh, of course, did most of the writing. He was assisted by the Teresians who took care of various routine but important details. Later some of the priests and students added their contributions. His long list of friends at home and abroad sent interesting letters. This all helped to fill the pages. It took much hard work.

Then came the day each month which Father Walsh set aside for paging the magazine. This was like the day at home which Dad set aside for his weekly shave. All had to be quiet, and the chief actor was as wrapped up and intent as a prima donna. When the work was done and the copy was off to the publishers, there was a sigh of relief all around.

The magazine, when it was printed, came back in bundles from the printer. Then we all pitched in to get it wrapped and out in the mails as soon as possible. These manual labor sessions were like old fashioned quilting parties. Later on, when the Sisters took over all the mailing, they said the rosary at their work, or listened to the reading of a pious book, and most likely got the work done more quickly and more correctly. For us it was an occasion to cultivate the social virtues.

Our repertoire of songs included most of those popular in the Gay Nineties, especially "Ta-ra-ra Boom-de-ray." When Willie O'Shea made his appearance, we had an appropriate "Strike up the Band! Here Comes the Sailor!" He was famous for his stories about the Brooklyn Navy Yard. He had owned a little boat of his own, the "May Queen," with which he had voyaged up and down the Hudson from Hoboken to Anthony's Nose and on to the unexplored North. George Cohan's songs, like "Mary, It's a Grand Old Name," were favorites, too, and we whistled or hummed tunes from Gilbert and Sullivan when we didn't know the words. Later on, we added "Over There," and "Keep the Home Fires Burning."

We often drifted back to "Maryknoll, My Maryknoll," especially when Father Kelly was there, because here he was sure of the words. The original two verses were written by one of the students the year before I arrived. A few years later, however, a lad in the West, hoping to come to Maryknoll, knowing nothing of our song, had picked the same melody of "Maryland, My Maryland," and adapted to it almost a dozen verses of his own which he sent to Father Walsh. His opus ends up like this:

> *"Live bravely on, play well thy role,*
> *Maryknoll, my Maryknoll!*
> *Help earth subdue with cross and stole,*
> *Maryknoll, my Maryknoll!*
> *Guard well thy trust, press toward the goal,*
> *God must be loved by every soul;*
> *His praise must ring from pole to pole.*
> *Maryknoll, my Maryknoll!"*

Father Walsh had perfected his system of gathering material, assorting it, editing it for publication, and so on. He was assisted by the Sisters, particularly by Sister Xavier, Sister Patrick, Sister St. John, the second Sister Xavier, and later by Sister Just. They all had a sense of what was required. Without their help, he could hardly have had the magazine out on time each month.

He tried to make it as interesting as possible. He used the best photos he could get, and followed the principle of the broken page, avoiding solid masses of printed matter. His work was a model of precise writing. He cut all unnecessary verbiage. He tried to make writers out of us, too. Our contributions would come back to us covered with his blue pencilings. At times his corrections would exceed the original text.

As the magazine grew, it passed through the hands of various printers. At first the Washington Press in Boston ran it off. Later the Paulist Press in New York printed it. Afterwards it was handled by Peter Carey and Sons. All the printers took an interest in it and tried to make it attractive. *The Field Afar* was Maryknoll's bread-winner, the source of practically all our material support.

Father Walsh introduced a number of his own expressions. He tried to popularize "stringless gifts." This meant that friends would leave their offerings free, not designated, and hence available for routine needs. People like to give a chalice, an altar, or a sanctuary lamp. This is good, of course; but boys also need potatoes and spinach, and they need brick and mortar for their buildings and coal or oil for the furnaces. Father Walsh introduced "brick cards" and "land slips," and he created "Dinny Dun," the little lad who went to friends through the mail to remind them that payment was due. All this took planning and lots of hard thinking.

Father Walsh always carried a little pad and a pencil. He wrote at almost any time and any place. He wrote while traveling and while waiting for a train; he jotted down notes at meals.

After World War I, Bishop Dunn of New York secured for him at bargain rates a carload of note paper used in the K. of C. wartime canteens. We used this paper in class, for our exams, for our notes, and for our letters home. We are still using it, but now in reduced quantities. Many of Father James Anthony's notes were written on this K. of C. paper. When on a trip, he would send back sheaves of these papers, all filled with his handwriting. This was material to be filed away and kept in reserve for coming issues of *The Field Afar*. Father James Anthony always did most of the writing, in those first years practically all of it, with the exception of letters from the missions.

In January 1917, the magazine was ten years old. "We are as proud as a ten-year-old boy," he wrote, "and about as big.

"The humor, (call it a light strain, if you prefer) that has occasionally appeared in our paper was not infrequently a forced remedy for some trouble from within or for an attack from without—real trouble at times, and oftener, perhaps, as is the case with most troubles, imaginary. It had a good effect on its producers, and it did not harm its victims.

"So far as we can observe, the New Year will not bring to Maryknoll a new building, but it will witness the organization of St. Joseph's Workshop. St. Joseph will not mind if we attach his name to what was only a barn. Meaner than this, our first barn, was the Cave of Bethlehem, and the carpenter's bench at Nazareth was perhaps not so well protected as is the building henceforth dedicated to the lowly laborer whose place in Heaven is next to its Queen.

"St. Joseph's workshop already has a fairly good supply of much, if not all, that an ordinary carpenter, mechanic, or electrician would need in order to take away from a poor landlord his month's gathering of rent. Never again will a plumber's bill unfold itself over the breadth of our treasurer's desk. Never again will "Elizabeth" (The Tin Lizzie) be asked to make an up and down trip to the village machine-shop for the sake of replacing a broken screw. Never again will an electrician and his hinderer be summoned at an uncanny hour to repair the pump in the woods at double the usual rate of wage. Never again—at least, we hope so.

" 'But,' you ask, 'have you mechanics?' Another foolish question! *Mechanics?* We sometimes wonder if there is anyone at Maryknoll, except the superior and the Teresians, who is not a mechanic, at least in his own estimation. Whenever an accident occurs, we have a series of diagnoses that would be infallible if they did not all disagree.

"It is a most reassuring experience to stand before a broken pump or a disorganized 'tin can' and to learn how simply the thing can be set to rights when certain portions are uncovered and the defect is revealed. And then when the trouble is located elsewhere, it is delightful to note how little affected are our cock-sure mechanics. Do they make excuses? Not at all. They have all the reticence of a brakeman on a train that is hung up between stations.

"More seriously speaking, however, we believe that our mechanics are no worse than those who criticize them and, besides, they charge nothing either for the time they waste or for the repairs they fail to make. But then, even at Maryknoll there are mechanics and mechanics, and after a while the job is done. In the meantime, something new has been learned by several of our future missioners, all of whom expect one day to be tinkers in their own establishments in a distant land."

This item about the workshop at Maryknoll is characteristic of the way Father Walsh kept his friends informed of doings here. Some of them said that when the mailman brought them the magazine, they turned to this page first.

He used to say that he would much rather have twenty thousand new subscribers secured by readers of the magazine than one hundred thousand subscribers brought in by the persuasive eloquence of professional canvassers. He inserted a note, entitled: "Compliments, squinting and straight: '*The* Field Afar *is dear.*' A Reader. —'*The* Field Afar *is a dear.*' Another Reader."

Father Walsh's classmates came to Maryknoll in 1917, to celebrate their Silver Jubilee of ordination. Some of them had died during the twenty-five years, but on that occasion eight of them got together at the home of Bishop Anderson in Boston and then made a pilgrimage to Maryknoll. Monsignor Thomas Duggan, of Hartford, Father Patrick McGivney, of Bridgeport, Father Stanton, of Stoughton, Mass., were there with Bishop Anderson and Father Walsh. Father J. A. Degan, of Beverly, Mass., Father Butler of East Cambridge, and Father F. X. Dolan, of Milton, also came.

Father Walsh wrote about this in *The Field Afar*. He told about the Mass and morning celebrations, and then went on: "Later in the morning the 'flivver' was dancing attendance again, accompanied by a more pretentious car, the property of a local undertaker whose identity was concealed until all danger was passed. These two vehicles conveyed the class—or what was left of it after a quarter-century —through beautiful Westchester County, over to Hawthorne, the cradle of Maryknoll, out under the hills that John D. calls his own, across the Briarcliff Manor grounds, to—must we confess it?—Sing Sing, where one of the class was being detained—by Father Cashin.

"On the way back to Maryknoll several interesting equipages were met, but none was more keenly noted than our 'Liz' the dear old mud-spotted truck, loaded to her neck with bags full of '*Field Afars*' destined for the suffering public of New York and around the orb of the earth."

Many of Father Walsh's followers were attracted to him by the sincere and very pleasant way he had of extending an invitation. Before he had any students at all, he wrote about "A Possible Vocation." He had been going through the schools talking about the missions.

"He was only a midget, twelve years of age, only nine in height," Father Walsh wrote, "but not afflicted with bashfulness. When the speaker referred to the need of English-speaking missioners in China and in a somewhat humorous vein called for volunteers, Master Midget evidently said to himself with more or less respect for his secular instructors,—'That's me!' The talk had been illustrated with slides.

"The following evening he called at the Cathedral residence and requested an interview with 'the priest that talked with the pictures.' Another boy, almost twice his size, a silent admirer, was with him. The twelve-year-old unhesitatingly stated the purpose of his visit. 'I heard yer yesterday at Sunday School and came to tell yer that I want to go away.' This was sudden, but after inquiry the following facts were learned:

"The family was poor, but the mother was willing to let the aspirant go to the ends of the earth. 'Me Mudder said I'd have to leave school when I was fourteen and go to work, but she'd let me go to China then if yer say so.'

"We commended the boy's fervor and good intentions, invited him to call at the office some Saturday morning, told him to say his prayers every day that he might know what to do later, and started him on his homeward journey. Then he spoke up again: 'But y'ain't sed nothin' to the other feller and he wants to go, too.' The 'other feller' was not brilliant in the replies which he made, but both went off quite elated. The future will tell the result."

Sometimes he would slip something like this into the pages. He had a drawing of a wee lad sitting on a pile of rocks and underneath were these lines:

"Seated atop a pile of stones
    And deep in thought was Billy Jones.
I wonder what—I wonder what—
    I wonder what I'll be?
A Fireman or a Soldier or
    a Sailor on the Sea—
An Engineer, a Trombone Man,
    Or how about a Cop?
Oh my! Oh me! It's something fierce;
    I'll have a talk with Pop.
And still I'd like to be a Priest,
    A Missioner, I mean;
But, gosh, I'm just a little kid,
    In fact, not quite thirteen.
It seems to me that Sister said
    The Venard College is the place

> *Where kids like me can study hard*
>   *And grow in missionary grace.*
> *Hurrah for me! Hi-Diddle-Dee!*
>   *I'd like to shout and cheer!*
> *I'll write today; Hurrah, I say!*
>   *That's where I'll be next year.*
> The problem is solved for Billy Jones
> Smiling atop a pile of stones."

His friends kept writing to show their interest in everyone at Maryknoll and everything, including the animals, and so he wrote this: "Did we tell you about 'Perky?' He *was* a pet rooster, but we don't know what he's doing now. A sprained ankle or some other trouble crippled him when he was young, and one of the Teresians, finding no other outlet for sympathy, bestowed much care on this particular bird.

"When our chicken house was moved, 'Perky' followed it. Then shortly after its establishment, a small coop was set up, in which edible roosters (otherwise useless) could be fattened for the Sunday table. Our students, who have been teaching at Sing Sing, referred to this annex as the 'Death Cell.'

"Imagine the horror of the Teresians, when on their first visit to the new quarters of 'Perk, the Proud,' they found their darling awaiting his doom. Since then the blow has fallen, and now 'Perky's' game leg, which is all that is left of him, is buried under the horse-chestnut tree in St. Teresa's garden.

"Our students have asked for a few old cassocks. As they are not accustomed to loose habits, this appeal will affect diocesan priests, rather than members of religious orders. We hope the latter will take no offense . . .

"One of our priests had been away from Maryknoll overnight, staying in a certain monastic establishment. He remarked, when he returned, that he had slept but little the previous night, because a mouse had actually pushed open his eyes.

"This brought forth from our latest arrival, a Dutch missioner with a huge beard just back from years of labor among the wild men of Borneo, the statement that not infrequently in that country a sound sleeper wakes in the morning to find all the hard skin removed from the soles of his feet by night-workers of the rodent family, all chiropodists."

Here is another of his poetical injections:

The Pigs

Ten little Jersey Reds getting nice and prime,
  Along comes Brother Hennery, and now they number nine;
Nine little squealers—My! But they feel great,
  Till Cook wants eggs and bacon, and now they're down to eight.
Eight little piglets think Maryknoll is heaven,
  But cherubs do have appetites—good master, we are seven.
Seven little ruddy-backs, full of pranks and tricks,
  Nosed too near the butcher's knife, and now they are just six.
Six little grunters, so glad to be alive—
  "Chops for the Fathers' table! So sorry,"—only five!
Five little snooters, fed on apple-core,
  Just the thing for Sunday, but this left only four.
Four little porkers, happy, fat and free—
  Kitchen larder's empty—too bad—only three.
Three little curly-tails roamed o'er pastures new,
  One went to see the wheels go round—it's sausage—now they're two.
Two little rooters each day ate a ton,
  Wanted: ham for luncheon! Good-bye, now only one.
One little piggy-wig, with not a place to hide,
  "No pork for Boston Beans," he heard, and committed suicide.

He told about our new laundry in one of the issues. "Why do folks wash on Monday?" Father Walsh asked, and then answered himself, "Because they've been thinking about it all day Sunday.

"While Maryknoll was expanding, the aboriginal tubs were congesting—till finally wash days were so multiplied, that even tramps lost track of the safe days for calling.

"Only a moving picture could do justice to what we saw on our last visit. The tiny stove would have melted a heart of ice, the water grew cold and hot by turns, and soap wasted away under our eyes. The wringer had no respite from its endless round, big lumps of starch were all broken up by the strain, and the temperature throughout reminded one of Dante. In the evening when the smoke cleared away, huge heaps of mangled clothes could be seen lying here and there in the twilight.

"Once a week was bad enough, but think of such a conflict spoiling even more days out of the seven—and incidentally holding up the office work!

"We don't know, but lately someone sent a wireless asking, 'Why do the Teresians wash also on Tuesdays and Wednesdays?'

"As Aesop had his dinner, we put it up to him.

" 'My child,' he said, 'a certain little ant went out one day to scrub an elephant, and do you know, it took him some time—longer than you'd think!' "

Along with these light comments on things that happened at the Knoll, there were likewise notes of a serious nature. Beneath it all the man's purpose could be seen: he was stirring up interest in the well-being of other peoples, interest in the great work of going to people in far-off places to make them happy, everlastingly happy. How well he succeeded can be judged by the growth of his idea. Maryknoll has grown and is reaching far and wide.

Sometimes I wonder if he foresaw this far in his vision of the future. If he did, he did not say so. Had he said in those days that within three decades there would be eight hundred American boys in Maryknoll's major and minor seminaries, with several hundred ordained priests at work on the missions, other people might have questioned his mental stability.

14

"Thank You!"

There are no poor in God's great cause,
Each heart in earnest, has its wealth;
The ill have silvers for His palm
As well as they who know but health.

The gold of "Aves" who has not?
Unloose now thy spirit's string,
And spend thy purse upon thy Friend
Whose love's above imagining.

— Mary Allegra Gallagher

One Sunday shortly after my ordination I was speaking on foreign missions in the church of St. John the Evangelist, New York City, invited by Father Francis Shea, who was then assistant to Msgr. Dunn, Director of the Propagation of the Faith. After the Masses I was in the rectory with the priests. Word came that I was wanted in the parlor.

A woman was waiting there, in her middle thirties perhaps, dressed very plainly. She said that she had heard the announcement the week before and had come to hear the talk on the missions. We conversed for a few minutes, and then she said that she wanted to do something for the missions; she had a donation with her. I felt that any little offering from this lady would be a sacrifice; she had told me that she worked as a charwoman, cleaning offices during the night. She handed me ten fifty-dollar bills.

It took me a second to get over my surprise. I told her it was too much, surely more than she could afford. "No, Father," she said, "I have been saving this for some time. If I am really going to show

God that I love Him I want to give all." I suggested that it might be more prudent to keep some, at least half, since as she herself said she had been putting it away against a rainy day. "No," she said, "I feel that if I am generous with God, He will certainly be generous with me, as He always has been. I trust Him."

Father Walsh used to tell us that during his years with the Propagation of the Faith and later as head of Maryknoll, he found that many, perhaps most, contributions come from people of moderate means and a great deal from the very poor. He had a great sense of gratitude. He insisted that we should have the same. We should thank God, he said, for all the benefits He gives us daily, for all the special helps and grace He gives us. We should thank our superiors and professors for all they do for us and we should thank one another, among ourselves as students, whenever we receive a favor. We should thank a friend for a two-cent stamp, and do so with a letter just as cordial as we should send in thanking someone for two thousand dollars. He realized that the two-cent stamp might have meant a greater sacrifice to the first giver than the two thousand dollars to the other.

People say that there is something in the American character which makes us feel it a weakness to express gratitude. Perhaps it is our love of independence: it's hard to admit that we need the help of others, hard to be under an obligation to someone. Actually, it is a sign of a well-balanced character to be able to receive and to thank gracefully. This was something Father Walsh stressed and which, I believe, he succeeded in implanting in us, that is, a conscious gratitude for all that the priests and Sisters and lay people of America do for us.

Father Walsh wanted us to keep in mind that the Catholics of America were building Maryknoll and were in a sense the owners of Maryknoll. Every time we sat down to a meal, every time we went into our chapel, every time we turned on a light or went to class, we could thank these tens of thousands, perhaps hundreds of thousands, of American Catholics who made all this possible.

These people, from all walks of life and all parts of the country, from the cities, and towns, from the farms, have built our seminaries and have built our missions overseas. They have paid for the training of our students. They have paid the passage for missioners to their fields of labor. They have kept the missioners alive and have supported their chapels, schools and dispensaries.

From their savings and their sacrifices come the funds to carry on the work of Maryknoll in our houses of training and in fields afar. Most of our friends are poor people. More than half of them are women. Almost all are wage-earners. The money we get comes from their weekly pay envelope. These good people earn their bread and ours by honest labor, labor that is nearly always hard and often humble.

An old man walked into our front door at Maryknoll one Sunday, just about dinner time. He asked to see a priest. He put fifty dollars on the table and requested a perpetual membership for an erring member of his family. He had already enrolled himself and his wife, who was dead, and, one by one he had enrolled the other members of his family, with the nickels and dimes he had saved over a period of years.

He would accept no lunch from us, not even a cup of coffee. He refused a ride back to the station. He had walked up from the railway, missing the turn and making a long detour by way of Briarcliff, and he would walk down again, smoking his pipe, to get the train back to the Bronx.

Some days later, one of our priests called at his home. He found the house, a rickety place pitched on the side of a steep rise at the edge of the city. There was no one at home. Though well up in his fourth score of years, our friend had to go out every day doing odd jobs. He was retired from one of the City departments, but his pension was insufficient to pay for his board and lodging. Meeting benefactors like this old man makes one pause before spending a dollar.

Father Walsh often told us about people like this, and told us that we should be praying for them always. He warned us of our obligation to fulfill promises made to persons who asked for prayers. "As soon as I leave a person for whom I have promised to pray," he said, "I always say immediately at least one Hail Mary. I know then that I have fulfilled the promise and will not burn in Purgatory for having neglected to pray for their intentions."

Only in the next world will we know how many of God's blessings came to us in answer to the prayers and sacrifices of these
friends. One such benefactor died not long ago in the poor house
of a New England town. As a child she had been adopted by a rich
family and brought up like a young princess. Later, she was married to a well-to-do business man of Chicago. In the years that followed, her foster parents, her husband, and her only child died.

She married a second time and was living in California. There is
no secret about her story; she told it to everyone who called on her.
She and her husband lost most of their money in a bank disaster.
They salvaged enough to buy a farm in Arkansas, which they
worked themselves.

A cyclone destroyed some of the barns, drought killed off the live
stock. Her husband, distraught by so many misfortunes, attempted
suicide. He repented before he died.

Alone in her misery, she struggled along for a time, but the farm
and the remaining stock were looted repeatedly. She leased the farm
to a neighbor who would have it free for five years, and then sold
some of her belongings to get her fare to Chicago. This money was
stolen from her by a ruffian who knelt on her throat while he seized
her purse. She was bleeding through the mouth when the neighbors
found her.

The robber was later apprehended and turned out to be the man
to whom she had leased the farm, but the money was never recovered. Penniless she went to Chicago and Buffalo but got no help
from relatives of her foster parents. She ended up in a city poor
house in New England.

She was a good seamstress and made herself valuable to the institution by mending the uniforms of the attendants and the clothes
of the inmates. For this she received no pay. Sometimes nurses from
outside gave her work to do and paid her. "And then," she said, "I
had something to send for your missions."

This was the widow's mite, precious in God's sight and of untold
value to our work. But most of all, we were blessed with her prayers.
In the advanced stages of creeping paralysis, her days and nights
were spent in suffering and in praying for us. The Lord has been
good to us. His own friends have been our friends.

Shortly after I reached Maryknoll in the fall of 1913, Father Walsh had an article in *The Field Afar* about "Little Mary Knoll." This was a doll, dressed by a little lady in Catonsville, Maryland, who sent a photo to Father Walsh and said she wanted to sell chances on the doll and send the earnings to the missions.

"Mary Knoll requires no feeding," Father Walsh explained. "She is filled for a lifetime with very fine board. She is out of long clothes and is in her first short dress (like her namesake, adds the observant mother). We are assured that her dress is white, her cap has blue ribbons, her shoes are blue, and she stands twenty-five inches in her 'shoesy-woosies,' whatever those are.

"Already she is quite accomplished. She walks with grace, rolls her eyes dreamily and expresses on her countenance various emotions. She is not 'up' in music to any considerable extent but—and here we pause to let this idea sink into the minds of our readers—she is 'up' on chances, and will go to some fortunate mortal before December 25, 1913. Will it be *you?*"

"Little Mary Knoll" went to a ten-year-old foster mother in Providence, Rhode Island, after winning $219.60 for the Big Maryknoll Seminary.

Many years have now passed since a little lad in Bethlehem, Connecticut, saved his spare pennies for the missions. He got the idea from two zealous young ladies of Bethlehem, who made house to house visits through the country collecting money to sponsor a Maryknoll missioner. He and his pals put on a small-scale circus for the sponsor fund.

Happy with the results, they made the trip from Bethlehem to Maryknoll to deliver the proceeds. Later this boy went off to fight for his country and was killed in action. The sponsor fund has been carried on faithfully over the years by the parishioners of the Nativity Chapel, at Bethlehem, very likely directed from Heaven by the little boy who supervised the circus.

"A dozen policemen in Lynn, Massachusetts, have shown that they mean to keep a close watch on us," Father Walsh said one day back in 1913. "They are reading *The Field Afar*." Almost at the same time, he got this note from a friend in Boston: "You will find enclosed one dollar—one bean from old Bean Town. I wish it were a plateful. I am satisfied to know that it is going to be planted in good rich soil."

Back in 1911, Father Walsh set apart the Friday of each week as a day of special prayer for all benefactors of the work. "We have set aside Friday of each week as a day of devotions to help us attain the several aims of our organization, to aid our benefactors, and to bring special graces to our missioners and their flocks.

"We shall gladly welcome, as cooperators in this form of help, any of our readers—religious or lay. The nun in her cloister can thus be of great value to this sublime cause, which is hers because it is that of Christ, her Master. It will be a distinct encouragement to many, and above all to the missioners themselves, if a record can be kept of such coöperation."

All Maryknoll priests throughout the world offer their Mass each Friday for all benefactors and their intentions. Every day, and especially on Friday, the various houses of training have prayers set aside for benefactors.

Employees of the New York Consolidated Edison Company have worked hard to do their bit. They have a mission-aid Club that has sponsored several priests now at work for the missions. The club has promoters who circulate among the workers to collect the contributions. Two of these promoters are Jews. One is a Presbyterian minister.

In one of the Edison offices, the Mission Club boys set up a "swear box." At a penny a word, they find that swearing is not profitable. One day the proceeds totaled eighty-six cents, including four nickels and a dime. The trooper suspected of depositing the dime also confessed to the four nickels,—"Darn it!"

There is a blind lady in a little town in Maryland. She has a news stand with which she supports herself and her family. She has been sending us a couple of dollars each week over a period of years. She got a friend to take over the news stand one week end and came to Maryknoll to attend a Departure Ceremony. She made the trip alone and had a near disaster in the Grand Central Station when she missed her step and started to slip down between the car and the concrete platform. She could see nothing of the Departure Ceremony, but she could listen, and one of the students beside her explained what was going on. She went away happy.

The burden of gratitude has been upon us throughout the years. It has been our task to sit down daily and write over and over again: "Thank you! God bless you!" But sometimes our friends, who have come to see Maryknoll, go home and write back to thank us. For what? For letting them be our friends, perhaps. Or maybe they were pleased to be asked to do something for God and thanked us for putting out our hand. Letters from the coming generation always have something special about them, like this one:

"Dear Father Superior:—On behalf of the baseball team, the girls, Sister, and all those that went on the picnic to Maryknoll last Wednesday, I wish to thank you for the sacrifices the students made to show us around the place. I also want to thank the boys for the wonderful game they played, even though they lost . . .

"We thank especially Carmen, Larry, Looney Rooney, Windy, Smokey and Red McGrath, and all the others who helped to make the day so pleasant for us. .

"The Seminarians acted so happy and carefree even though they will be probably martyred some day. Yours sincerely, . . ."

God seems very near when a note comes like this one, which is not rare; "Dear Fathers: Sorry that I am not in a position to be of much help in your noble work, as I have been out of work for more than twelve years on account of asthma. What little income I have is the twenty-eight dollars a month for Blind Relief for my wife who is now eighty-three years old, and my own railway pension of sixty dollars a month. That's a total of eighty-six dollars a month and we have to watch every penny to keep on top of the water. We were raising ten children and we had a little money saved, but I took a heart attack, and my wife had one the following year. That took all our savings . . . May God bless your noble work." There was a gift enclosed with this letter.

I remember hearing, or reading, a conference some years ago in which the speaker put forth an idea which went something like this: "The world does not know it, but its safety is in the hands of our good people whom God has tried and found not wanting in complete fidelity. If the world today is not plunged into total paganism and collapse, it can thank these generous souls who hold back nothing in an all-out effort to do what He holds dear. . . ." This thought keeps coming back.

The Angels in Heaven must rejoice at the generosity of such a soul as revealed in this letter. It was written in the scrawl of an elderly person in poor health:

"Dear Maryknoll Fathers:—I hope you have some other way to get help for I can't do any more. I have nothing for myself—I had this dollar towards getting a pair of shoes but. . . . no more to go with it so you can have the dollar. I can't work. My brother that I was keeping house for has been out of work since last March. I am sorry. But thanks for your prayers, as I hope God will help us all. I can't do anything. So long, Rev. Fathers. ."

15

Friends at Home

"Oh, it's just the little homely things
The unobtrusive, friendly things,
The 'Won't-you-let-me-help-you' things
That make our pathway light."

— Grace Haines

"We have a million little friends, and they're wonderful." A confrere, who ought to know, made this remark. It's true: we have a multitude of friends who have helped us in a little way; in their numbers they have been our mainstay. There are other friends who have helped in a big way, but their number is small. Big and little, friends were a consolation and a support to Father Walsh and to Father Price.

As I think back now over those first years, there are certain faces which remain clear in my memory, as frequent visitors, or as friends upon whom Father Walsh leaned with trust and gratitude. Still, no one individual friend can be pointed out as standing above the rest; they were all wonderful. No one took possession and identified himself as the patron and protector. Our patrons and protectors have been legion. A fitting dedication of the seminary and the entire mission work would be: "To the Bishops, Priests, Brothers, Sisters and Laity of America. To them Maryknoll owes everything."

When I arrived in August, 1913, the other students spoke of Cardinal Farley's visit the previous May. He had come up from New York with Monsignor Carroll just a few months after the seminary was started here. I remember reading Father Walsh's account of the visit:

"There was no white spread of fine linen, but His Eminence apparently did not observe its absence as he took his fast-day dinner from our well-scrubbed board. After a short sit-down following dinner, His Eminence walked over the property, down hill and up hill, along the brook, on soil that was by turns dry and oozing, through briars and blackberry bushes, and across stone walls, without a stop for one good hour and a half. Can you ask a finer tribute to the food and air of Maryknoll,—and to its milk?

"On the way to St. Teresa's Lodge, the dairy was honored with a visit, and as the Cardinal neared it, Mr. Proud Turkey Gobbler fluffed out his breast, spread his tail feathers and stalked off like a stern propeller sailing up the Hudson. A Cardinal was nothing to him. His Eminence was snubbed on this occasion, but he will have a chance to get even with Mr. T. Gobbler if he will dine with us next Thanksgiving.

"At St. Teresa's Lodge the Maries of Maryknoll, who habitually, during the day, disturb the peace of the Knoll with the sound of typewriters and other villainous machines, were waiting to make full amends for Mr. Gobbler's bad manners.

"They were glad, indeed, to see their spiritual father and they greeted him arrayed in the new gray uniforms that he himself had suggested.

"His Eminence remarked the apparent weakness of these Maries for the episcopal cape, on which they had unconsciously modelled their own. But he left them happy with his blessing and a good, bold autograph written in their guest book.

"Then came a brief rest on the piazza, a final glimpse of the great river, a blessing for us all, the promise of two free days for the students, and a hearty good-bye.

"As the big auto lumbered carefully over our rocky drive, carrying away our distinguished guest, all felt as if a Pentecostal wind had swept Maryknoll, leaving behind it a storage of strength for our young aspirants and their superiors, and for all, the sweet memory of a blessed day. Long life to the Archbishop of New York, Cardinal of the Missions!"

Father Joseph Bruneau was on the first board of the Catholic Foreign Mission Society, when it was formed in Boston, in 1906. His presence was a guaranty of its success. He was a sworn enemy of procrastination. "Killing time" was something no one should do, he said. He would appear at his lecture desk in Saint Mary's Seminary just one minute before bell time, never before that.

Once, we are told, on the way to the railway station in Baltimore, he pulled out his watch and discovered that he still had ten minutes. He told the friend with him that he had ten minutes to spare and was going to buy a hat. He hurried into a hat store, bought himself a straw hat and made his train, exulting in the fact that he had rescued ten minutes from complete loss.

Father Bruneau commanded the respect of everyone, even though at times he aroused the ire of those who sat at his feet in the lecture hall at St. Mary's. He was easily one of the greatest educators of priests we have ever had in this country, a man of most intense life. His mind was keen, and it was difficult for him to refrain from sarcasm in the face of pretense and bluff, and frequently he did not refrain.

One day in class, the boy called upon to recite hemmed and hawed while everyone could see that he was not prepared to answer Father Bruneau's questions. Father took out his watch, looked at it and said: "So, you have talked for two minutes. You have said nossing. There are sixty-five persons present. You have wasted two minutes for each; that is over two hours. It ees a grave mattair! Sit down."

He suffered from severe headaches, but he kept on working. He had been seen working in his room with an ice bag on his head. One day when I visited him in the old Seminary on Paca Street, he handed me two books in French and told me that I should translate them in my spare time. One was a book of meditations for priests, by Father André, who had taught Father Price at St. Mary's and Father Walsh at St. John's. Father André was then rector of the Seminary in Avignon. The books are still on my shelf in Fushun, Manchuria. I wonder if the Red invaders read them. Father Bruneau tried to translate a book, or write one, each time he crossed the Atlantic, and that was frequently.

Father Bruneau's interest in Maryknoll never diminished. He came often and gave good talks. He rarely missed a Departure Day. Perhaps two dozen or more of our priests were encouraged by him to come to Maryknoll while they were seminarians at St. Mary's. He attended Father Walsh's consecration in Rome in June, 1933, and then went for a visit to his home parish in France where he fell ill and died.

Archbishop McNicholas, of Cincinnati, came to Maryknoll many times. His friendship started in 1906 when he met Father Walsh in Washington, D. C. He himself had hoped to go to some Dominican mission field. In the *Dominican Year Book,* which he was editing in 1906, he published an article which he had asked Father Walsh to write, "An Apology for Foreign Missions."

Before he was appointed secretary to the Master General of the Dominicans at Rome, he had helped the Teresians in getting started as a religious community and it was he who received them as Tertiaries of his Order. As Bishop of Duluth he started the Diocese of Duluth Maryknoll Burse. In Cincinnati, he had Maryknoll start its junior seminary right beside his own archdiocesan seminary. He was a close friend and adviser of Father Walsh through the years. He tells of a day spent with Father Walsh just a week before the latter's death:

"He insisted that I remain throughout the day; I promised to do so, provided I could pay him very brief visits whenever he wished to see me. He sent for me six times on that day, which stands out so clearly in my memory . . . He spoke little of his illness and of the end of his earthly life, for which he was preparing with that calmness and thoroughness that we are apt to attribute to the saints. He spoke at length of opportunities other than those of the missions, which he considered important for the Church of the United States. He manifested special solicitude for the Catholic University of America."

Archbishop Dowling of St. Paul came East sometimes with Archbishop McNicholas, and the two would journey to Maryknoll. As Bishop of Des Moines, Archbishop Dowling had watched Maryknoll grow. Father Bernard Meyer was one of his boys. He was a friend and counselor. When the seminary was being built, he was fearful at one time lest we were moving too rapidly. He sent back word with one of our priests passing through St. Paul: "Tell Jimmy to take it easy."

Archbishop Dowling died poor, as those who knew him well were certain he would. Personal effects and a checking account that allowed enough for his funeral expenses made up the subject matter of his will. The checking account would have had a few thousand dollars more if he had not been mindful, as the end approached, of Maryknoll's struggling Japanese Mission in Seattle.

Monsignor John Dunn was New York Director of the Propagation of the Faith, when Maryknoll was started. He was a member of the corporation from its beginning in 1911. As Bishop, he ordained one hundred and six Maryknoll priests. He was with Father Walsh when the property on which the seminary stands was purchased in 1912. We usually referred to him as "Uncle John."

Cardinal Hayes delegated Bishop Dunn to be ecclesiastical superior of the Maryknoll Sisters. It worried him to see the Sisters living in scattered houses, old wooden houses dating back years and years, and he hoped for the day when they would have their own Motherhouse that would keep the Sisters all under one roof. After a wait of twenty years, he encouraged them to put their trust in Divine Providence and erect their Motherhouse. He gave a beautiful altar for their chapel, a monument to his goodness.

Bishop Dunn made two trips to Eastern Asia and visited as many Maryknoll missioners as he could. After one of these trips he wrote a letter to the *Catholic News,* asking help for the immediate erection of a rest house in South China for American missioners there. He found a kind-hearted layman, Sir George McDonald, who provided a good part of the wherewithal to build the rest house. He introduced to Father Walsh a generous Catholic lady whom he called "Lady Bountiful." He found other good friends for the missions. He was a real "Uncle John."

After the first general Chapter at Maryknoll, in 1929, Bishop Dunn came for our second Bishop Walsh—Bishop James E.—just back from China, and took him down to his own home at the Church of the Annunciation on Convent Avenue, in an attempt to build him up physically and find him some friends for Kongmoon.

Back in China, Bishop James E. wrote a long letter of gratitude poetically extolling Bishop Dunn's big heart. He ends like this:

"The minarets of Manhattan are powerless to thrill an oriental. He sees too many cities, and suffers too many woes to feel deeply about most things; least of all, about houses made with hands. The canyons of trade and the cathedrals of barter are nothing to signify, in his perspective.

"But there is something in New York not made with hands, or if with hands, then with those unique Hands that once were pierced in order to bring this gift to men; and that is its charity. Who knows this, knows New York, for is it not spoken of in the whole world? And when its palaces shall have crumbled into dust, is it not this characteristic that will be remembered?

"A certain Chinese missioner is guarding a warm souvenir of Convent Avenue, as he climbs the mountain trails of Kwangtung and pauses to rest at its wayside tea houses . ."

It seemed that everyone was good to us. Archbishop Hanna invited us to San Francisco, Archbishop Cantwell wanted us in Los Angeles. Archbishop Glennon gave us many vocations. Bishop Dougherty of Buffalo, later Cardinal of Philadelphia, was interested. Bishop Nilan of Hartford appealed to his priests to help the missions. Bishop Harkins of Providence did the same. Bishop Feehan of Fall River, himself in need of priests, let two of his come to us, Father Morris and Father Paulhus; both of them genuine apostles, who have spent their whole lives in the East.

Bishop Swint of Wheeling is the kind of friend that prompted Father Walsh to say, "Maryknoll owes all that it is to the priests of America." Bishop Muldoon of Rockford gave us our first priest, Father Daniel McShane. Archbishop Ireland said, "The time has come when no excuse may be offered for further abstention from a participation in this holiest of works. A Foreign Mission Seminary will be of inestimable value to seminaries having as their prime object the formation of priests for the ministry in America itself."

Bishop Shahan wanted us to take a chair of missiology at the Catholic University. Bishop Busch of Lead, South Dakota, said, "I have always felt and maintained that the mission spirit is a vital element of a healthy condition of religion and that it largely determines the supernatural vitality of the individual as well as that of a religious society." *

One of our most frequent and best known visitors was Father James Kelly, of Hough's Neck, later of Newton, and later still of Jamaica Plain, Massachusetts. He has been a friend to many and in many ways, but perhaps his greatest benefaction to Maryknoll was his ability to help Father James Anthony relax. He would swoop down on us from Boston, find Father Walsh a bit tense under the strain of debts and appeals, builders and professors, students and what not, and he would bustle him off for a ride during which he usually kept him laughing all the time. He was Father Superior's jongleur, sent by the Lord to help him forget his problems. He also had a way of helping him to bring home many gifts.

For years Father Kelly would take no other vacation but the two weeks during which he carried Father Walsh in his car, from rectory to rectory around the Boston Archdiocese. Father Walsh had many friends among the pastors and assistants in this area. Together Father Kelly and he would descend on their prey, and their approach was irresistible. At the end of two weeks, Father Kelly would

---

* It is hopeless to try here to list all our friends, the Bishops, who came to Maryknoll or who wrote from their dioceses: Bishop Ryan of Alton, Bishop Richter of Grand Rapids, Bishop Glorieux of Boise, Bishop Doran of Providence, Bishop Canevin of Pittsburgh, Bishop Chatard and Bishop Chartrand of Indianapolis, Bishop Janssen of Belleville, Archbishop Prendergast of Philadelphia, Bishop Hogan of Kansas City, Bishop Northrop of Charleston, Bishop Fox of Green Bay, Bishop Van de Ven of Alexandria, Archbishop Moeller of Cincinnati, Bishop McGolrick of Duluth, Bishop Dunne of Peoria, Bishop Gunn of Natchez, Bishop Keiley of Savannah, Archbishop Blenk of New Orleans, Bishop Grace of Sacramento, Bishop Colton of Buffalo, Bishop Cunningham of Concordia, Bishop Conaty of Los Angeles, and his brother Monsignor Bernard Conaty of Pittsfield, Mass., Bishop Garvey of Altoona, Bishop Donahue of Wheeling, Bishop Garrigan of Sioux City, Bishop Gabriels of Ogdensburg, Bishop Maes of Covington, Bishop O'Reilly of Baker City, Archbishop Christie of Oregon, Bishop Curley of St. Augustine, later Archbishop of Baltimore, and so on and on and on, with so many others. They all had a share in building Maryknoll.

point his ship in the direction of Maryknoll, and the two would roll homeward with their little bag full of gifts.

Another who merited a distinct place in building up Maryknoll was Father Henry Borgmann, the Redemptorist. He came often, gave us talks, and preached some of our retreats. "If I were free and able to join up," he once said, "it wouldn't be 'Walsh and Price'; it would be 'Walsh, Price and Borgmann.'" He liked to be called "Uncle Henry!"

He insisted that we should make the most of the name, MARY-KNOLL, principally because it was such a beautiful name, embodying our dedication to the Queen of Heaven. He pointed out that it had an appeal that we must not overlook, and that we should be wise to keep this same name for all our establishments. It would be a mistake, he maintained, to give our colleges and schools in other parts of the country different names, reserving Maryknoll for the seminary and the center. They should all be known as Maryknoll. The name would bring us friends and followers. He was right.

In his later years he sent us some verses, written after he had received *The Field Afar* with a cover picture entitled, "The Road that Leads to Maryknoll."

> "There's many a road leads up and down,
>   Out to country or in to town;
>   But the road I love the best to stroll
>   Is the Road that leads to Maryknoll.
>
> "Young lads and sweet young lassies there,
>   I saw them meditate in prayer;
>   The field afar, that was their goal,
>   Down the road from Maryknoll.
>
> "Oh, I love to go there oft and moon,
>   Auld Lang Syne sped away too soon;
>   I want to dream of the young who stole
>   My heart on the road to Maryknoll."

We had countless other "Uncles," hundreds of them, even thousands, I suppose. Monsignor Chidwick, of Dunwoodie Seminary, was a good neighbor. He also found good friends for us, including

Mr. Robert Cuddihy, owner of the old *Literary Digest*. Father Florence Halloran and Father Joseph Lynch Early both joined Maryknoll, and then had to return to their diocese because of poor health. Father Stanton, whose brother was Doctor Stanton, chief of staff at St. Elizabeth's Hospital, Dorchester, was one of the first four members of the Catholic Mission Board. He came one evening and spoke on Ruskin, quoting long passages by heart.

Other good friends and frequent visitors were Doctor Aiken, professor of Apologetics at the Catholic University, Father Vieban, and Father Havey, of the Sulpicians, Father Charles Crane who accompanied Father Walsh to the far East in 1925, Father George Caruana, who later as Archbishop Caruana represented the Holy See in Mexico and Cuba, and Father Peter O'Callaghan, classmate of Father Walsh, who established the Mount Melchisedech Seminary for the Home Missions.

Father Paul Francis of Graymoor was our neighbor. Father Walsh liked him particularly, because Father Paul always had an interest in the foreign missions and helped them through his publication, *The Lamp*. When Father Paul got enough students together, he used to bring a baseball team to Maryknoll each year on Ascension Thursday. It was amusing to see the interest he and Father James Anthony would take in the game, egging on their own teams.

On one such occasion we made a bad mistake. We had beaten Graymoor year after year. We became presumptuous and booked two games for Ascension Thursday, one with the Josephite seminarians at Newburgh, the other with Father Paul's team. Graymoor beat us. Father Paul Francis wrote about it in *The Lamp*. Father Walsh warned us never to let that happen again!

Father Hudson, of *The Ave Maria,* and his successors were very sympathetic. *The Ave Maria* always boosted mission work. The Holy Cross Fathers at Notre Dame welcomed our students in quest of degrees, and offered scholarships to a number of students whom we brought from Asia. Catholic editors helped.*

---

* *Our Sunday Visitor* solicited funds for us. Father Noll, later Bishop Noll, never tired campaigning for us. The *Providence Visitor,* the Hartford *Catholic Transcript,* the *New York Catholic News,* the *Brooklyn*

Perhaps it is a mistake to try to list these friends of the early years, because I know I am missing many of them. But then there were many who insisted that their tokens of friendship be kept secret, that their names never be mentioned. The Lord, the Master of Apostles, will give them full recognition for their goodness, in a way more worthy and more effective than we can give it here.

I recall a letter written back in 1911 by Father Francis Kelley, later Bishop of Oklahoma. He was then President of the Church Extension Society. He wrote to Father Price and Father Walsh, saying that the Board of Governors of the Society were in sympathy with the idea of a foreign mission seminary and hoped to be able to assist. Bishop Kelley used to stop at Maryknoll on his trips to New York. He was an interesting talker.

Mother Alphonsa, foundress of the Rosary Hill Home for cancer patients at Hawthorne, was the daughter of Nathaniel Hawthorne. Anyone who has visited the Rosary Hill Hospital knows that the charity found there suggests, and even rivals, the work of Father Damien and his successors at Molokai. It is a shining example of latter-day heroism.

In the Hawthorne days, the little group of Maryknollers had many proofs of interest and kindness from Mother Alphonsa and her Sisters. The cancer patients prayed for us and offered their suffer-

---

Tablet, and other Catholic papers of those days sought news items about the missions, that they might help in putting the work before the eyes of the public.

Father Alexander Doyle, Father Elliott, Father Bradley, Father Elias Younan, and many Paulist Fathers of later days, did all they could to help Maryknoll get on its feet. Father McQuaide of San Francisco was largely instrumental in launching our little seminary on the West Coast. Father Costello of Fort Wayne, like Father Kane of Scranton, went around begging for us.

Monsignor Van Antwerp of Detroit, a classmate of Father Price, Father Guinevan of New York, Father Donovan of Kenrick Seminary, St. Louis, Father Danner of Pittsburgh, Monsignor Dionysius O'Callaghan of South Boston, Father Hally, Monsignor Deegan, Monsignor Lenihan, Monsignor Dolan and Monsignor McGivney, of the Knights of Columbus, were all familiar acquaintances.

ings for us. Some sent little gifts, all entailing sacrifices of course, since only the poor are admitted to Rosary Hill. Mother Alphonsa taught her entire "family" to love the missions. She welcomed the Teresians as her own daughters, threw open her chapel to them, did them frequent kindnesses, and, on feast days, sent them portions of the dainties she had prepared for her dear sufferers in the hospital. At a crucial period, she intervened and came to the rescue with a very large thank-offering which solved a vital problem for the little Maryknoll group and made possible its further development. Mother Alphonsa's name will always be held in benediction at Maryknoll.

Father Walsh's brother, Mr. Timothy Walsh, the architect, and his partner, Mr. Charles Maginnis, were frequently with us, laying plans for the seminary. Mr. Maginnis was always a most entertaining talker. His sparkling flow of English kept us smiling.

There were stories about him, too, most of them centering around his absentmindedness. Someone recalled how he had started to board a streetcar in Boston. He threw his satchel on the car's platform, then suddenly saw a friend getting off the car. He stopped to talk, and during the conversation the car rolled away with his bag. Conductors on the trains were instructed to check Mr. Maginnis and all his belongings when they neared his destination, so as to make sure that he and his effects were completely assembled before he left the train.

Mr. Cuddihy, of *The Literary Digest,* Sir George McDonald, Judge Talley, Judge Victor Dowling, and Judge Michael Maginnis, Major O'Rourke, Mr. John K. Ewing, Mr. Lewis Britt, and other laymen were all good friends.

Dr. Horatio Storer, of Newport, gave Father Walsh most of the oil paintings which adorn the walls of the new seminary. Dr. James J. Walsh, the writer, Doctor Lynch, the oculist, Doctor Tyson, Doctor Perrault, Doctor Edgerton, all said they wanted to have a hand in getting things started. Katherine E. Conway, the authoress, was active in her interest. Miss Elder, related to Archbishop Elder of Cincinnati, went through New England making friends for *The Field Afar.*

Scranton was outstanding for its friends. Their names would fill a book. Mr. A. J. Casey, Mr. Edward Lynott, and Mr. James M.

Boland represented us as lay members on the civil corporation. Mr. Ed Connerton was ever ready to lend a hand.

In those first years we began to receive letters from Mary Donovan, Father Walsh's secretary in *The Field Afar* office in Boston, who had joined the Immaculate Conception Sisters in Montreal, and as Sister Mary Angeline, had just been sent to Canton, China.

Father Walsh told us every now and then how grateful we should be to the Sisters in schools and hospitals all over the United States. "Sisters of Charity, Sisters of Mercy, Sisters of Notre Dame," Father Walsh said, "Sisters of the Immaculate Heart, Poor Clare Nuns, Sisters of St. Joseph, Sisters of the Holy Cross, Sisters of the Visitation, Dominican Sisters, Franciscan Sisters, Madames of the Sacred Heart, Sisters of the Holy Child Jesus, Sisters of the Blessed Sacrament, Cenacle Nuns, Carmelites, Franciscan Missionaries of Mary, Sisters of the Good Shepherd, Sisters of the Precious Blood—all these have proved their wish to coöperate with us. There are others, too, and we do not forget the Little Sisters of the Poor, who surely have given us a right to rejoice in the title—'Beggar of Beggars.'

"There is no body of women in this country, I believe, that has a stronger and more personal interest in Maryknoll," Father Walsh said, "than the Carmelite Nuns, wherever they may be found." He invited them to a Sisters' Day at Maryknoll one summer, knowing of course that they could not leave their cloister. They wrote back:

"There are eighteen of us, and, being bound by the laws of Enclosure, we can come only by 'heirship.' That allows us the privilege of being present at all your Masses and spiritual exercises. Please do not send us home when evening comes, for we wish to stay in your prayers and share with you the Banquet of Life. You have been so long our guests, we trust you will pardon our liberty in choosing the name, your grateful—Coheredes Christi."

Many of our students came from Holy Cross, Boston College, Fordham, Regis High; and in later years some of them went for degrees to St. Louis University. We had good friends among the Jesuit Fathers of these schools. Father Wynne, Father Francis Donnelly, Father Weber, Father Fox and many others. One of them, to whom Father Walsh was especially devoted, was Father Michael Earle. Father Walsh used to quote Father Earle, and these lines from the old professor give partially the motive for these chapters of retrospect:

"As you build your edifice of Today, put your front door on the Avenue of Tomorrow, and a few windows on the Backyard of Yesterday."

16

Friends Afar

*"I have lived thirteen years in the depths of China.
I would have liked to be able to say that America has
a Catholic Foreign Mission Seminary, so as to impress
the Chinese with the universality of our holy Church.
My successors can do so now, thank God."*

— Rev. A. Roulland, January 1913
(The missionary 'brother' of St. Therese of Lisieux)

Père Robert wanted to see the water works. I was delegated to show him the new Croton Dam, the great conduits that carry the water to New York City, and to find someone that would explain the Water Supply System of the metropolis.

Père Robert had been a missioner in China for many years. In Shanghai he was active and so well known that they named a street after him. In Hongkong his knowledge of men and matters and his shrewd foresight made him much sought after by civil administrators and business men. Once a week he dined with the Governor, Sir Reginald Stubbs, who at this weekly meeting sought his advice on various problems. Water was getting to be a problem in Hongkong. The supply on the island might soon be too meager. In a bad year it might fail. Père Robert foresaw the need of reservoirs on the mainland with an aqueduct under the bay. On this trip to France, the Governor had suggested that he look into the way New York handled its problem.

On our trip to the Croton and Kensico Reservoirs, Père Robert asked endless questions. We went down into the filter shafts, inspected the overflow, watched the operation of the water gates, examined the aerating system. Mr. Frank Palmer, a Maryknoll friend, was in charge of this section, and he arranged our tour. We learned that this aqueduct ran from the Ashokan reservoir, under Croton Lakes, to the Kensico Reservoir, and from there on to the city. It was a hundred feet underground in many places. If the conduit were empty, you could drive a load of hay through it. The lakes were nearly full that day, and the sight and sound of the water going over the spillway impressed Père Robert and myself as well.

When the Dam was finished in 1905, the water of the Croton Lakes and Croton River backed up through the valleys. Several villages had to be abandoned. They were soon deep under water. Old Katonah, Whitlockville, and Woodsbridge now lie in the bottom of the man-made lake. The village of Pine's Bridge, our neighbor up the road, which had been popular as a summer resort and famous for its exciting political conventions, was submerged.

Père Robert made voluminous notes and brought them back to Hongkong. The administrators of the colony decided a new prison was more urgent, and so they used their funds for a prison. That year Hongkong had its worst water famine in history. Fresh water had to be brought by boat from Shanghai and other ports. The next year they began work on Père Robert's project.

Père Robert was keen. When our first missioners went to China he gave them helpful advice, and from his experience they were able to avoid some mistakes. Later, he became Superior General of the Paris Foreign Missions. I once asked him if he ever made a mistake. "Oh," he said, "I suppose I am right about seven times out of ten. Not bad, you think?"

Another friend overseas, whom Father Walsh mentioned frequently in his talks to us, was Sister Xavier Berkeley. When he was Director of the Propagation of the Faith in Boston, he had many letters from Sister Xavier. He helped her work among orphans. They started a system of godmothers. The godmothers in America paid for the babies' support; in return each received a photo of her godchild and periodical notes on the child's health and progress. Once she wrote: "You must not only send American money to the Foreign Missions, but also train American missionaries to come out and work for souls." Sometimes Father Walsh spoke of her as "the Co-foundress of Maryknoll" or as "Maryknoll's big Sister."

He visited her orphan homes at Chusan on his first trip to the Orient, and later called on her mother, Lady Catherine Berkeley, in England. Sister Xavier Berkeley was born in England, joined the Daughters of Charity, and went to China in 1890.

When she came to America in 1923, on her way to England, she was here at Maryknoll for an ordination ceremony. Father Walsh said that he would like to have all our Sisters spend some time at Sister Xavier's mission; she would infect them with her missionary zeal. "Your house is my ideal;" he told her, "simple, modest build-ings for the Sisters, with the poor Chinese around you all day long. It is real mission life such as I wish our Sisters to live."

Father Arsenius Mullin, a Canadian Franciscan Father, one of the first missioners from America to the Far East, was among our friends and wrote from time to time.

Father Conrardy, who was in charge of a leper island near Can-ton, was an American citizen, though born in Belgium. The Sisters who worked among the lepers were from Canada. Father Conrardy used to write to Father Walsh, and in 1913 he sent this:

"I am well pleased to know that you have started an American Seminary for Foreign Missions. Indeed, it will not be long before many people will ask: 'Why was it not begun sooner?'

"We are all Catholics, but each nationality has something peculiar to itself. There is need here of Americans, men with their eyes and ears open, up-to-date, as they say in the United States.

"How I long to see an American priest in Canton! It is true that here, or even in Hongkong, there are very few Chinese who under-stand English, but the presence of American priests will place the Church on a higher level . . ."

These lines make me think of the day when as a boy in Lawrence, I saw Father Conrardy when he spoke at St. Mary's School.

Almost at the same time, Father Walsh had a letter from the apos-tolic Father Vincent Lebbe, who did so much over the years to help the Chinese hierarchy and clergy get started on their own. He wrote: "A writer . . . speaks of the good that American missioners could accomplish in India. What he says of that country is a thousand times more true in the case of China.

"Here America is more popular, more admired than any other country. But Protestants take care to give you the impression that it is exclusively Protestant and anti-Catholic. What can we do? Is it any wonder that we long to have American missioners?"

The issue of the *The Field Afar* coming off the press when I reached Maryknoll in 1913 had a photo on the cover, a group picture of the hierarchy of Japan and Korea. It showed Archbishop Rey of Tokyo, Bishop Combaz of Nagasaki, Bishop Chatron of Osaka, Bishop Berlioz of Hakodate, Bishop Mutel of Seoul, and Bishop Demange of Taikou, Korea. All these Bishops wrote frequently to Father Walsh, and we listened to their letters at spiritual reading or we read them ourselves later. Some of them visited Maryknoll on their way to France, or on a trip through America collecting funds for their missions.

Archbishop Rey was here. Father Walsh took him to see the sights of New York. He had a few minutes left one evening, and decided to conduct his guest to the top of one of the skyscrapers to see the Big City lighted. They were high above the streets on an open roof. Archbishop Rey was amazed. Suddenly a gust of wind lifted the hat from his head and carried it off into the blackness of the night. He clasped his hands over his head and called to Father Walsh. "Don't mind," said Father Walsh, "that's a frequent occurrence here." The Archbishop was not at all reassured by his companion's nonchalance. A few seconds later, there was a swish against the parapet beside them, and lo and behold—there was the black hat, back like a boomerang! "Oh yes," remarked Father Walsh, "a frequent occurrence here."

When I was in Mukden in later years, the young French priests had a collection of letters written by Saint Therese of Lisieux. They were letters addressed to her adopted missionary brother, Père Roulland, who had been in Szechwan, China. Later he returned to France, was procurator at the seminary in Paris, and while there he let the boys make copies of the letters he had received years before from Sister Therese.

These young priests said that Père Roulland had to take no end of teasing from the other priests and from the students, because Saint Therese had frequently addressed him with the devoted language of a real sister. Here are a few lines from some of these letters:

"You wanted me to say a prayer for you and ask Our Lord not to let you be appointed to a seminary. I know that such an outlook is not a pleasant one for you. I will ask Jesus to be kind to you and let you realize your dreams of a hard-working missionary in the field . . . but I will add, with you, 'May God's will be done . . .'

"O my brother. . . . I must say that I was truly envious when I read that your hair was going to be cut and that you were going to have a Chinese pigtail. Maybe you think I am very childish in my requests. No matter. I want just one little strand of those locks. Why? You won't need them any more, and when you are up in Heaven, carrying the martyr's palm, those hairs will be relics. . . . You're laughing at me, I know, but I don't mind that, not one bit. If, in return for this bit of pleasure I am giving you, you won't mind paying with the hair of a future martyr, I shall truly have a real bargain!

"You will like this: some kind person sent us a little lobster, tied up in a basket. We had not seen one in our convent in a long time, but the cook did remember that you have to toss them alive into hot water. She did so, lamenting that she had to treat a poor innocent creature so cruelly. The innocent creature was apparently asleep, but when it reached the hot water, its meekness turned to rage; it knew it was innocent and without so much as a 'Beg pardon,' it hopped out onto the floor.

"Sister went after it with her tongs and they had quite a race. Finally, she ran to Mother and told her the lobster was surely possessed. . . . Poor lobster; a moment ago it was so innocent, and now it's possessed by the devil. We must never trust the praise of any 'creatures.' Mother corralled the lobster which, not having the vow of obedience, protested vigorously when it was being brought back to the pot. The poor little lobster gave many a laugh to our little Carmel. Next day we all enjoyed a mouthful.

"I have read the lives of several missionaries . . . Among others I read Theophane Venard's, which was very interesting and touched me beyond words . . . I wrote some verses about him and I am sending them to you . . . I say I should be happy to set out for Tonking. . . . No, indeed, it is not just a dream. I really want to go and if Jesus does not come soon to bring me to the Carmel of Heaven, I will depart some day for the Carmel of Hanoi. . . ."

Père Roulland, who received these letters, was in correspondence with Father Walsh. He had spent many years in the Province of Szechwan. In 1913, he wrote to Maryknoll: "I have lived thirteen years in the depths of China. I would have liked to be able to say that America has a Catholic Foreign Mission Seminary, so as to impress the Chinese with the universality of our Holy Church. My successors can do so now, thank God . . ." In spite of his prayers, and those of St. Therese, he did get a seminary appointment in France. He was procurator at the Paris Mission Seminary, where he helped to train candidates for the missions.

Lady Herbert of Lea was another friend esteemed by Father Walsh. She was the daughter of General a'Court, born and brought up in England. She married the Right Hon. Sidney Herbert, and was mother of Sir Michael Herbert, British Ambassador to the United States, Lord Pembroke, Baroness von Hugel, Lady Maud Parry, and Lady de Grey. Her husband was British Minister of War. She was a convert, received into the Church by Cardinal Manning, who was a classmate of her husband. She wrote *Cradle Lands, Impressions of Spain, Children of Nazareth,* and the *Life of Monsignor Dupanloup.*

Father Walsh visited her in London. He found her at the time busy with a huge correspondence, practically all of which had to do with her many charities at home and on the missions. Lady Herbert brought out the first English translation of Theophane Venard's letters. Had it not been for this work of hers, Father Walsh admitted that his own edition of the life and letters of Theophane Venard, which he called *A Modern Martyr,* might not have been published. She died about two years before I went to Maryknoll, but Father Walsh spoke periodically of her pioneer work of writing about the missions.

Eusebius Venard, brother of Theophane Venard, wrote regularly to Father Walsh. He was a parish priest of the village of Assais and had entertained Father Walsh there and at their old homestead. He was still living in 1909 and on May 2nd of that year, had the privilege of attending his brother's beatification at Rome. That same night he wrote to Father Walsh:

"The great day has just come to an end and I wish to tell you my joy and how much I have thought of you and prayed for you. Yesterday and today, I have had emotions beyond all expression . . .

"The Holy Father wished to receive me alone and to give evidence of his fatherly tenderness. He asked intimate details about dear Theophane. . . .

"Today was the great day of the Beatification . . . The assemblage was immense, the great Basilica filled to overflowing. All the Papal Court was present. . . . When the Pope and his court had left the church, from the tribunes next to me there rushed towards me an avalanche of people, most of them unknown to me, who offered congratulations, shook my hands, and kissed them with visible joy. In treating me thus, they believed that they were in relationship with Theophane himself, as if he were living. . . . Very affectionately yours in Christ, L. E. Venard."

We felt that we knew these people personally. Father Walsh used to bring in their letters and read them to us. All this had an effect on us. We idealized the missions through these letters, and built up our vision of the perfect missioner. He made them all live for us.

Father Aimé Villion was another interesting friend. He spent sixty-eight years in Japan and was ninety years old when he died. When he arrived in Japan in 1866, Christians were still being persecuted. He never returned to his homeland. He used to say: "When I am called to Heaven, I want to draw my last breath shouting, 'Banzai!'"

He was several times decorated by the Japanese Government. The police used to annoy him with their repeated and endless questionings about himself, his work, and his homeland. They asked to see his passport. He devised a way of hanging his passport, spread open, on his back. When a detective accosted him and demanded his credentials, he would gravely turn around and let the plain-clothes man read the vital information from his back. While he was still alive, his statue was set up in the city of Yamaguchi, beside a monument to Saint Francis Xavier.

I was in Japan in the summer of 1924, having gone there from Hongkong to welcome the first group of Sisters of Notre Dame de Namur, who were to open a school at Okayama. I met Father Villion at Father Fage's mission in Kobe. He walked up close, peering at me through his bushy eyebrows, and asked: "Are you one of Father Walsh's new missioners, what?" Then he threw his arms around me.

"Look," he said. "Look at me. My bishop has stopped me from working. I am now too old. Too old! Look at that!" And he stamped around the room with all the vigor of a twenty-year-old.

"See that!" He pointed to one of his ears, which was scarred and had a part of the lobe missing. "My horse bit that off. Too old! Ha!" After that the bishop sent him to Nara. At this last post he set about building the present beautiful church.

Bishop Mutel, of Seoul, Korea, had been in correspondence with Father Walsh for a dozen years when the latter visited him in Korea. He was every inch and every moment a bishop, Father Walsh said. Large in heart, large in view, he was Catholic through and through. His beautiful life was like an open book, making an impression on all who came in contact with him. He wanted Maryknollers to take part of his mission.

When Father Walsh visited Bishop Mutel's house, in 1917, he wrote back to us: "The house within is physically cheerless, with its floors of wide boards filled with the dust of years, its bare walls, its poor oil lamps, and the general lack of small comforts; but the spirit that pervades it, I soon learned, is so warm, so pure, so unconsciously spiritual, that I realized more fully than ever how small an influence material comforts exert in the life of a Catholic missioner . . ."

Father Larribeau, who later became Bishop, read this letter when it was printed in *The Field Afar*. Maryknollers ever after, passing through Seoul and stopping at the Bishop's house, would invariably be greeted by him: "See—we still have the house that Father Walsh wrote about. And here are the wide boards and here is 'the dust of years,' still here, only some more has been added."

Bishop de Guébriant, of Kien Chang, China, afterwards of Canton, who later became Superior General of the Paris Foreign Missions, wrote to Father Walsh: "We missioners can't help shouting for joy on seeing the great new American Church, brimful of youth and hope, rise up in its turn and call upon its sons to send them to the field afar! I was all set to send you my offering, when I saw your notice: *Only Prayers accepted from missioners!"*

Sister O'Sullivan used to write from her hospital in Shanghai, telling her difficulties with attendants and with all sorts of vermin—beetles, flies, fleas, mosquitoes, and crabs. She wrote about a crab that got into the chapel one night. "He was making the stations and didn't want to get out when I went after him; said he hadn't finished. He tried to hide under the benches. As he was a stranger, I didn't try to lead him out by the hand but coaxed him, instead, with a few judicious kicks. He got as far as the door and then pretended that he could not climb over the sill—from which you can see what a lying race those crabs are. I reached my pencil towards him; he thought it was my finger (so slender and yellow!) and nipped it. Thus I had him and I slung him from the veranda into the sugar-cane plot."

I wish I could tell you about all of them. There were so many friends overseas, and all so good and so interesting: Father Verhaeghe, the Belgian priest in Shanghai; Bishop Vidal and Father Helliet from the Fiji Islands; Fathers O'Leary and Reilly, two young Irish priests in China; Bishop Rayssac in Swatow, Father Jackson and Father Wachtner in Borneo, Father McNeal, a Jesuit missioner in the Philippines and later in Tokyo, Bishop Hurth of Nueva Segovia. When Bishop Hurth visited Maryknoll, Brother Benedict spilt some hot gravy down his neck. He didn't take his eye off Brother for the rest of the meal. Can you blame him?

Letters from the "Bishop of Too-Gay-Gara-Oh" were frequent in those days. Father Maurice Foley, a Boston priest, a friend of Father Walsh, became Bishop of Tuguegarao, in the Philippines. We soon learned that this was among the northern islands and that the diocese took in three provinces—Cagayan, Ysabela, and Nueva Vizcaya, besides the islands of Batanes and Babayanes. These became household words with us, and we could say Too-Gay-Gara-Oh just as easily as you would say Far Rockaway.

Poems and various contributions from Father Thomas Gavan Duffy poured into our mail box. Thanks to him, we knew about mission life in Pondicherry, India. He sent us what he called the Latin translation of a manifesto which he wanted presented to the Archbishops and Bishops of India at their next meeting:

"In view of the heavy loss of life caused by lack of experience with regard to native rules of the road, we request that your Graces and Lordships consider the advisability of printing the following rules and their motives for the enlightenment of the newly landed missioners in those parts of the country where the bicycle is in use.

Rule I: Never ring your bell. (Latin *scararium*). Reasons from experience:

1. The native on the road will probably not hear the bell, and then you will be left to the last moment in uncertainty as to his intentions, eventually running into him and being killed. Whereas, if you pass him quickly and silently, he will awake from his reverie when you are one hundred yards away.

2. If, however, he hears the bell, he will stop and turn around. As you approach, he will hurriedly cross the road in front of you.

3. If he is leading a bullock by a rope, he will not stop, but, crossing the road as in rule 2, he will stretch the rope across the road, the bullock remaining on the original side.

4. If he is a Christian, he will wish to get your blessing; accordingly, he will join his hands before his forehead, bowing suddenly forward in such a way that your handle-bars will necessarily crack his skull.

Rule II: Don't stop for a puncture. (Latin, *exhalatio*). Reasons from experience:

1. There is no water wherewith to localize it.

2. As every tree has thorns, you will get another puncture ten yards further on.

3. Either you will catch a sunstroke, or else night will fall—and so will you, into the ditch.

We beg your Graces and Lordships, etc. . . . (signed) The Elders.

Many friends wrote or visited Maryknoll from Ireland, England, France, and from Germany, Italy, Holland, the Tyrol, Austria, and the East.

Brother Dutton, Father Damien's assistant at Molokai, wrote to Father Walsh in 1913 and sent him a dollar bill. "The blessed offering of the poor to the poor," Father Walsh called it. He wrote to explain his title of "Brother."

"I, myself, a convert, was baptized on my fortieth birthday, April 27th, 1883. Not really under vows at all. After about 20 months at Gethsemani, Kentucky, with the Trappists, I came here to help Father Damien, in July, 1886. I helped him three years. He died April 15th, 1889. The Sisters came that year (Sisters of St. Francis from Syracuse, N. Y.).

"I thought to explain about the 'Brother,' as applied to self. Father Damien always called me Brother. After the actual Brothers came to assist, it looked more regular, I suppose, to call me Brother . . .

"At first I corrected many correspondents about calling me Brother, at least told them how it is (that I'm Brother only in the Third Order of St. Francis), but a good share straightway began to write 'Father,' so I hushed up. . . ."

Brother Dutton's home was in Vermont. He read in *The Field Afar* about Tim Mahoney, one of our lay workers at Maryknoll whom Father Walsh described as "the man who could cut his own hair." "That's nothing," wrote Brother Dutton, "I have been cutting my own hair for years. It's not hard."

Father Fraser, a Canadian priest working with the French missioners in Ningpo, visited at Maryknoll and was a frequent correspondent. When he returned to China in 1912, he brought with him a young Irish-born priest from Brooklyn, Father Galvin. Father Galvin became the pioneer of the Maynooth Mission to China, the present St. Columban Fathers. In 1912, Father Galvin wrote back to us:

"Chinese has been called the 'lingua diabolica.' Well, I won't make any comments. One of the students in the seminary gives me about an hour a day, and one of the servants gives me two hours a day. Of course, he doesn't know Latin but with the help of the dictionary you sent me, we get on very well.

"I wrote an appeal to Maynooth. I had a letter from one of the Fathers who said: 'Some of us may follow you to China.'

"My beard is growing at a terrible rate. Father Ibaruthy said it will soon be under the table. . . ." Father Galvin, later Bishop Galvin, directed great mass conversions after the floods of the Yangtze-Kiang and built up a large flourishing diocese.

Father Fraser's letters and photos of his Chinese boys seemed to bring the missions of Ningpo and the Province of Chekiang very close to us. He was the precursor of the Canadian society of Scarboro Bluffs, having been in China long before the Society was founded. He has spent almost his entire life overseas. One of his photos was very popular. It was of a Chinese boy whom he called "James John Everywhere-Fruitful-Grove." This little Jimmy John, and about seventeen others like him, were good beggars for Father Fraser's orphanage.

Sister Catharine Buschman was perhaps the first American nun in China. She wrote frequently, telling about her orphans and her hopes for the future. She added this: "I read that an experienced priest had said, 'I hold firmly that for every vocation to the foreign missions, God grants three for the home missions.' An elder brother of mine was a Redemptorist when I came to China. A younger brother and sister, who seemed to have no intention at that time of becoming religious, both left home, before I was in China one year—the one to enter a Benedictine monastery in America, where he now is, and my sister to become a Sister of Charity. Soon after, one of my nephews entered a Redemptorist seminary. Later, a niece entered a convent of teaching nuns, and another niece hopes to enter a religious community soon . . ."

She was a Sister of Charity, from Baltimore. A photograph of herself and her orphans in China appeared on the cover of *The Field Afar* in 1910. Later, after Maryknoll was started, she wrote to Father Walsh: "May God bless your Seminary and may your good missioners carry the cheerful Maryknoll spirit to distant lands in the near future. I have been most anxious to have a little spot of land in your interesting Maryknoll. I was going to send an American 'greenback,' when it occurred to me that it would be more business-like if I sent you the enclosed Chinese bill. . . . I am sending some photographs. The cats are for my friends, the Teresians. . . ." One of Sister Catherine's relatives followed her to China, as Sister Rosalie of the Maryknoll Sisters. She is now a member of the Maryknoll Cloister.

An endless procession of friends wrote to us from afar and visited us from afar, during those first few years.

Bishop Berlioz, of Hakodate, Japan, was among them. His cathedral burned down three times. Bishop Chatron of Osaka was another. When he came to the States he slept on the floor; after years of Japanese habits, he found it more comfortable. Bishop Breton had worked among the Japanese in Los Angeles, as Father Breton, before returning to his missions in Japan. Bishop Espelage, the Franciscan Bishop of Wuchang, was the first missioner from the United States in China. Bishop Henninghaus, of Shantung Province, Bishop Boeymaen of Honolulu—we knew them all.

The Baroness Van Hoffmann sent us relics from her estate at Meran in the Tyrol. She also helped to support the missioners. Some of the relics at our Martyrs' Shrine at the seminary are gifts from the Baroness.

Dr. Agnes McLauren, a graduate of Edinburgh University, the first Catholic to devote herself exclusively to Catholic Medical Missions, told us about her work.

Father Andrew McArdle—born in Glasgow, educated at Blairs, Aberdeen, Valladolid, Bearsden, Glasgow, and All Hallows, Dublin, —joined Father Fraser and Father Galvin in Chekiang Province and wrote regularly to tell us about this English-speaking trio.

Father Paul Manna, founder of the Missionary Union of the Clergy, later Superior General of the Milan Foreign Missions, wrote to us and visited us. His book, *The Workers Are Few,* was translated by Monsignor Joseph McGlinchey, Father Walsh's successor in the Propagation of the Faith Office at Boston, and did much to stimulate missionary vocations in the United States.

Father Kennelly, S. J., an Irish missioner at Shanghai who edited a series of volumes on *Chinese Superstitions,* sent us reports on the situation in China. His American nephew, Father Robert Kennelly, joined Maryknoll and has spent a quarter of a century in the missions of Kwangtung.

Father Nicholas Walter, and his brother Augustine, were among the first Americans to go to Japan. They wrote regularly. Augustine was tutor for the children of the Japanese Emperor. He taught the present Emperor.

Father Cothonay, who had been superior of the Dominican House in Hawthorne and became Bishop of Longson, in Indo-China; Father Henry, Superior General of Mill Hill; Bishop Murel of Pondicherry; Bishop Benziger of Quilon, India—all these names were familiar to us. There were others, too numerous to write about here, though all are well remembered.

Christian de Bretenières, whose brother, Just de Bretenières was martyred in Korea, was a friend of Father Walsh. Another French friend, who wrote regularly, was Père Basil Huctin, a missioner from the parish of Father Eusebius Venard, brother of Blessed Theophane Venard.

There was Father Hopfgartner, of Borneo, short of stature, long of beard, gentle in manner, and altogether lovable. We had fun with him, as he told us tales of the Wild Man of Borneo. He told us that when he investigated Barnum and Bailey's "Wild Man from Borneo," he discovered he was an Irishman born in Cork.

Mother Paul in Uganda wrote interesting letters.

Then there was Bishop Gauthier, who as Father Gauthier, was Father Walsh's guide through Kwangtung Province in 1917, and who later, as Bishop, gave Maryknollers their initiation into mission life in the Kongmoon area, our first Maryknoll Mission. He had been French but, as Father Walsh described him, he became Chinese to the backbone and preferred chopsticks to a knife and fork, liked rice better than French bread. He visited Maryknoll and spent some months with us.

Father McAloone, one of the Irish White Fathers in Uganda, was on our mailing list. He wrote about a visit to his out-missions where he told all his people about Maryknoll. It was their duty to pray for us, he said. On the first day of the trip he had no sooner finished Mass when his head catechist, Danieli, jumped up and addressed the people: "Father McAloone wants us to pray for that good priest in America who has charge of a great big house, where white boys study to become priests. When they have finished, they will come out to teach people like us the one true religion. Now let us all, young and old, say a prayer for this good priest and another for those good boys who are going to become priests." Danieli made the same appeal in all the chapels.

I could go on and on, recalling these friends who beckoned us to come and welcomed us to the missions. I must not forget the Rogans.

Letters from the Rogans made good reading. Their father was in the British Army. The children—five boys and one girl—were all raised in military cantonments. They all entered religion.

The mother of the Rogans died in 1896, when Laurence, the eldest, was twelve years old. The father brought up the whole family. Peter, the poet of the family, was born on the Rock of Gibraltar, when Mr. Rogan was stationed at the garrison there. Kathleen became Sister M. Seraphina in the enclosed order of Redemptoristines, at Dublin.

When his friends remonstrated with Mr. Rogan, saying that he should not let all his children leave him to become religious, he replied, "God has given me these children; if He wants them for Himself, He shall have them." In later years, back in the County Kildare, Mr. Rogan's house and farm were three miles from church, but he kept up his practice of years and was at Mass and Communion daily.

Father Laurence Rogan had a difficult mission in the Philippines. There were rats and more rats under his little mission. "But the rats are used to me now," he said, "so used to me that they talk with a brogue." Some of the Rogans were in Africa. The "Little African Limericks", by Father Peter Rogan, who afterwards became Bishop Rogan of the British Cameroons, are mixed here with other of his lyrics:

> *This missioner who, to give him his due,*
> *Had labored in deadly climes,*
> > *Without much ado*
> > *Said, 'Glad to meet you,'*
> *And delivered the following rhymes.*

> *Mary sent a little lamb*
> *To Maryknoll P. O.;*
> > *It gave three squeals—*
> > *Grace after meals—*
> *'And it's gone where the good niggers go.'*

> *Jack and Jill climbed up a hill*
> *To see the Hudson water;*
> > *Where's Jack today?*
> > *A student—eh?*
> *And Jill? Teresians caught her.*

If modern apostles had nets
They could manage to pay off their debts;
  But a missioner now
  Who 'puts hand to the plough!'
Into trouble and woe deeper gets.

Please look for the moral in each little verse,
The meter, I know, could hardly be worse;
But then you must pull all the verses apart,
Reflect on the moral and take it to heart.

17

Brother Henry and Company

"Their individual names also are so given as to sig-
nify the kind of ministry wherein each is powerful.
Michael signifies: Who is like unto God?"
— Pope St. Gregory the Great. Sermon on the Angels

Brother Henry was dying. The news came to me while I was in the midst of collecting these memoirs. At irregular intervals in years past he had made occasional false starts in that direction. This time it was the real thing. Everyone knew it; Brother Henry knew it. The thought of death worries some people. I have known persons who were afraid of dying; others were afraid of being dead. Brother Henry made it clear that he was not afraid of dying because he knew that he would never really be dead.

He was living in our little seminary at Mountain View, California. The night before he died one of the Fathers called on him. Brother Henry was sitting up in bed, wearing his white nightcap, his glasses on, smiling. He was reading the paper. After a half hour, during which they talked mostly of old times, the priest got up to go. Brother looked at him with a big smile: "How would you like to see the latest racing sheet?" he asked. "Years ago in Boston I took two quick looks at the racing news with a friend of mine. We each put fifty cents on a horse named 'Canon Law,' and fifty cents on another called 'Doctor.' Both forgot to move!" Then with another smile he said: "Good night. Thanks for the visit." He died a few hours later.

I had been associated with Brother Henry, off and on, at various periods, ever since the day he arrived at Maryknoll in 1916. My chief recollection of him is his unfailing ability to make people laugh. He demonstrated daily that "Joy is the echo of the life of God within us." He is buried now at Mountain View, and the stone on his grave carries the same text inscribed on the graves of all our departed Maryknoll Brothers, *Quis ut Deus*—"Who is like unto God?"

From the very first days of Maryknoll, Father Walsh and Father Price felt that besides accepting students for the priesthood, it would be well, in imitation of the European congregations, to provide for other helpers, auxiliaries, or whatever you might wish to call them, who would do the work of Brothers. There were already three Brothers at Maryknoll when I arrived in the summer of 1913. Brother Henry came three years later, but I mention him first because he is uppermost in my thoughts now.

He was the son of Doctor Corcoran, a man who still lives in the memory of many, because of all he did to assuage the pains and relieve the misery of the people of Brooklyn. Brother Henry was the last of fourteen children and was the last one in his family to pass away, but many nephews and nieces survive to laugh over the stories told them by Uncle Henney. One of his nephews wrote to me after Brother's death:

"My fondest memories of Brother Henry, or 'Henney' as my saintly mother used to call him, picture him dancing an Irish jig in his favorite room—the kitchen. Then with appropriate gestures and waving a teacup he would regale us with yarns of his earlier days as a knight of the road.

"Did he ever tell you about the time he almost died of thirst, while crossing the Mohave Desert under a flatcar? He was indulging his avocation of moving about; that of course was before he became a monk. Somehow, I am sure if anyone gets right into Heaven it will be Henry. He can get in anywhere—a born gate-crasher. But I hope they have movies there.

"I bet he never did tell you about his letter-carrier brother, my Uncle Joe, and how he was almost buried in Cardinal Hayes' old pants, which happened to be lying around the house on the way to your mission shipping room.

"I know you will forgive these informal phrases. Perhaps I inherit a wee bit of Henry's love for the amusing aspects of this sometimes too serious life. I have an idea that he is all ready to bring a smile to the stern visage of St. Peter and the other apostles of whom you, as Bishop, are one of the successors."

Something must have moved Henry to make a big sacrifice. He enjoyed moving from place to place and he realized that once he entered the religious life he would have to give up all this. Before he came to Maryknoll he wrote: "Dear Father Walsh,—I shall be with you in spirit November 21st, on the feast of the Presentation of the Blessed Virgin Mary, and if in your estimation I am a fit subject to join your dear community, pray accept my application as a lay brother and present it to the Queen of Heaven and Earth as a love token on her feast. This is the wish of one who feels himself most unworthy of such a vocation."

His letters must have brought joy to Father Walsh, because his humor was of the type that would please Father James Anthony. His numerous letters, all in the same vein, are proof enough that Father Walsh never discouraged Brother Henry from writing. Right after one of his false starts towards the next life, Brother Henry wrote back: "Dear Father Walsh,—If I push off and am fortunate enough to make the big grade on high, for which I feel the least worthy, rest assured I won't forget Maryknollers and our benefactors, nor your loving kindness and care . . ." Later he wrote: "One doctor said I have the flu, but some of those heartless fellows say things sometimes just to see a fellow shake. Anyway, I feel all right now, as I took the proverbial ounce of prevention. Affectionate greetings to all."

Brother Henry could get a dollar for the missions where most men would hesitate even to try. His file at Maryknoll is filled with letters to his various superiors over the years with suggestions on ways and means of boosting support for the missions. Father Walsh wrote to compliment him on his good work, and he wrote back: "You have been a kind considerate Father to us all. I know I am unworthy of the compliments. I feel I have not measured up to the trust and confidence you have placed in me, but with the help of the Immaculate Mother on whose feast you saw fit to accept me into

your good society I shall strive both to atone and to reach the goal
of eternal life. The past two years have indeed been the happiest moments of my life and anything the world could offer would be as
nothing in comparison."

Brother's letters are filled mainly with reports on his work of
winning friends and reports on his narrow escapes from death. "The
hills seem to have no terrors for me now," he wrote, "and my heart
action has received only three thrills since I arrived: first, a chase
by a wild country dog; second, caught in a blinding snowstorm a
quarter of a mile from home; and last, the shock when a lady
handed me a check for fifty dollars for perpetual membership, and
said she may help educate a student later on . . .

"I had an operation, you know . . . The sixth day after the big
wind, and the compass tells me I am still a few points off the coast
of Hoke Poke where they serve arsenic ice cream cones. I feel lonesome but I suppose that is only natural after being separated from a
couple of my organs. I hope the good doctor had the presence of
mind to substitute some other music in place of them—an old Stradi-
varius or a baby grand—so that I might be able still to charm people
to subscribe to *The Field Afar*. If they neglect a substitute, with
my nerve and gall gone, I'll feel like a blooming blighter . . .

"The doctors, Sisters, orderlies, and students were great. Thanks
for your intercession at the throne. John Chang is in the same room
with me and is to be operated on Wednesday, August 31st." John
Chang, whom Brother mentions here, was a Korean student at Manhattan College, spending his summers at Maryknoll. He later became first Ambassador from Korea to the United States, and he
represented his country at the United Nations.

Towards the end of that particular siege of sickness Brother
Henry reported to Father Walsh: "The doctor finished giving me
twenty-four hypos of iron about ten days ago. He advised me to
come back if it did not pep me up and he would shoot some more
into me. I am on the job every day doing what little I can and,
please God, I shall have a few more perpetual members to write
home about before I am given the last shove. Father Keller's perpetual smile has me grinning from 'year to year.' I felt a little lonesome
after Father McCarthy and Brother Edward left. For several days I

left some oats in the feed bag but now I am clearing up all the grain. Praying that this finds you well."

Father O'Shea, whose association with ships and yachts and the Brooklyn Navy Yard, as already mentioned in a previous chapter, retained for him to the very end the title of "Cap," got this letter from Brother Henry during one of his periods of convalescence. "The climate here is much easier on the arthritis, and I am looking forward to a ripe old age in this lovely mountain home with its pure spring water. Just what the doctor ordered for old joints. The scenic beauty of this Santa Clara valley is marvelous, carpeted as far as the eye can see with pink and white fruit blossoms; it's beyond any poor words of mine adequately to describe. All the time the rippling sunshine dances on the whitecaps of San Francisco Bay for fifty miles as the crow flies. The Tanforan Race Track is only a hop, skip and a holler away, and with my field glasses in the tower I can pick the winner every day before the bookie. . . ."

After my ordination in 1920, I was in charge of our Brothers. From time to time Brother Henry would come looking for me. His smile would be worn a little thin, and his general air would be a bit bluish. This would indicate that he "felt like breaking glass." I always knew what this meant: Brother wanted to get on the road again, and the search for new and helpful friends would make his journeying well worth while.

Only a few months before he died, I visited him at Mountain View. That was our last meeting. On a previous visit to California, I made the mistake of bringing Brother Henry and Father John Morris on a visit to the Carmel at Santa Clara. Father Walsh had instructed me to visit the Prioress. In the parlor, while I tried to engage in holy conversation with the Lady Prioress, who was behind the curtained grille, Brother Henry and his companion went through their repertoire of monkey shines. Their object was to embarrass me by making me laugh. They had unexpected success when, trying to concentrate on what the holy lady behind the grille was saying, I moved close to the screen and pushed my nose into one of the iron spikes of the grillwork. My two attendants were convulsed.

Brother Henry and I went to Atlantic City one Sunday to take up a collection for the missions. It was at the Church of St. Nicholas. I talked from the pulpit, and Brother went around with the basket and smiled at the people as they left the church. When we counted the returns we saw that we had sixteen hundred dollars. Afterwards, I learned that Brother Henry had said rosary after rosary while I preached.

It was a morning of hard work, and we had hardly let ourselves sink into the soft seats of the train for New York when Brother was fast asleep. He woke up as we were pulling into the Penn Station, just in time to see the porter come in for the bags and pick up the one with the sixteen hundred dollars in it. Brother Henry sprang out of his seat as if propelled by springs and clinched both the bag and the poor porter in one leap. It took me some minutes to convince him that it would be just as well not to show too much special interest in that one bag, lest someone make a real attempt to make away with it.

Another day, we went together to Camden, New Jersey. The parish had a sort of mission attached to it, or rather, there was a Mass for the people in the chapel of a cloistered convent within the parish limits. I spoke in the main church, and Brother went to the other Mass. The chaplain there spoke on the missions and asked the people to contribute. He had Brother Henry sit in the sanctuary while he preached. Henry was terribly embarrassed because the good chaplain spoke mainly of the hero sitting in the sanctuary who was giving his life for the poor benighted heathen, and so on. If Brother looked up, he was staring into the face of the community of nuns on the other side of the grille facing the altar. If he looked to the right, there was the congregation admiring him. He couldn't turn left and put his back to the people. He was like a hen on a hot griddle until the sermon was over.

For a time, Brother Henry was caretaker of the little office and tenement we had on 57th Street in New York City. We had a Spanish missionary Father visiting us. This missionary had what was thought to be, and could likely have been, an original Velasquez, a painting of one of the Isabellas of Spain. The painting had been unearthed in a monastery where it had been disguised purposely; a Carmelite habit was painted over the robes of the Queen. It was found by an expert, restored, and given to this missionary, whose plan was to sell it and use the proceeds to start a foreign mission seminary in Spain.

It was Brother Henry's job to guard the painting at night. He had been solemnly instructed regarding the value of the painting and what a treasure was left in his keeping. One night, not long after retiring, he heard a sound coming from the other side of the room. He was naturally nervous. He thought of the art treasure. Others knew about it. Such things had been stolen before. That noise sounded like someone filing on iron window bars. "Good night, Queen!" he said, or something like that, "every man for himself!" He dashed up to a room on the floor above and barred himself in. Next day he discovered the source of the noise. The telephone receiver had been left off the hook, and the operator was trying to attract attention. It was a long time before Brother heard the end of comments on his unchivalrous conduct when the Queen was in peril.

Brother Henry is remembered most of all for his ability to make friends, and also, as already indicated, for his ability to make people laugh. Stories by him and stories about him would fill a small volume. One day, just before an exhibition ball game between the students and the Brothers, he had someone paint the features of a face, with eyes, nose, mouth, etc., on the back of his bald head. The effect was startling if you stood on the side lines and looked at the fellow up at bat with his head swiveled around at you. Running from second base to third, he tripped and fell flat on his face, that is, on his own face, and the grotesque face on the back of his head stared with a foolish impassive grimace up at the sky, giving the impression that his head was twisted completely around. I suppose that now, up there in Heaven, he is carrying on just the same as ever.

Father Walsh's idea, in founding the Auxiliary Brothers, was to attach to the seminary a body of earnest, bright young Catholic men who would serve at home or on the missions, wherever they might be needed, as helpers and companions. His dream was gradually realized; the number of Brothers grew and they were banded together under the patronage of St. Michael the Archangel.

The *New York Times,* reporting a Departure Day at Maryknoll, printed photos of the ceremony. One of the pictures showed the Departure Bell being rung to announce the beginning of events. A

Brother stands at either side of the huge bell, swinging a wooden mallet. One, tall and elderly with white hair, is Brother Xavier. The other is dark-skinned. This is Brother Aloysius, born in Cuba.

In 1889, the year of the great Johnstown flood, the same year when the first automobile was exhibited at the World's Fair in Paris, Brother Aloysius was born at Limanor, in Cuba. His name then was Horace Moliner. In later years he deserted Havana in favor of Brooklyn. He learned about Maryknoll through the Sisters of the Precious Blood Monastery, on Fort Hamilton Parkway. He came to us in 1916.

He has been a painter at times, a carpenter at other times, and always a gardener. Once, as charioteer in charge of the rubbish disposal, he backed his dump cart a little too close to the brink of the gully. Horse and wagon, rubbish and Brother Aloysius went head over heels down into the ditch. Saint Michael, ably assisted by a corps of Guardian Angels, hauled him out all in one piece, fortunately. Brother Aloysius was a bit chagrined but still smiling.

As senior Brother at Maryknoll, Brother Aloysius has preached to everyone every day, not with wordy eloquence, but rather with the way he does things and the way he says things, which is a pretty good index of why he does things.

Brother Xavier Lambe, born eight years before Brother Aloysius, came to Maryknoll a year after him, in 1917. When his parents died, he and his sister carried on with the family farm at Fairfax, Vermont. Later they sold the farm; Brother came to Maryknoll, and his sister joined the Mercy Order and became Sister Celestine.

We students marveled at his size and strength. On the farm, making hay, cultivating, cleaning up—no one could keep up with him. One day Doctor Bradley, the Veterinarian, came to inoculate our hogs. The doctor hesitated to approach the big animals with his needle. Brother hopped calmly into the pen like a master of judo. He reached under the belly of the hog, grasped the off leg and in a twinkling had the animal on his back. If necessary, he held it quietly in place with a sort of half nelson or hammer lock. In student days he was our hero, and he ever remained such.

Visitors to the Seminary find special interest in the oriental kiosk, which stands in the center of the quadrangle, built as a canopy over

Our Lady of Maryknoll. It is the work of Brother Albert Staubli. As architect and builder, Brother Albert supplied most of the brains and a good part of the brawn for several mission buildings in South China, into which he worked various details of Chinese art.

Brother Albert was born among the Swiss Alps. He spent eight long years as apprentice to a wheelwright, living with the master's family on the side of a mountain in Switzerland. He came to Maryknoll in 1917 and went to China four years later. He is also a good farmer. During the war with Japan, when armies overran the provinces of China interrupting the people's life line of food and supplies, he turned to farming and supplied his fellow missioners with the vitamins they needed to stay on in the land of the living and keep busy.

When Jim Coffey, the "Roscommon Giant," was training for his bout with Frank Moran, he had his camp at Kelley's Pinesbridge Hotel, about an hour's walk from the Seminary. Passing back and forth on their way to the railway at Ossining, Coffey and his trainers got to know Maryknoll. One of the trainers, Martin Barry, joined us. Later, at the Japanese Mission in Seattle and after that in Hongkong, Brother Martin taught Oriental youngsters the useful art of jab and self-defense.

Besides training prize fighters, Brother Martin had worked in his younger days as an undertaker's assistant. He had been also with the Internal Revenue Department. One of his missions of investigation took him to Kentucky, where he was to localize the source of a big flood of moonshine. His identity was soon established among the gentle mountaineers, and when he heard that some long-barreled guns were getting his range, he forthwith got a timetable and looked up the next train for New York.

When St. Conrad of Parzham was canonized, the Holy Father Pope Pius XI said in his address to the pilgrims that in every religious community the two most important posts are held by the Superior and the Porter. There may be hundreds of holy monks dwelling within the monastery walls, but to the new arrival and the casual caller the Porter represents them all. To the outside world that comes knocking at the gate, to bring gifts in kind, to ask for a bowl of soup or to sell oil, insurance, and patented can-openers,

Brother Porter is the outside guard reflecting the warmth, joy, and kindly feeling from within. He is like the eyes, which, we are told, are the windows of the soul.

For years we have been blessed with another Conrad of Parzham who answers our doorbell and wears out much shoe leather in quest of self-effacing souls whose presence is urgently awaited in the parlor or at the end of the telephone line but who, yearning for the quiet life of Simon at the top of his pillar, strive to suppress their identity and conceal their whereabouts. Our St. Conrad is Brother George Lannen, who came to us from Waterbury, Connecticut, when Maryknoll was only nine years old.

How far can a man walk in a day? We have an authority. Brother Vincent Parkinson, who came to us from Preston, England, says that it depends partly on how much a man can eat in a day, either before or after the hike. Brother Vincent is an expert farmer and experienced maintenance man, a source of information on chickens, roads, and the reigns of all the King Georges.

From Scoutmaster to Editor is the life story of Brother Theophane Walsh who grew up in Roxbury, Massachusetts, where an especially strong and hardy stock of Catholics is known to thrive. For thirty years he has been showing Japanese youngsters how to grow up big and happy in the sunshine of the Faith.

Jersey City may wish some day to raise a monument to a local boy who made good. Brother Joseph Donahue, who has been with us since 1916, lost a leg when only a boy. He was always reminding us that he had one foot in the grave. Compensating for his restricted footwork, he became an expert stenographer and bookkeeper, and for many years in Korea, kept accounts straight for our missioners. As a missioner, he has an easy entree with the youngsters. One of his bag of tricks is to go into a store, ask for a thumbtack and then bend down in the presence of "the gang" to adjust a sock by pressing the tack into his cork leg. He might ask a youngster to help him pull off his shoe; at the same time he releases the strap that holds the artificial leg in place. The youngster's eyes open wide as saucers when he finds not a shoe but a leg coming to him gently from the trousers.

He was in trouble one day in the Bay of Wonsan, Korea, when a storm overturned the small boat in which he and other missioners were crossing to the mainland. The cork leg, which might normally have been expected to help keep him afloat, drifted away. Father Leo Sweeney helped him to the side of the capsized boat and stayed with him until a rescue party arrived. One of the party drowned.

Remember the story in the Book of Kings about Jehu, who became King and drove his own chariot? "And the driving," says the Holy Book, "is like the driving of Jehu, the son of Namsi, for he drives furiously." We have had many followers of Jehu in the early gigs, later with the "Tin Lizzies," and more recently with the streamlined models. But one driver we have who goes, not furiously, but gently and well. Instead of Jehu, we call him Brother Charles. He was James Fowley in little old New York, but he has been Brother Charles for well over a quarter of a century. Most of this time he has spent behind the wheel, and if he had his own personal odometer it would show a record of hundreds of thousands of miles accumulated during years of driving bus loads of oriental school children or truck loads of mail sacks filled with *The Field Afar*. Rain or shine, he sees to it that the mail goes through.

The Brothers have grown in strength and numbers. At this moment we have a good hundred of them. Some are at work in practically all of our mission fields—China, Japan, Africa, Hawaii, South and Central America. Maryknoll's houses of training have multiplied rapidly, however, and these schools have absorbed the greater portion of the Brothers, who keep the wheels moving and the home fires burning. They help keep the wolf from the door, laboring generously in the home land as carpenters and painters, masons, chauffeurs, farmers, mechanics, bookkeepers and accountants. The value of their service mounts immeasurably. Eventually, more of them, we hope, will be made available for service in our mission fields, and with this in view we are endeavoring to train them now with specialized courses in agriculture, animal husbandry, arts and crafts, etc.

Perhaps I have unfolded this chapter in reverse, since I began it with the most recent of the Brothers to die, Brother Henry. I come at last to the Brother who was the first to die. This is Brother Bernard.

Brother Bernard was Eastman Alfred Bobb, a stocky Negro, born in Grenada, British West Indies, in 1890. He gave up his job as fireman on a sugar plantation and moved to Wakefield, Massachusetts. He came to Maryknoll in 1919, but before that he had been helping the missions, writing to Monsignor McGlinchey in Boston and to Father Walsh at Maryknoll. He sent ten dollars every week for the education of students for the priesthood. Since, as he felt, he could not become a priest himself, he would do what he could to help others on their way. He said in a letter to Father Walsh: "All my desire is to devote myself to our Eternal Father. I am not worthy to serve at His altar. I shall labor honestly in assisting His blessed servants in all good works. That is what I am here for, and nothing else."

Brother Bernard was with us only two years, but everyone that knew him still remembers him. He was cheerful and most affable. He was modest, humble, industrious, pious. He sent a note to Father Price about consecrating himself to Our Lady: "Since last November I wanted to approach you about consecrating myself heroically to our sweet and loving Mother for the remaining portion of my life . . . What I have experienced myself of the advantages received through our loving Mother is more than I can describe. She it is who induced me to leave the world and its pleasures and amusements. I thank God in the first place for being here, and then her, and finally you, dear Father. Please excuse me for giving you this trouble and wasting your precious time . . ."

I shall never forget the day he died. It was February 25th, 1921. He had served my Mass that morning in the little chapel of the Brothers, at St. Joseph's, the converted barn. It was Lent. He was fasting; all he had taken for breakfast was a cup of coffee and a piece of bread. All morning he had been working at the pump house down in the woods, getting the motor in order. It was noon when he got back to the seminary, almost time for the noon visit in chapel, but he still had an adjustment to make in the boiler room.

He hurried over to the other building, down into the pit and then climbed up on the Dutch oven. He was probably weak to begin with, having gone the whole morning with hardly anything to eat. Then, too, the sudden change from the cold outdoors to the hot boiler room may have made him dizzy. Blowing out the tubes of the boilers would have released some coal gas. Whatever it was, he drew back, caught his heel in the pipe that ran along the edge and fell to the concrete pavement below. The force of the fall fractured his skull. He never regained consciousness. We took him to the Ossining Hospital, and that night he died.

Only the day before, one of the Sisters had brought her father to the boiler room. "I wished to show my father the heating plant," she said afterwards. "When we went down we found Brother Bernard busy at the furnace preparing for the night man. I knew that what he was doing was extremely heavy work. I remarked it and said it was too bad he did not have more help.

"Brother smiled and then he said, 'It's like this, Sister. I have given myself to God and have consecrated my life to Mary.'"

From the way he worked and the way he talked, it was clear that he lived and worked in the presence of Jesus and Mary. And, doubtless, in their presence he died.

18

The First World War

"The aircraftsmen of our Army, now being trained to fly the skies, are symbolic of the times in which we live. As they rise from the ground and tread the by-ways of the birds, they better realize how small is that part of the world's acreage from which they came. . . . They get a wider horizon."
— James Anthony Walsh. November, 1917

It was June 29th, 1914. We were commemorating the third anniversary of Maryknoll's foundation. The front pages of the newspapers carried the story of what had happened the day before at Sarajevo. Gaurillo Princip, a Serb student, had killed the Archduke Francis of Austria and his wife. Perhaps some people realized the seriousness of the incident and guessed the aftermath. I'm afraid we didn't. Two years previously Serbia and Montenegro, Bulgaria and Greece had waged a war against Turkey, and for us this latest incident was just another sign of the usual unrest in the Balkans.

By the time we returned to class in September, Austria had declared war on Serbia, and Germany had invaded Belgium, Luxemburg, and France. Russia had attacked Germany and, in return, had been ignominiously defeated by the Germans at Tannenberg. The Battle of the Marne was raging.

Father Walsh warned us not to discuss political questions. Tension was increasing daily. We had such a representation from European countries, either by origin or by descent, that any expression of indignation or condemnation would be more than enough to touch off the hair trigger of sensibilities and cause an explosion.

During the first years of the war, before America got into it, we made an innocent blunder which caused us trouble. We published in *The Field Afar* a letter from a missioner in India, in which the writer used a disparaging term at that time in quite common use to designate one of the belligerent nations. It caused quite a tempest. Several scores of letters came from our readers, accusing us of unfairness, taking sides, prejudice, and violating our Catholic neutrality. In our little world it became a *"cause célèbre."* Some of the letters were violent, some even insulting. Subscriptions were canceled. It all indicated how inflamed spirits were at that time and how difficult it was to avoid taking, or seeming to take sides. All this, of course, was before the United States had been drawn into the war.

The war was thinning the ranks of European missioners. Bishop Combaz of Nagasaki wrote to say that he had lost eleven of his priests. The French laws of conscription made no exception for the clergy. The Bishop of Canton, too, described how mission work there had been sadly slowed down by the loss of priests. So it was all over the East and Africa and the islands of the Pacific.

"Blessed be the Divine Providence, which at the propitious moment inspired the thought of establishing an American Seminary for Foreign Missions!" wrote Bishop Bertreux of the Solomon Islands in 1916. "This work becomes more than ever necessary on account of the terrible European war and its consequences.

"Religio depopulata! Alas, how well the words apply today to the Catholic countries that up to the present time gave to Holy Church legions of missioners! And what will these countries be able to do on the morrow of the cataclysm which has wrought universal destruction? . . .

"Fill up quickly all your ranks at Maryknoll. *Intende, prospere, procede et regna!* But I warn you that when the first band of your apostles going to China or Japan, passes near our islands, I shall stop a half-dozen of them that they may work here with us for the conversion of our poor savages. . . . We have four thousand Catholics. There are still one hundred thousand cannibals to be converted."

Father Walsh received a letter from France, edged with a heavy black border. It was an announcement that read: "Killed on the

Field of Honor, September 21, 1915, in his 56th year." It bore the name of Father Compagnon, who was rector of the Paris Mission Seminary when Father Price and Father Walsh stopped there in 1911. Father Walsh recalled the long walks they had together in the seminary garden, during which the saintly missioner had given him many useful suggestions.

"For a man of little faith this is the hour of despair," wrote Father Manna of the Milan Missions in 1916, "but for us it should be the hour of great sacrifice and heroism. If we have in our hearts an ounce of love for God, we ought to save the missions. Patriotism places no limits to the sacrifices it imposes on nations at war. May zeal for the establishment of Christ's Kingdom—which is the patriotism of Faith—inspire a like generosity in Catholics of those nations that have been spared the war."

Bishop Demange of Taikou, Korea, which in later years has been spelled Taegu and figured prominently in the news of 1950 when the Reds invaded South Korea, wrote in April 1916: "This terrible war is so prolonged that I begin to despair. If it continues it will mean the ruin of many missions. We certainly hope that American Catholics will realize how dependent we have been on Europe."

During the war, missioners were caught now and then at Maryknoll, either on their way to Europe or trying to get back to their missions. Two of them were with us for a long time, Father Verbrugge from Borneo and Father Poirier from India. At the end of the war, when Father Poirier was able to set out on his way, we hurried together a little skit in his honor. Written, rehearsed, and staged all in less than a day, this entertainment made Father Walsh laugh more than anything else put on in all my years at Maryknoll.

The theme of the comedy was Father Poirier's send-off at Maryknoll and his welcome in France. We dug up some frock coats, silk hats, and a few beards. We put on our best French accent to practice "Bon jour, Monsieur! Mais comme vous êtes bienvenu! Mais, oui, la, la!" Et cetera, et cetera!! and we represented the great men of France—Poincaré, Foch, Clemenceau, Joffre, and the rest. As Father Poirier stepped off the boat, he was greeted by each in turn and given the traditional French bear hug. Each of us carried a huge placard on his back bearing the name of the great man we impersonated.

The war was having its echo in China. The country was thrown into confusion while various provincial factions struggled for the supremacy. Late in 1916, we received this letter from South China: "The troubles in Canton are increasing, and the city has been terror-stricken since last July. Shells and bullets are raining here and there, but the danger is not excessive. In Tungkung last week there was a fight which lasted through the whole night. Yet, although about thirty thousand rounds were shot, only a few civilians were killed or wounded. The Chinese soldiers are not very anxious to kill, but persons may be killed by accident. Hongkong is full of Chinese refugees—about two hundred thousand."

When a city like Canton changed hands, as each succeeding war lord came into power, it was a strain on the diplomatic prowess of the Bishop of the place. I know a French Bishop who had the reputation of accompanying the retreating Governor to the North Gate of the city, and then hurrying over to the South Gate to welcome the new master of the place.

Early in 1917, Germany had informed America that it was returning to unrestricted submarine warfare. This practically barred American vessels from entering European waters, since the German "Safety Lane" admitted only one American vessel a week to the port of Falmouth. The United States broke off diplomatic relations with Germany on February 3rd. In March, the President gave orders to arm our merchant ships. On Good Friday, April 6th, we learned that the United States had declared war on Germany. American soldiers were in France by the end of June, and in October casualty lists were coming back from the American lines.

Father Walsh used these war days to push home lessons on foreign missions. "Prepare," he said, "This is the country's watchword and it applies not only to immediate needs, but to the future. Even now the business world is looking ahead to after-war conditions and actually planning for those days.

"Prepare. Catholic missioners are groaning under the strain of increased responsibility and diminished numbers, but this condition will be yet worse because the supply of men from Europe has been stopped, and years must elapse before it is resumed. . . .

"They say, whoever they are, that small nations must disappear. We are no prophets at Maryknoll, but we see the ends of the earth drawing together so steadily, and strange peoples getting to know one another so easily, that we believe that even big nations may yet lose their identity.

"A long way off, you say? Well, nobody knows anything these days except that God is in His Heavens, and the earth is ablaze, and great changes are coming rapidly.

"We wish, however, to add this word. Without the Prince of Peace there can be no lasting peace, and those of us who follow His standard must learn to look upon the man who walks at our side as a brother, whatever may be the country of his birth, or the color of his skin." Father Walsh wrote this in the summer of 1917. Later he went on with the same subject:

"In the wake of our World War which seems to be slowly finishing its course, there will follow a host of theories on permanent peace. Statesmen and poets will theorize, but few will strike at the root of the evil; few will find the cause of war in the violation of God's great command, 'Thou shalt love thy neighbor as thyself for the love of God'; fewer still will seek the remedy in the Foreign Mission ideal.

"Yet the Foreign Mission ideal is the antithesis of restricted nationalism, of prejudiced provincialism, of narrow racial barriers, of social exclusiveness. The Cause of Foreign Missions is the Cause of the Universal Brotherhood of Man. The apostolic spirit makes men equal on God's earth and kin to all the world,—no longer Jew or Gentile, Greek or barbarian, but all children of God, our common Father.

"The Court of Permanent Peace was set up in Galilee, when Jesus Christ sent forth His chosen men to preach the Gospel to every creature, to bring peace to men of good will. This spirit, once thoroughly grasped, would override all national prejudices that blind us to the good in other peoples. If Governments were actuated by the principles behind the apostolic mission work, if Christians the world over were enrolled under the standard, 'Going, teach all nations,' if rulers, spiritual and temporal, kings and bishops, priests and congressmen, had minds and hearts big enough to embrace the welfare of their fellow man without regard to his color, the racial hatred that rules today in Christian hearts would be swept away, and men would see in every other man a brother.

"This is admittedly ideal, but ideals should be the gauge of our actions. Every act that furthers the cause of Foreign Missions is a step nearer the ideal of Christian life, a blow to jaundiced nationalism, and another link in the bond of the universal brotherhood of man."

These words of Father Walsh, written and published in 1917, are striking now in the light of what actually took place ten years later, twenty years and thirty years later. It seems that we shall never learn. How futile and fruitless have been the billions spent on defense, squandered in making the world safe for democracy, waging wars to end wars.

Although we were generous with our Marshall Plan, American lawmakers at Washington were miserly in voting support for the Point Four Program to maintain world peace and freedom, a plan that would have relieved great misery in undeveloped regions of the world and at the same time would have brought happiness and good feeling to multitudes in distress. What excellent returns would have been brought by substantial support of UNESCC and other efforts of this kind. Yet, when war clouds threatened again in the East, threatened our economic security, again the lawmakers voted billions for arms, again for arms and munitions, that accomplished so little for us in two world cataclysms in one generation. It seems true, we shall never learn.

In July, 1917, Mr. Herbert Hoover became "food dictator" and the next month Mr. Garfield was appointed "fuel administrator." Every possible step was taken to expedite the production of munitions, war supplies, and foodstuffs, and to get these supplies to Europe as quickly as possible for the relief alike of the armed forces and of the civilian population. Placing American grain, meat and money, as well as munitions, at the disposal of the Allies was an important step in hastening the end of the war.

Our attempts to Hooverize brought complications, as described by Father Byrne in the winter of 1917-18. "Thinking we were subscribing to the wishes of Mr. Hoover, and anxious to do our bit in saving our bites, we placed 'ice skating' on the menu as the regular afternoon dessert; but experience shows that this practice, instead of being an economy, defeats its purpose by increasing the appetite for supper.

"We've noticed this hitch in other spheres as well. For instance: to save coal, we burn wood. But cutting the wood develops pangs of hunger so enormous as to demand for their quieting more than the price of the coal saved.

"Again, we get up earlier to save daylight, but it is so dark we have to use electricity which means more coal gone, of course.

"Finally, we find the disease contagious, for the chicks and the moo-cows have entered so whole-heartedly into the economy propaganda that we don't get enough milk now to float our weekly egg.

"Meatless days? The idea! Of course we have meatless days— every week. We've always had them. The kind, y'know, where you can't possibly get both ends to meet, no matter how you stretch them."

Whatever its other results, the war was broadening our outlook on life. Instead of being definable as a number of continents separated by water, the world was coming to be regarded as a number of continents connected by water.

All during this time Father Price continued to be an inspiration. At times he was on the road to make mission work better known and to secure support for us all. Back at the seminary, he directed our spiritual life. By his own command his name was withheld from all publicity, so that again and again his friends asked for him, wondering where he was.

In the spring of 1918, he composed a Message of the Immaculate Conception, Patron of America, to American Catholics. Instead of his name, he signed the usual "M.B.", for Mary Bernadette. "Pray and work for the conversion of souls now perishing—this is the message which the Immaculate Conception gave to little Bernadette and bade her convey to all.

"How can it be possible that God should give to America the Immaculate Conception for its sole National Patron and that the greatest and most wonderful and most important message of the Immaculate Conception should have no particular interest for America? Are we not justified in concluding, are we not forced to conclude, that of all people on earth American Catholics are most bound to heed and obey that message. . . ?

"Not only has the Great War taken away missioners, but it has cut off missionary effort of almost every kind from almost all the nations except America. Today, America is practically the only nation on earth in any condition to help the missions.

"We are the wealthiest nation on earth . . . Nowhere else on earth do wealth and luxury of life appear as in America. But we are paying and must pay more and more the penalty for all this luxury and worldliness. Day by day our Catholic life is going down perceptibly under the corrupting influences surrounding us . . .

"To resist these corrupting influences, to keep our Catholic life pure and untainted, to spread our Catholic faith throughout America, there is no possible way except to build up and increase among our people the apostolic spirit. . . ."

Day by day, month by month, Father Price was getting his "boys" ready for the Chinese front. The Maryknoll cantonment was being quietly drilled. He was giving us the fruits of his own experience, the wisdom of his years, getting us ready to win back for God His neglected "no man's land"—China.

When American boys were dying in the Belleau Woods and around Chateau-Thierry, Father Walsh issued a little reminder: "The parents of the nation are sacrificing their sons to cross the Atlantic, and to die, perhaps, as every true patriot is willing to do for his country, and the world applauds the sacrifice, as it should.

"But remember—when a youth, your boy possibly, volunteers to cross the Pacific so as to fight not men but Satan and his legions, do not keep from him the encouragement which he deserves."

As the year 1918 progressed, the war in Europe went better and better for the Allies. The apathy and defeatism of Western Europe disappeared, and martial enthusiasm ran high. The tide was definitely turning. In June, Father Walsh had us take note of President Wilson's Memorial Day Proclamation:

"And whereas, it has always been the reverent habit of the people of the United States to turn in humble appeal to Almighty God for His guidance in the affairs of their common life:

"Now, therefore, I, Woodrow Wilson, President of the United States of America, do hereby proclaim Thursday, the thirtieth day of May, a day already freighted with sacred and stimulating memories, a day of public humiliation, prayer and fasting, and do exhort my fellow citizens of all faiths and creeds to assemble on that day in several places of worship and there, as well as in their homes, to pray Almighty God that He may forgive our sins and shortcomings as a people and purify our hearts to see and love the truth, to accept and defend all things that are just and right and to purpose only those righteous acts and judgments which are in conformity with His will; beseeching Him that He will give victory to our armies as they fight for freedom, wisdom to those who take counsel on our behalf in these days of dark struggle and perplexity, and steadfastness to our people to make sacrifice to the utmost in support of what is just and true, bringing us at last the peace in which men's hearts can be at rest because it is founded upon mercy, justice, and good will."

Events moved fast in September 1918. The Allied offensives were bolder and more determined. They were attacking all along the front. American troops were advancing east of the Argonne and in the valley of the Meuse. The German Chancellor resigned. The new Chancellor set his program before the Reichstag in which he stated Germany's reply to the Pope's note of August 1st, and he said Germany was ready for world peace. The next month he appealed directly to President Wilson for a cessation of hostilities.

The war had worried and wearied practically every corner of the United States. At Maryknoll we were sheltered, in a way, from many of its harsher aspects, but some effects were inescapable. It was depressing to read the casualty lists that came from the battle front week after week. A very evident tension was wearing on men's nerves. A heavy weight oppressed the spirit of every man and woman, and of every child old enough to realize what was going on; mothers and wives felt it most.

All of a sudden this weight was lifted. Word went around on

November 7th that the war was over. The announcement was premature, but people took it as authentic. Men left their work, schools sent home the children, people filled the churches to offer prayers of thanks. We were at manual labor in the afternoon. Suddenly the air was filled with the ringing of bells, the clamor of fire sirens and factory whistles. From the railway yards at Harmon came an earsplitting din of innumerable locomotive whistles, all unleashed in wild abandon.

We lost our heads and started a parade, carrying whatever we found next to us—picks, shovels, axes, hammers, saws. As we marched, we sang and shouted and pounded boxes and tin cans. Joe Sweeney drove his wagon in the procession and had the mule pirouetting in front of *The Field Afar* building, when Father Walsh emerged just in time to see the wagon bog down in one corner of the hedge while the mule was left straddling another part of the same beautiful hedge. I would rather hurry over the speech that Father Walsh made to us then and there, with a picturesque appraisal of our judgment, or lack of it.

Back on the steps of the seminary, we cheered everyone from the Holy Father down to the least of the doughboys, including all the heads of nations and the great generals one by one. Exhausted we went back to our rooms and later learned that it was all a false alarm.

But peace was on the way. The Armistice was signed at five o'clock in the morning of November 11th, and hostilities ceased six hours later. Owing to the difference of time, it was all over and announced to the world before most Americans were up. We were allowed a free day in New York to see the demonstrations.

"The war is over," Father Walsh said in November, 1918. "Why stand gazing back on the gaping ruins, the blood-stained earth, the fields banked with the graves of young men? The past is useful only as it urges us to something higher today and for the future.

"The hour has struck for great movements, and the clarion call sounds for another kind of war—an unbloody one, the sole object of which is to draw by love from under the standard of Satan the millions who serve him because they know not Christ. Big as we Americans thought ourselves, we can never again be as small as we were. Henceforward, we shall be satisfied only when doing great things, not alone for our country but for the world.

"The world-wide spirit is sweeping over us and the more deeply we breathe it the better we like it.

"The world for Christ should today be the slogan of every man whose heart is Catholic."

19

The Search

*"O you American youths, what an opportunity is yours
to lay out the ghosts of Americanism and Modernism
that have floated from Europe over to the Far East
and found cozy corners and fresh waters here and
there in this distant land!"*
— James Anthony Walsh, *Observations in the Orient*

"Good-bye, New York,—mine of activities, breeder of vice, stimulant
to heroic virtue, home of the good, the bad, the indifferent, where
legions of devils roam and where angels follow the souls of men or
keep guard under the lights that twinkle in hundreds of sanctuaries
where Jesus dwells unseen." From the rail of the Hoboken ferry
Father Walsh looked back at the Manhattan skyline, and that evening on the train to Scranton he penned these lines in his diary.

It was Labor Day, September 3rd, 1917. He left Maryknoll that
morning and was on his way to the Far East in search of a mission
field. There was a tug at the heart-strings when we said good-bye.
We were excited, of course, over the idea that soon we would have a
mission field of our own. Nevertheless, there was a definite touch of
sadness about the departure because this would be the first time that
the Father of Maryknoll was to be separated from his family for so
many months, and that family was as yet quite small.

The war was still going on. American boys were in France. More
were leaving home for the battlefields. As Father Walsh crossed the
Hudson River from New York, he saw the big German liner, the
Vaterland, which was being re-conditioned as a troop ship. Flying
the Stars and Stripes and given a new name, the *Leviathan*, it was

soon to return to service and carry thousands of American soldiers to Europe.

"A poor time to travel," you might say. But the Pacific Ocean seemed safe. Besides, the family was growing, the boys were sharpening their scythes for the harvest in fields afar, and the "Father" had to find an outlet for their holy ambitions.

"In the last few weeks I have been asked many times who will guide Maryknoll while I am absent," Father Walsh said on the eve of his departure. "There was only one answer to this question,— God. God has guided Maryknoll so far. This work is His. Daily we have here the opportunity of seeing His Providence, His hand directing the work. The consciousness of this is enough to make a man realize that he is nothing but an instrument, and often he fears lest he prove an unworthy one."

The Tenyo Maru, a Japanese liner, sailed out through the Golden Gate on September 15th, with Father Walsh aboard. There had been a pretty little ceremony of departure at the dock, which he then saw for the first time and which practically every Asia-bound missioner since then has seen. Scores of passengers lining the upper decks held in their hands ribbons of colored paper, each of which had been caught at the other end by some one standing on the dock. The distance was too great for ordinary conversation, but every ribbon served as a silent wire to carry unspoken messages from friend to friend. When the ship swung away and moved out into the bay, the ribbons snapped, one after another.

Meanwhile, back at Maryknoll, we waited expectantly for letters from Father Walsh. The first to come told about his trip to Scranton and then on across the country, the big welcome at San Francisco by Archbishop Hanna and Father Joseph McQuaide, who was Chaplain of the Coast Guard. The next letters were a long time coming, since they had to travel all the way back across the Pacific. They told about the ocean voyage:

"Practically all the officers, deck stewards, cabin stewards, and seamen are orientals. The waiters in the dining room are divided between the two races, Japanese and Chinese, each 'shinnying on his own side,' and we were assigned to that of the Chinese.

"Our 'boy's' name is pronounced like 'tack,' but there is nothing in him to suggest either a hard cracker or the pointed instrument of torture that needs the blow of a hammer on its head. We will write him up as plain Tak, and he is worthy of mention.

"Tak was born of Chinese parents, somewhere near Canton, that portion of the Chinese Republic that contributes to the United States most of its laundrymen. Tak looks young but he assures us—and his countenance compels belief—that he is twenty-four years old.

"At breakfast he appears in a neatly laundered dark blue affair, that hangs well below his knees and has long slits on either side. If it were not for a standing collar and the fact that the garment fits the body rather closely, I should boldly say that Tak and his fellow waiters serve us in their night gowns. At noon the shade of blue grows lighter, and at the evening meal Tak is in immaculate white, as are all the others except the headwaiter who retains the blue. We like Tak.

"There is one group of pretty little live Japanese dolls on board, and I have had a talk with their father. He is by no means wealthy, but, like every other Japanese ocean traveler, intelligent and aspiring. His babies were born in San Francisco and he is taking them back to Japan for their education, doubtless also to get them saturated with the full strength of Japanese patriotism.

"My opening came when he asked where I was going. When I reached the end of the Asiatic rope, I said that I should try then to get to Europe and see the Pope at Rome. His eyes sparkled and he asked, 'Are you an American?'

"I nodded assent and in turn inquired if he had seen French priests in Japan. He had, of course. 'Well,' I went on, 'I am on my way to visit them. They belong to my Church, and we are all under the great head at Rome. It happens,' I added, 'that most of the priests in Japan come from France, but the great Church of Christ may be found everywhere.' Did he know that in the United States, where he had been for several years, there are seventeen million and more Catholics?

"Just as I asked the question two of the children demanded his immediate attention, but as soon as he returned to the steamer rail by which he had been standing, he asked in surprise, 'Do you really mean to say that there are so many Catholics in the United States?'

It was evidently a revelation to the man, as it is to so many orientals.

"I met a keen Japanese last evening. Together we were leaning over the rail watching the spray, and an unexpected wave showered us into talking. His English was so much more perfect than my Japanese that there was no choice of languages. He had lived several years in the United States and had observed much. His questions were direct and earnest, following the discovery that I am a Catholic priest. He knew the great metropolis of New York and had often visited the Cathedral which he admired much. He realized that there are in America great men who belong to the Church—Cardinals, Archbishops, Bishops and noted priests—and that all are under the Pope at Rome.

" 'Is the Pope an American?' he asked.

" 'Why not?'

" 'Can an Irishman be Pope?'

" 'Has the United States Government a representative from the Holy Father?'

" 'Why don't we see American priests in the Orient?'

" 'Why have not some gone to Japan?'

"These were some of the questions asked, and on that of papal representatives at the courts of the world, he expressed very clearly his conviction that, as the Pope has children in all countries and is a spiritual father, he should be properly represented everywhere and his priests should be listened to with great reverence.

"I was bold enough to tell him in answer to his questions about American priests going to Japan that we had very little hope of impressing the Japanese at present, because they are too much preoccupied with material advancement to raise their thoughts to spiritual things. He smiled and admitted the truth of the statement.

"As he had recalled the early persecution of Japanese Christians, I repeated the story of their perseverance, without priest or altar, in the faith of their forefathers, and added my belief that people who could show such steadfastness of purpose must be worth while, and I expressed the hope that some day, and soon, Japan, less absorbed in her attempt to be materially great, would examine seriously and for her own good the revealed truth of Christ.

"Before parting, the young man told me that he himself is a Presbyterian.

"Not all on board except the orientals are missionaries, as I first thought, although the numbers of preachers and teachers is considerable,—twenty-five, I am told. There are several businessmen, and some women, with or without children, going to join their husbands. I catch occasional conversations from these travelers, who do not hesitate to ventilate their opinions on all kinds of subjects. Some of them certainly need religion more than the oriental pagans, for the simple reason that they have none at all. Money, clean bodies, health, frequent feeding, 'good times,' and a respectable position summarize their philosophy of life. God and the future mean practically nothing to them. They seem to have got beyond the idea, to have had their chance and missed it. I often hear the objection that there are plenty of heathens at home. Most certainly there are, and the pity of the situation is that they prefer to remain such.

"Hanging over the rail of an ocean liner when one is well may appear a fruitless occupation, and yet it has decided advantages. There is inspiration in the great expanse of sky and water and there is freedom from distraction fore and aft, if one happens to be at the side rail. It is under such circumstances that I usually talk with people.

"What has happened? Yesterday, so far as I recall, was Tuesday, September 25th, and today is Thursday, September 27th, and everybody is literally and otherwise at sea.

"My companion should have celebrated his ordination anniversary on the twenty-sixth, and we had no twenty-sixth. Our Spanish friend, who sleeps like a log every night and takes a short afternoon nap daily from two to five o'clock, is almost convinced that he did not wake up at all on the twenty-sixth.

"For many the mystery is not cleared, but the fact stands that out on the Pacific Ocean, when the 180th meridian is passed, a day is dropped on the western voyage and on the eastern trip a day is added.

"I picked up a Korean today but did not recognize his nationality until a good-natured Chinaman enlightened me. The Korean hailed from Honolulu and told me his life story, which can be summarized in these two chapters: 1—Left Korea as a boy fifteen years ago. 2—After many struggles became the respected owner of a moving picture outfit in Honolulu.

"The third chapter is opening with the wanderer's return to find what is left of his family; and the fourth will be to establish another 'movie parlor' in Shanghai. I like this Korean, and I have an idea from all that I hear of Koreans in general that their country, watered with the blood of martyrs, in whom Maryknoll has been interested from the beginning, must be an inviting field.

"Already we are in sight of Japan, and as I make these few notes I can see the Land of the Rising Sun. The sun happens, however, just now to be setting, and it sinks gracefully over the Island Empire, whose interesting people we shall soon see in their own unique environment.

"For lack of something better to do, I went again to the rail and watched the moon during the space of a half-hour.

"It hung barely visible, back of a small group of inky clouds, with the sky perfectly clear in every other quarter. Occasionally, as the clouds thinned, it would show the strength of its light.

"Did it symbolize the difficulty which the pure Gospel of Jesus Christ finds in penetrating the soul of this ambitious little empire?

"I wondered how long the clouds would remain and how long it would be until the Soul of Japan should scatter the mists like ashes."

These letters which Father Walsh wrote back to Maryknoll during his months of absence in the Far East were published regularly in *The Field Afar* and called "The Pioneer's Log." Later they were compiled in a large volume, *Observations in the Orient,* and were illustrated with photographs which he took along the way.

Meanwhile, back at the seminary the school year was in full swing. We felt at times there was an artillery duel going on in the neighborhood. The Palisades directly across the Hudson were being blasted by some enterprising road-makers with quarry rights. Fortunately, thanks to the intervention of Mr. Rockefeller, an end was put to all this by the State, before the majestic beauty of the spot was irreparably marred.

In our plan of cooperating with the Government and "Hooverizing," we acquired some new workers for the family,—one hundred thousand bees. We engaged them to make wax for our chapel candles and provide honey that would substitute in part for the sugar that was so hard to get in those war days.

Late one afternoon the phone rang. It was a call from St. Teresa's Lodge: "Have Brother Bee come over right away with his bird cage and gloves. His bees have swarmed our community room." When Brother Bee arrived with his paraphernalia, he found the bees had landed and had the situation in hand, while the Teresians, calling orders from behind closed doors in other parts of the house, gave instructions for a counter offensive to regain the salient.

While Father Walsh was in the East, Father Patrick Byrne took over some of his duties. Years later, Father Byrne became first superior of our mission in Korea. He started the Maryknoll mission in Kyoto, Japan, and was able to remain in Kyoto all through World War II. In 1949, he was made a titular Bishop and appointed by the Holy See to be the first Apostolic Delegate to Korea. When, in 1950, the Communists from the north invaded Seoul and South Korea, Bishop Byrne became their prisoner, together with his Secretary, Maryknoll's Father William Booth.

In 1917, while Father Walsh was absent, Father Byrne edited *The Field Afar*. The "Votes for Women" campaign was pushed harder than ever while so many of the menfolk were overseas, and their promoters even came to Maryknoll. "We know that Maryknoll is on the map," noted Father Byrne, "for the suffragettes have found us out. One day while the back door was locked, a delegation swooped down, under the camouflage of two henpecked Fords. They wanted to know if we didn't believe women could rock the cradle with one hand and steer the ship of state with the other. We gave three woofs for the Goddess of Just Rights and apologized for the crack in our mirror. Leaving, they left.

"How the hens got wind of it we don't know, but they haven't been the same since. The Reverend Manager soliloquizes vaguely about 'moulting', but it's an even bet that we get no more eggs till those hens get club privileges, moving pictures, and Saturday afternoons off.

"Being some distance from our nearest neighbors, we felt comparatively safe in incorporating at Maryknoll an imposing Symphony Orchestra. All told, it must weigh nearly two tons.

"The programs are heavy, too. At times, the united efforts of all the virtuosos are unable to carry a single bar, but the pieces are generally executed about the same as in an ordinary sawmill.

"Though an occasional halt is necessary, to unwind a fiddle string from the neck of some innocent bystander or to put a depth charge in the French horn, yet progress is constant, and the next time you visit Maryknoll we'll entertain you with an inimitable rendering of Beethoven's, 'Rag in Flat G.'

"We stop the press to announce the house warming at St. Joseph's barn. The finishing touches were given to the last straw, the heating plant that badly bent the camel's back, precisely at two on a freezing Friday afternoon. Within forty-five minutes after kindling the first fire in the furnace, several of the students had been all but overcome by the heat, while others leaned far from the windows, fanning vigorously and begging for ice water.

"Like Gibraltar, St. Joseph's could stand a siege of seven years without a wrinkle of anxiety. St. Martha's, too, is about ready for its diploma, and expects to be operating in full blast by New Year's. It is indeed quite fitting that this, the great feast of the Chinese should inaugurate our beautiful laundry. Doubtless, it is their natural idealism that inspires the Chinese in this country to elevate us above the gross materialism of the day, and to teach us their horror of the sordid by purifying our shirts and collars of all that is earthly.

"The cost of the laundry was moderate. The reason is simple. Our fields are separated by long walls of loose stones, erected by our ancestors before the movies came to play so prominent a part in the killing of time. Now, when we need a building, we just go out into the fields, take so much wall, so much cement, and so much fuss— and behold, a splendid modern mansion with everything but elevators and a soda fountain!

"The expectation of soon engaging in that work for which they have been many years preparing has naturally rippled the usually placid surface of life at Maryknoll with many little waves of excitement. Something is in the air. This spirit is one of happy anticipation,

A feeling of gladness and longing
Not the least akin to pain;
That resembles sorrow only,
As the sunlight does the rain.

"This eagerness has shown itself in rather unexpected ways. A consuming desire to follow Father Superior to China inspired several of his sons at the Knoll to acquire the essential Chinese and whiskers without delay. Everyone knows the Chinese don't talk with chopsticks, but very few understand the need for whiskers on a foreign missioner.

"Whiskers are a strange prepossession. A man without them doesn't want them, while he who has 'em is proudly embarrassed. They must be a great aid to memory, for stroking them always brings a far-away look to the eyes. 'Why do missioners wear them?' Many such inquiries have reached us. To tell the truth, we think it is because they can't get anyone else to carry them instead.

"When we asked Padre Julio, who has a heavenly set, unearthed in Borneo, he said: 'For the same reason as a rooster crows. They keep people from thinking he's a hen, and besides they lend a great reputation for dignity, sobriety, and useful knowledge.'

"Whiskers are all right in their place, but they often have a hard time getting there—judging by some Maryknollers, at least."

For three months we waited, as Father Walsh went on through the East in search of a mission field for us. He was in Japan, visiting missions, schools, colleges, seminaries, orphanages in Tokyo, Osaka, Kyoto, Sendai, Kobe, Nagasaki, and so on along the line.

"I decided to remain over at Yokohama," he wrote back, "so as to get introduced gradually to new surroundings. Archbishop Rey left for Tokyo in the afternoon. This gave me an opportunity to talk English to myself, to take some photographs of the sacristan's children, and to make a sortie through the town.

"I found my way back to the wharf and then summoned a rickshaw. It was a lucky chance because the driver understood the three words I spoke to him: 'Kelly and Walsh'! Not to mystify you, 'Kelly and Walsh' is the name of a book and stationery firm that has stores in several cities of Eastern Asia. I attempted to trace relationship to both members of the firm, so as to secure reductions, but learned that the originals had long since disappeared. It was presumed that they had come to the East from the Island of the West, but no one could tell me if they are over or under the old or the new sod.

"As I left the place I breathed a prayer that some day we should have more 'Kelly's and Walsh's' in the Orient, and that they would come not to sell books but to break the Bread of Life."

Father Walsh crossed from Japan to Korea, to Fusan, now written Pusan. He found his friend, Bishop Demange, at Taikou, later spelled Taegu and often in the news during the Red invasion of South Korea. He visited the Cathedral of Seoul and the missions roundabout, and went on to Manchuria.

Mukden, Peking, Tientsin, Chengtingfu, Hankow, Chusan were all stopping places on his long line of march. He spent many days in Shanghai visiting the Catholic hospitals, university, colleges, and the charitable establishments of Mr. Lo Pa Hong. This astounding Catholic layman founded and directed a model hospital, a vast orphanage, and in later years had a hospital for the mentally ill.

Bishop Paris, of the French Jesuits, was in charge of the missions in that part of China. Father Walsh visited him. "I met several Jesuit Fathers on this occasion, and they, like the Bishop, were most affable. Bishop Paris has, however, an idea that American priests will not be able to accommodate themselves to Chinese life with its quaint customs and slow movement. He has never been in the United States and is quite willing to admit that his experience with priests from that country has been very limited, but his idea persists.

"I assured him that possibly he was right, but I reminded him that possibly also he was wrong; that, given strong faith with charity broad and deep, the grace of God could make an apostle out of even an American.

"O you American youths, what an opportunity is yours to lay out the ghosts of Americanism and modernism that have floated from Europe over to the Far East and found cozy corners and fresh waters here and there in this distant land!

"Not every American priest who comes to work in China will succeed. No nationality has had so enviable a record, and we have no right to believe that ours will be the exception. American priests will make mistakes, and we who send them out shall find that our judgment will not always be true, but our hope is strong that American Catholic missionary effort, with God's help, will prove well worth while. We are young in mission experience and have much to learn. If, in return for the lessons ahead of us, we can give something more than money, so much the better. God knows the future. We will do our best, but we must remember His kingdom in every effort that we make for souls. The glory of our young Society and that of our nationality will take care of themselves and need not concern us."

Father Walsh filled his letters with all sorts of little incidents that he found interesting and that he knew would amuse us. He sometimes had difficulty finding a mirror when he wanted to shave and remarked that many missioners had perhaps not seen their faces in years, and if by chance they suddenly had that experience they would ask: "Is that really my face?"

Once in a priest's house in Boston he could find no mirror so he used the brass ball of a bedpost while he shaved. A looking-glass is not indispensable, he said, but it can be very convenient when in the process of shaving you would like to explore your countenance. Once while spending a week at a seminary in Italy, he ran into the same difficulty. "Then," he said, "I found that I could follow a line by the use of the dormer window."

Another time, while touring an oriental town in company with the Bishop, he decided he needed a haircut. The Bishop took him to a barber shop, told the barber that Father Walsh had only twenty minutes to spare, so the whole family got busy. "The cutting was followed by graceful and rapid strokes of the hair," he wrote, "the artist striking an attitude occasionally and listening, as if to assure himself that my head was really empty. Just as all kinds of lotions came into view I borrowed the brush, patted the pate, bowed to the Bishop, paid my ten cents, and said 'Good-bye'."

Father Walsh was beginning to get worried. He had visited a good part of the Far East and when, after reaching Shanghai, he had not received a single invitation to take over a section of existing mission territories staffed by other societies, he was candidly concerned. It was evident everywhere that while financial and other material help from the United States would be most welcome, the Bishops were loath to be the first to invite this new society to their missions. Americans as missioners would not succeed; that was the idea. Besides, they might stir up trouble.

Christmas, 1917, stands out in the memory of many. Some veterans of World War I recall it as the Christmas they spent in the trenches. For countless American homes it was a sombre feast, with one or more of the boys "somewhere in France." A coal famine threatened to leave many homes cold, and we at Maryknoll spent long hours in the woods gathering fuel for our stoves and furnace. The Bolsheviki were just beginning to take over in Russia. The Allies were hammering away at the Hindenburg Line.

Father Walsh spent Christmas in Canton. When he had arrived in Hongkong a few days before, Père Robert, his friend of many years, met him at the dock. In Canton he also met the man whom in all China he was most anxious to see, Bishop de Guébriant, the Vicar Apostolic of Canton.

When Maryknoll was just getting started in 1911, Father Walsh received letters from three Bishops in mission lands, offering their congratulations and suggesting that there would be a welcome for his priests in their missions, some day in the future when Maryknoll would have priests ordained and ready. One of these letters came from China, from Bishop de Guébriant, then in the province of Szechuan. Before starting out on his trip, Father Walsh had received word indirectly that he and his priests would be welcome to a section of the Canton mission territory.

"I had hardly met Bishop de Guébriant," he wrote, "before I realized that Maryknoll's first mission in the Orient had been found, and a few minutes later my eyes were on the map of China, riveted to a point marked YEUNGKONG."

Father Walsh celebrated the Midnight Mass in the Cathedral of Canton. In the morning he said his Third Mass at the Convent of the Sisters of the Immaculate Conception, where a young lady, Miss Mary Donovan, formerly his secretary in the Propagation of the Faith Office in Boston, was now Sister Mary Angeline. Later, he assisted at the Pontifical Mass celebrated by Bishop de Guébriant.

"I thought much that day of Maryknoll's future field," he wrote. "From several points of view it is not attractive. It lies in the south of China, where everybody swelters in the summer months. The entire province has been and is yet upset through political conditions which seem to become more and more hopelessly involved. On the seacoast along which one portion of the mission extends, and on the West River, its northern boundary, there are many pirates; while in the interior bandits have been allowed to go even to the extremes of burning villages, shooting their fellow men, and looting everything they could lay their hands on. The Mission contains not one considerable city, and has at present only a thousand Christians scattered among a million heathens. Even this thousand is an outside calculation, and probably exaggerated, because, since the European war began, no priest could be spared to watch this portion of the vineyard. Picking up from my desk the report for the preceding year, I read its concluding paragraph:

" 'Numerous troops raised to defend the Republic continued to operate on their own account. They held the country districts, pillaging at will. Nearly all the mission districts suffered from these soldiers, and some of the priests ran real dangers. On July 4, 1916, the Christians at Lantung were attacked and seven were killed.' And Lantung lies in Maryknoll's new mission!"

Later in the day, when the excitement of the Christmas festivities had subsided for the moment and the Bishop was free, Father Walsh went to Bishop de Guébriant's room. There, in the presence of Father Fourquet, the Vicar General, and Father Souvey who had accompanied Father Walsh to Canton from Hongkong, after a prayer to the Holy Ghost, the agreement was signed by which Maryknoll should be entrusted with its first mission, that of Yeungkong and Loting in the province of Kwangtung. A little later a cablegram went overseas bringing the news to Maryknoll.

We were in the midst of Christmas when the message arrived, "FIELD FOUND."

"It was the Christ Child's gift to our young Society," Father Walsh said. "May we put it to the best possible use and prove worthy of the responsibility which its possession will carry!"

20

The First Departure

"Tell Father Walsh my last thoughts were for them all, and that I died in the love of Jesus, Mary, Joseph, and of Maryknoll."

—Father Price's last words

The big bronze bell, which Father Walsh had brought back from Japan, was hanging from a beam of the seminary porch. For fully a hundred years it had summoned Buddhist pilgrims to their pagan shrine. On September 7th, 1918, it began its new role as Departure Bell. It was just growing dusk when the old bell started its solemn tolling. It was a discordant sound, far from agreeable, but all who heard it realized that it signaled the hour for our First Departure.

We crowded our small chapel. We were eighty then, dwelling at Maryknoll, and that night we had a score of friends taking part. It seemed hard to realize that within six short years some of us had grown from boys, were ordained, and were starting out for the Far East.

Since Christmas of the year before, when word came from China that we had a mission, there had been constant speculation as to who would be in the first group. It was June before we knew. Father Price would lead the pioneers, and he would have with him Father James Edward Walsh, Father Francis Ford, and Father Bernard Meyer. By that time we had a dozen priests, so there were various conjectures until the names were definitely announced.

Father Price was like a child in his excitement, getting ready for the big event. For him it was the fulfilling of a dream. His long years in North Carolina, and the difficult pioneering days at Hawthorne and Maryknoll were to have a climax that would be the reward of all: he would lead a band of American missioners to China.

He even allowed us to take his picture. Such was his excitement on that last day that he forgot his usual decorum, and I met him making a hurried trip through the upstairs hallway divested of his cassock, which he regarded as the minimum of dignified and modest attire which he so stringently insisted upon in our regard. Suspecting my thoughts, he turned to me with a broad smile: "Brother Raymond, there are times when all of us forget, and this is one of them."

Cardinal Farley had planned to have this first Departure in St. Patrick's Cathedral. He himself would preside, and a Bishop would preach, because the occasion would be historical. But when September came the Cardinal was gravely ill, within the shadow of death. He could not even see the missioners to lay his hands upon them in blessing. When he was told that our priests were about to leave for the East, he brightened for a moment and murmured, "Tell them that I bless them."

Though a simple ceremony, it was impressive. The words of the Canticle of Zachary, which are part of the Church's prayer for those going on a long journey, were strikingly appropriate:

"Blessed be the Lord God of Israel; for He hath visited and wrought the redemption of his people. . . .

"For thou shalt go before the face of the Lord to prepare His ways . . .

"To give knowledge of salvation to His people unto the remission of their sins . . .

"To enlighten those who sit in darkness and the shadow of death. . . ."

Father Walsh addressed the departing missioners. He referred to the importance of their work and its timeliness. He reminded them that they were the pioneers and on trial before the Catholic world— soldiers of Christ, as yet unknown, untested, and in some respects lightly esteemed, as were the soldiers of the nation before their appearance in Europe. He said that they had yet to prove that faith, humility, self-denial, and zeal were not lacking in the American priesthood.

He pointed out their duties: their own personal sanctification; their reliance on Divine Providence and the careful use of whatever money should be sent to them; their love for the crucified and patient Christ; their devotion to the Holy Ghost as the source of light and strength, to Mary Immaculate, and to their particular patrons; their loyal union with the Society that was sending them forth. He assured them of constant prayers and close interest in all their successes and trials.

There was a thrill of excitement mingled with joy and with some sorrow as the refrain of the Departure Hymn filled the chapel, the hymn that Charles Gounod had composed for the Paris Seminary:

"Go forth, farewell for life, O dearest Brothers;
Proclaim afar the sweetest name of God.
We meet again one day in Heaven's land of blessings;
Farewell, Brothers, Farewell!"

At the front steps after the ceremony, there were more good-byes, handshakes, singing and cheering by the light of camera flashes and lanterns. Two automobiles which had brought visitors from New York carried the missioners out into the night, down the highway that led to the city. By midnight, they were on their way to Baltimore.

At Baltimore, Cardinal Gibbons greeted his old altar boy, Freddie Price, and sent the missioners on their way with blessings and prayers. In Washington, the Apostolic Delegate, Archbishop Bonzano, who had spent the first six years of his priesthood in China, recalled for them his days in the Province of Shansi.

When their train reached Cincinnati, they were met at the station and immediately whisked out into the suburbs to bless the new establishment of Father Peter E. Dietz, whose brother, Frederick, had been ordained at Maryknoll two years before and was engaged in teaching at the Venard.

Father Peter Dietz, while still a seminarian, had spent some time with Father Price in North Carolina, helping with his cornet to attract villagers to Father Price's impromptu sermons for non-Catholics. When Father Price was starting out for China, Father Dietz had been engaged for about ten years in social work on a national scale, and he asked Father Price, when the latter was passing through Cincinnati, to bless his newly founded Academy of Christian Democracy.

The aim of this Academy was to counteract the venom of socialism by inculcating and applying the true remedy for existing social evils, that is, by applying the teachings of the Papal Encyclicals, particularly the *Rerum Novarum* of Pope Leo XIII, "On the Condition of the Laboring Classes." Nurses, settlement workers and others interested in promoting the cause of social justice could look to the Academy for proper schooling and preparation.

This building, blessed by Father Price, later became the headquarters of the Catholic Students Mission Crusade, and at the present writing still serves that purpose.

On September 21st, the group sailed from San Francisco on the SS Ecuador. As the boat left the Bay and headed out across the Pacific, the little band gathered on the after deck and sang softly the "Ave Maris Stella."

There were a hundred Marines aboard, for the war was still going on. Destined to land on some disputed but undisclosed terrain, they would soon have the situation well in hand, but in the meantime they were anything but warlike. The land swell, disturbed further by a choppy sea, was taking its toll among the passengers. Many of the Marines were moaning in their bunks, apprehensive at first lest the boat should go down and sorry the next minute that it didn't.

Storm-seasoned sailors aboard seemed to take comfort at the Marines' distress in which they could see a timely retribution for the belittling chanty:

> *"Ten thousand gobs*
> *Laid down their swabs*
> *To lick one sick Marine. . . ."*

Leaning over the rail and meditating on the majesty of the tossing blue ocean must have stirred the muse in the soul of Father Francis Ford. His first letter to cross the seas to Father Walsh carried some verses on "The Pacific."

> *O depths of mystery,*
> *How can you calmly sleep*
> *And sluggish stretch your breadth*
> *Of shining, peaceful deep*

> *Between the East and West,*
> *Between the Day and Night,*
> *Between the Heathen Dark*
> *And God's all-saving Light?*

Their letters began to arrive, and we learned that in Japan the group divided. Father Walsh and Father Meyer continued on the boat to Shanghai. Father Price took Father Ford overland by train through Japan, Korea, and Manchuria. When their train passed from Korea, over the bridge of the Yalu River, and stopped at Antung, they were on Chinese soil for the first time. Father Price left the car, knelt down in the railway station, and kissed the ground. This was the land of his dreams. He suggested to Father Ford that he do the same.

As they went on their way, they understood that they were going to be watched. It was no secret that many Europeans believed that Americans would never make missioners. One man, though treating them kindly, said he would see them at the boat a few months later to say good-bye to them on their way back to America.

We may suppose that these observers were genuinely pleased when they found they had been wrong in their estimate. After three decades and more, the three young pioneers were still in China and hard at work. Father Price died in China.

They wrote back to us about their new language. "We are still engaged in the Chinese exercises analagous to the *rosa, rosae, rosae* . . . of our early Latin days," wrote Father Meyer. "It is a poor analogy, however, because there is no declension in Chinese. There are tones galore, and so we repeat over and over—*sin, sin, sin, sin, sin*—each in a different tone.

"There are only seven hundred eighty words in Chinese, that is, words as we know them, or rather as we represent them by letters of the alphabet. To get the thousands that are necessary, there are nine tones in which each of the seven hundred eighty sounds may be uttered. Then there are aspirated and unaspirated initial consonants, long vowels and short vowels, each device changing the meaning completely.

"In English we use tones for emphasis. In Chinese tones affect the meaning, so that one may not use the tone he pleases. If one uses the

wrong tone, he thereby uses the wrong word and so may be misun-
derstood.

"There is the short sharp tone, the rising tone similar to the ques-
tioning inflection in English but not at all interrogatory in Chinese,
and the drawling tone, and all these in a higher or lower scale. . . ."

It did not sound easy to us. Even the description was fairly in-
comprehensible. Perhaps they were trying to make it look hard. We
would go some day, please God, and find out all this for ourselves.

These first impressions of Chinese language study remind me of
Father Patrick Byrne's description of the Korean language.

"The Korean language," said Father Byrne, "is especially designed
to confer merit upon its students. In the national folklore it is told
how once upon a time a certain gentleman of vigorous parts, though
tongue-tied, was chased by a royal bull around the sacred tango tree,
whereon was perched a shorthand artist who with great presence of
mind did take down the remarks uttered on this auspicious occasion.
The king, being presented with a copy, fell into a deep trance, from
which he was with difficulty awakened; whereupon he proclaimed
the discovery of the long-sought national tongue."

By Christmas of that year, 1918, Father Price and his companions
were finally established in their own mission at Yeungkong. He
dated his letters from "The Church of Our Lady of Lourdes, Yeungkong." "Such a Christmas!" he wrote, "a Christmas we never experienced or conceived of in all our lives.

"The Christians made a gala day of it, pouring in on Christmas
Eve and all day during the feast, in delegations from all the villages,
celebrating both the feast and our arrival in one great outpour. We
had a Solemn Midnight Mass and a Missa Cantata at eight o'clock
in the morning.

"A Chinese band, hired by the Christians, played Chinese music
nearly all day while the Christians shot off loads of firecrackers.
They insisted on giving us a banquet, which they were considerate
enough to let our 'boy' prepare,—and such chickens, and ducks,
and shrimps, and meats, etc.! It would be difficult to match!

"All day long these good people flowed through the church and
reception room and bedrooms and office and kitchen and every
nook and corner imaginable.

"Many had clubbed together, bought an ox and killed it, camping here on Christmas Eve and eating the ox with all the concomitants on the feast the next day. . . .

"We are bottled up here, at least in a sense. Though Canton is not very far away, about two hundred miles by boat, it takes one week to make the trip and return. We have two boats a week to Canton and none to Hongkong, which is less distant. Mails are delivered at any old time whenever the Chinese feel like it, and they don't feel like it very often. . . . Affectionate greetings to all, T. F. Price."

As the months went by, our missioners' letters came regularly. Meanwhile, at Maryknoll another year was passing. More land was acquired. It was the top of the hill, adjoining the farm we already had, and was to be the site of the permanent seminary. Plans were made.

The 1919 Departure Group was announced: Father Daniel Mc-Shane, Father William O'Shea, and Father Alphonse Vogel would leave for China in September.

Then we got a shock. It was on a Sunday morning, late in September. A cablegram came from Canton, signed by Bishop de Guébriant, and it said that Father Price had died of appendicitis.

For me personally it was sad news. Father Price was one of my greatest friends. He had been my spiritual director for years, and I had spent much time with him, particularly during the last weeks when he was getting ready to go to the East.

I recalled how hard he had worked to finish his life of Bernadette Soubirous, *The Lily of Mary,* and get it published before he left for the missions. We never really knew how many hours he spent on his knees praying for us, for all Maryknollers, praying for the salvation of souls. He told us many things that have helped us all through the years, and he communicated to us some of his own loyalty to Our Lady and devotion to her Bernadette.

It must have been hard on the three young priests in China. He had gone to the East principally for their sake, that they might have an older head among them. They had learned to lean on him and look to him for guidance.

The details of his death came by letters. We began to realize that his year at Yeungkong had been difficult. He suffered from the climate. It was hard to adjust himself, fifty-eight years old, to new food, customs, and surroundings. His greatest trial perhaps was his inability to master the language. He was bursting with eagerness to talk to these people, to tell them about God, Our Saviour, Mary, and Bernadette. After a couple of months he began to realize that, because of his age and because of the peculiar difficulty of the Cantonese tones, this great joy would never be his.

It is told how the children would gather around him. He would take out his watch and put it to their ears, smile at them, and try in some way to convey the affection of his heart to these youngsters.

Two of his letters reached Maryknoll after the cablegram announcing his death. They were both from St. Paul's Hospital, Hongkong. "I have appendicitis and must be operated on in a few days. The doctor says there is not great danger. Please pray for me and have all pray for me.

"We have been waiting to know who are coming this fall. It is important to know as soon as possible, and the date of their arrival at Hongkong.

"I am writing this in bed suffering and must ask you to excuse what is wanting. Love to all. Thos. F. Price.
P.S.—All well on the missions."

No Maryknoller was at the bedside of Father Price when he died, and none was present at the funeral. The nearest were at the mission in Yeungkong, unable to reach Hongkong on time. Father Jean Tour, of the Paris Missioners, was with him during his illness and at the moment of death. He wrote immediately to Father Walsh.

Father Price was operated on, September 8th, the Nativity of Our Lady. He died September 12th, the Feast of the Holy Name of Mary. On September 15th, the Feast of Our Lady of Sorrows, the Bishop of Hongkong had a Solemn Requiem for him at the Cathedral. The day before he died, he said to Father Tour: "I expect to die tomorrow, the Feast of my Heavenly Mother."

Father Tour knew with what impatient interest Father Walsh and all of us at Maryknoll would be awaiting the details of Father

Price's last hours on earth. He did not disappoint us. The details as recorded in his letter gave us a picture of Father Price, dying as he had lived.

"Today, at precisely ten a.m., your young Mission has received its second consecration, and a lasting blessing, by the happy and holy death of the venerable and saintly Father Price," wrote Father Tour. "What we feared yesterday is now a sad reality.

"The good Father did not feel well yesterday. He passed a good night, but at three this morning awoke feeling unwell again. At seven he asked for the last Rites. He was told there was no hurry, that he could wait for me, but he insisted on receiving Holy Viaticum, Extreme Unction, and the Plenary Indulgence.

"Father Lemaire, a missioner from Canton who is convalescing here, yielded to his wish. All the Rites were received in the most edifying manner.

"When I arrived at nine, good Father Price gave me a sweet smile and a hearty handshake. He spoke very low, but quite intelligibly. I helped the best way I could during a full hour. His hands and forehead were dead cold: had it not been for that, we would have felt no anxiety for the day. He was very quiet and even somewhat hopeful. Still, there was no doubt but that he was sinking.

"I spoke to him of all things dear to him: of Jesus, Mary, Joseph, of Our Lady of Lourdes, of Bernadette, and he was smiling and giving assent all the while; then of dearest Father Walsh, and of all the beloved Maryknollers, Maryknoll proper, Scranton, San Francisco, Yeungkong. At each name, he lifted his eyes heavenward and prayed according to the thoughts and intentions I suggested.

"At about nine-thirty, I understood that he was sinking more rapidly. 'Dear Father Price,' I said, 'you will kindly bless your friend Father Tour, and, in his person, dearest Father Walsh and all beloved Maryknollers of Maryknoll, Scranton, San Francisco and Yeungkong, won't you?'—

" 'Most willingly and from the depth of my heart,' he replied.

" 'You offer now your sufferings, and even your life, for the prosperity of your beloved Society, and you pray and will ever pray that they all may do the work of God in a truly apostolic spirit, don't you?'—

" 'Most certainly.' And as I bowed before him at the side of his bed, he placed his weak hand on my head and blessed me, making the sign of the cross on me and praying at the same time, as I guessed, the blessing form.

"Up to nine forty-five he repeated after me all the ejaculations, but his tongue was no more free. Till then he always gently smiled at the Holy Names and at the name of Maryknoll. I started the prayers for the Commendation of the Soul, in English, which he seemed to follow throughout. When these prayers were over, he could see no more. Then he felt very distressing pains in his wound and moved pitifully to the right and to the left a dozen times, while his breath was more and more hard and scarce.

"At ten o'clock, he opened wide and wild eyes and was shaken most painfully: the good Sister on one side and I on the other helped him the best we could, holding his hand till he breathed his last quite peacefully, after some five minutes of rest.

"I had the sad privilege of closing the eyes of your venerable friend and devoted coöperator in the great work of Maryknoll. I felt that I was representing you all, and I could not stop my tears.

"I can assure you that his death was in very truth the death of a just man, and even of a saint. His last words were: 'Tell Father Walsh my last thoughts were for them all, and that I died in the love of Jesus, Mary, Joseph, and of Maryknoll.' "

21

The Altar

*"Bestow, then, we beseech Thee, Almighty Father,
the dignity of the Priesthood upon these Thy servants. . . ."*

— The Rite of Ordination

The fighting in France took the lives of one hundred and twenty-
six thousand American boys. Influenza killed four times that number
among the people in the United States alone. This terrible pandemic,
sweeping over the entire world in 1918 and 1919, crept into almost
every home in America. Doctors said that about one third of the entire population had been infected by it. I caught it.

I was lying in bed on Monday morning, March 10th, 1919, with a
splitting headache, nauseated and sore all over. The seminary bell
was tolling slowly, mournfully. They told me that Father Massoth
was being buried. Burning up and muddled with fever, I half told
myself: "It will probably toll for me tomorrow or the next day."

When the first epidemic hit the country in the fall of 1918, it
passed us over, both at Maryknoll and at Scranton. No one caught it.
It came back again in the spring, and this time almost thirty of us
caught it, but recovered. We were deeply thankful. Then, in March
our turn came.

One of the students at the Venard, Richard Fitzgerald from Albany, died of the "flu" in the Mercy Hospital at Scranton. Father
John Massoth, who was teaching at the Venard, showed symptoms
of the fever while on a trip to New York. He was hurried to Maryknoll and put under the doctor's care. He made a strong fight, but
complications set in, and he died Sunday, March 9th.

John Considine was infirmarian during the epidemic. After Father Massoth's Mass, he came to my room, took my pulse, rolled up his sleeves and proceeded to give me an alcohol bath. I began to feel better. The will to live came back to me. In a couple of days I was sitting up and enjoying the tea and toast and soft-boiled egg served to me in bed. That was just about the beginning of the final twelve months before ordination.

"Why so many years of study?" is a fair question for wondering observers, who are still mystified by the long years spent by students in black behind heavy seminary walls. It is a long preparation. Twelve years normally pass between the grammar grades and ordination. To speculate on what depths of preternatural alchemy is practiced by these apprentices in priestcraft is still a choice indoor sport in some corners of the American backwoods, and also in the not-so-backwoods. Even to some Catholic parents, the course of studies is not too clear.

An old legend, which I have already mentioned, centers around two elders of Irish origin, both with sons in the seminary. Meeting at wakes and funerals, they would greet mutually as members of a special caste and each would inquire about the progress of the other's son. According to the story, one of them thought that the seminary course instructed the student chiefly in saying Mass, starting off in the first days with the opening prayers and then proceeding onward. After some years he would reach the prayers after Mass. The "place where the priest cries" was a revealing observation on the ability of the priests in Patrick's parish to sing the Preface and the Pater Noster.

So let's step into the visitors' gallery, and watch a priest-in-process move along the assembly line.

After completing his college courses, the last two years of which are given to the study of scholastic philosophy, the student takes four years of theology. During these four years, he studies the teachings of the Church, that is, the doctrines we must all believe, as summarized in the Apostles' Creed. He learns also to dissect the fallacies and the attacks of unbelievers and he investigates scientifically the historical and logical supports of all that he believes and has to teach.

He studies also the rules of moral conduct which Catholics must observe, as laid down in the Ten Commandments and in the Precepts of the Church. At the same time, he is instructed regarding the liturgical worship, the ceremonies of the Church, particularly the Mass and the administration of the Sacraments. He learns the main events of history, in their relation to the Church, and he learns something about Church Law.

These are the principal studies. The others vary according to the policy of the particular seminary, more or less time being given to public speaking, languages, and the social sciences. At Maryknoll, we have had courses on introduction to oriental languages, medicine, first aid, and other subjects useful to a missioner.

Meanwhile, as the student advances towards his goal, he receives what are known as the minor orders. At the end of his first year of theology, he becomes a porter and lector. After the next year he is made an exorcist and acolyte.

Translated, porter and lector mean doorkeeper and reader. Exorcist and acolyte mean, respectively, the one who drives out devils, and the attendant. Practically, these minor orders are reminders that we are getting along towards the priesthood, stepping stones to ordination. They are pats on the back to keep us plugging ahead through those long years. They refer to offices in the early Church, and empower the student to perform certain minor functions.

To be porter, or doorkeeper, for example, is nowadays a full-time job for the sexton or the housekeeper in a parish, and, in monasteries, for a lay Brother. The lector, or reader, exercises his office somewhat during the ceremonies of Holy Week, and at rare special festivals, but practically all the "reading" is done by the priest celebrating Mass, or by the deacon and subdeacon.

The exorcist, or "driver-out-of-devils," may not use this authority until after his ordination as priest, and then only with the specific permission of his Bishop, given for each case. Obviously, this is a wise arrangement. Besides, at that stage of our training we are busy enough driving the devil out of ourselves, without turning elsewhere.

The office of acolyte, literally the attendant, is generally performed by that little elf you see running around the altar of your parish church, tripping up the steps with a huge book, splashing water on the priest, and shaking the life out of the poor little bell.

One year before ordination, the seminarist has his last chance to turn back to the world of householders and fathers of families. At this point he makes up his mind definitely to follow Our Master. With Him he must choose to give himself wholly, body and soul, to his life's work, free from family ties, going on singly and alone until his work is done and his ministry ends in death. The order conferred at the end of this third year is that of subdeacon. This is one step lower than deacon, which the student becomes as he begins his fourth and final year of preparation. This latter order, differing from the office of deacon as explained in the Acts of the Apostles with the election of Stephen, means that the student may now assist the priest more closely at Mass, even handling the Blessed Sacrament.

My years of theology were nearing completion. In June, 1918, I had received the final minor orders of exorcist and acolyte. The ceremony took place in the chapel of St. Joseph's Seminary at Dunwoodie, Yonkers. On that day Robert Cairns was ordained to the priesthood.

Father Cairns was later pastor of the mission on Sancian Island, off the South China coast, where Saint Francis Xavier died. He restored the shrine of Saint Francis and the Memorial Chapel there. To many he became known as "Father Sandy of Sunny Sandy Sancian." When the war started in December, 1941, he was taken from the island by an enemy patrol and never heard of again. We have set December 14th as the presumptive date of his death, but it is not certain. Nor do we know how or where he died. We suspect that it was at sea, off the coast of China.

The following year, June 14th, 1919, I was ordained subdeacon. Again the ceremony was in the chapel at Dunwoodie. On that day Archbishop Hayes conferred various orders on thirteen students from Maryknoll. Among them was Father Anthony Hodgins, who died in China only three years later.

In September, I was ordained deacon. Together with Frederick Fitzgerald, who had come to us from St. Bernard's Seminary, Rochester, we received this order from Bishop Gibbons, successor of Bishop Cusack in Albany. The ceremony was in the Franciscan monastery at Rensselaer, where we had made our retreat.

There is a word, "retreat," that may need explanation. A non-

Catholic friend of mine, coming in contact for the first time with Catholics "on retreat" was mystified. His friends, when questioned, could give him no help. He looked up the word in the dictionary, and found: "Retreat: An act of withdrawing from what is difficult, dangerous, or disagreeable; a place of seclusion, privacy, safety; an asylum for insane persons, inebriates, etc." With this light from the dictionary, his wonder only grew.

For us a retreat means a period of days, a week more or less, during which we aim to observe silence, cut off as much contact as possible with the world about us, and spend the time thinking and talking things over with God. We look back over the past, examine our present ways and habits, and make definite plans for the future. All this we do in the light of four solemn facts: Death, Judgment, Heaven, and Hell. We decide, or we re-examine the decision if we have already made it in the past, whether we are going to give our life interest to what the world about us has to offer, or whether we will make provision rather for the life after death. Will our heroes be the great men of the world, or will we follow the Man who chose the hard way, the way of insult, obstruction, and death, because it so happened that it was the only way He could bring men back to God when men had forgotten that they came from God and did not want to be reminded about the law of right and wrong which God had written in their hearts. Ordinarily, a preacher, or "Retreat Master" gives a series of talks covering the period of retirement. This is supposed to stimulate thought and self-examination, but the main work of thinking and praying and determining a plan of life is done by the individual "on retreat."

So, in the fall of 1919, I began my last months of preparation. Almost ten years had passed since the day I cut the item from the Boston *Pilot* in the library at Danvers. The priesthood was in sight, and China lay just over the horizon. Meanwhile, life at the seminary went on as usual.

Dom Pedro was dead. He had passed away some months before, and his successor was duly installed. Dom Pedro, I should mention, was a mule, one of the team that had walked all the way from Brooklyn in reply to Father Walsh's plea for a horse. A kind lady benefactor, as I have already explained somewhere in the foregoing pages, offered a mule instead of a horse; but Barney Meyer insisted that if she wanted to give a mule, it would be a better balanced gift to give two.

They were a valuable acquisition, those two mules. They worked hard and ate frugally. They seemed to take much less care than the jalopies. There was no rust on their hinges, no dirt in their carburetors. But then Dom Pedro died. There were conjectures and suspicions, but the only sound conclusion was that Dom Pedro just turned up his "toes" and died. We planted him out in the fields beneath the shade of the horse chestnut tree, or where we had hoped a horse chestnut tree would grow and cast its shadow. Father Walsh suggested that with Dom Pedro planted there, we might reap a donkey engine.

His successor was Jack, also a mule, and like Dom Pedro, born and brought up in Brooklyn. He, too, walked all the way to Maryknoll, having had lots of practice in walking on week-end trips from Flatbush to Coney Island pulling after him a heavy-duty sulky, not unlike a jaunting car.

We had our usual run of entertainments that year. Our plays were made to entertain, not to educate. Father Walsh would have preferred something more uplifting. This, however, would take time, talent, and hard work. We disposed of a minimum of the first, had little of the second, and we felt that the hard work should be limited to road building and breaking rocks. Important to us was the element of spontaneity, a minimum of rehearsals, and a maximum of laughs. We succeeded in a fair way, but one evening after the curtain dropped, Father Walsh's appraisal was critical. "It smacked of the gutter," he said.

Brother Henry figured in the plays. He was scenario writer, director and star. I recall one time when he begged to be excused from the regular weekly walk. His arthritis was paining him terribly, he said. With the permission granted, he hopped into bed with a pile of favorite literature by his side. Not many minutes later, Joseph Sweeney who had run into trouble planning the evening's entertainment, sought the professional advice of Brother Henry. Henry became so enthused in working up the script that he jumped out of bed, and the two rehearsed the act together. Imagine Father Rector's surprise that night to see the poor arthritis victim doing a jig, just as bright and nimble as a youngster as he capered on and off the stage.

In one of these entertainments, Brother Henry was to impersonate an ancient missioner and make a dramatic entry on a pair of crutches. He was made up in authentic invalid style, with white gown and nightcap, but the crutches were much too high for Brother Henry's four feet and a fraction. He made a flying leap on to the crutches, and they lifted him high in the air like a youngster on a ferris wheel and then dropped him near, ever so near—almost in the lap of Father Walsh who was sitting in the front row. So the tradition grew. Our plays were entertaining, never too deep, rarely serious, preferably relaxing, and designed to stimulate a laugh.

The Catholic Students Mission Crusade was being organized at that time. The inspiration for this organization came from Father Clifford King, a priest of the Divine Word Society, at Techny, Illinois. It spread rapidly. Father Frank Thill, now Bishop of Salina, who became Secretary-Treasurer, directed the first General Convention at Washington, D. C., with delegations from schools in all parts of the country.

The program of the Crusade included the education of students in mission facts and ideals. This was to be achieved through lectures, correspondence with missioners in the field, and by writing books and pamphlets on mission subjects. The Crusade also promoted prayers and sacrifices among students for the spiritual support of missioners. It also encouraged financial support for mission work, and had pledged itself to raise a million dollars the first year.

Branches of the Crusade were called "Units." We had a unit at Maryknoll, called "The Academia." This title was suggested by Father Walsh, who had in mind the student organization at St. John's Seminary, Boston, which was called by that name. The Academia has continued to this day, and our students have tried to do their bit to carry out the program of the Crusade.

I remember one of the first meetings. It was a venture at audio-visual education regarding the needs of missioners in the vast continent of Africa. Brother Bernard Bobb, who came from the West Indies and was dark-skinned, introduced the session when he walked slowly and solemnly out on the stage, turned to the audience and announced: "I represent one hundred million souls!" Student ingenuity and talent went into these Academia meetings. They were entertaining as well as instructive.

Some events of that year stand out in my memory. One was the death of Father John I. Lane. The news came as a shock to us. We knew he was ill, but not seriously. He had gone back to Boston when his inflammatory rheumatism made it impossible for him to continue with us. He never lost interest in us. I called on him several times during his illness. He died at St. Agnes Hospital, in Baltimore.

He longed to return to the work at Maryknoll, hoping to do so up to within a few months of his death. He was received as a member of the Society. Father Walsh made a special trip to Baltimore for the purpose; Father Lane had never actually joined the Society while he was with us, for then he was simply helping Father Walsh and Father Price to get started. He had a lovable personality and made friends everywhere.

When I was practicing the ceremonies of Mass, Father Joseph Early helped me. Father Early had come to Maryknoll from Boston, already a priest. He was one of the most brilliant students that had gone through the Brighton Seminary. He was an inspiring teacher, but his health was poor. Eventually, suffering night after night with asthma, he had to give up and go back to Boston. He was one of those rare souls whom God seems to have designated as a victim. Without a doubt, his sufferings helped the work of Maryknoll immeasurably.

Do you remember how it snowed in February, 1920? Most of the Eastern States were buried in snow for a week, the first week of the month, and that was the week before our ordination, on February 8th. My companion in retreat was Joseph Sweeney, the same who in later years gathered a flock of lepers about him in the cemeteries outside the town of Sunwui, in South China, and afterwards, migrated to an island in the West River Delta, where he still lives and works for them.

As a student, Big Joe—he is well over six feet tall—got a lot out of life, a lot of fun. He enjoyed "living dangerously." Half way through the retreat, when the snow kept coming down, I began to have visions of being ordained alone. He and some other students had a toboggan slide down the hill of our new property. Its special feature was a jump of thirty-five feet from the top of a fieldstone wall to a runway leading into the woods. They found that flexible flyers could be guided more easily and made better time than the toboggans. They also found that the sleds and their riders could get damaged. One student was carried to the infirmary with broken ribs. It is still a mystery how my classmate, Joe, survived until ordination day and could appear that morning unencumbered by slings, splinters, or casts.

For three solid days it snowed without a letup. The morning of ordination the country about us and beyond the Hudson was a fairyland of white. Maryknoll was beautiful, but the question was would our relatives and friends be here to enjoy its beauty. Walking for some of the guests was surely out of the question, and automobiles, that ordinarily could make the trip from the station to the seminary in fifteen minutes, were useless.

The snow was so heavy on the last day before ordination that retreat had to be broken while the students shoveled the snow to break a path from the old seminary, Rosary House, out to the main road and down the hill to the end of the trolley line. The path was about a mile long. It had to be wide enough for a team of horses and a sleigh.

We tried to clear the roads with a pair of horses and a snow plow, but Brother Xavier and Brother Martin were afraid of breaking up the horses rather than the snow. We were expecting twenty-five guests, including Bishop Gibbons of Albany, who was to ordain us. It was a memorable experience. The village stables had all been transformed into taxi garages with sleighs for hire. The few available horses in Ossining were and would be engaged.

But, as in all such emergencies, the situation was saved,—thanks this time to some of our guests who loved a brisk walk in the snow, and thanks also to Buck and Nig, the two mules, who took their responsibility seriously during those days of passenger service and never once kicked.

Buck and Nig solved one problem, but there was another—the conveyance. The small cutter was too small. We had to use one of the farm sleighs. A few rough boards made a good floor, and we dug some fur robes out of moth balls.

I learned later that when my mother was leaving Lawrence she had to ask the milkman to give herself and my brother a lift to the railway station. They arrived at Ossining just when the train from Albany was pulling in with Bishop Gibbons. They all piled aboard the sleigh. The Bishop occupied a sort of throne which had been fixed up on the sled behind Brother Martin, the driver. My family had places in the rear. So they started out for Maryknoll.

Without a toot of the horn or shifting of gears, Brother Martin and his team began the journey at slow speed. There were no traffic policemen out and speed laws were discreetly overlooked. The distance was just as long then as it is today, but the two mules did it in forty minutes, more or less.

"The only cloud that appeared for Buck and Nig in the next forty-eight hours," as Father Walsh wrote afterwards, "was the positive refusal of the Bishop to use the royal mules on his return trip. When this decision was announced, Nig was brave, but a solitary tear fell from Buck's eye and turned into a salted peanut on his hoof—where it yet remains."

The ordination was for me, of course, something never to be forgotten, as it is in every priest's life. The small chapel was crowded. It was one of the last ordinations held in the old farmhouse, our first seminary. The following spring, ground was to be broken for the new seminary. Once a temporary chapel had been set up in the new seminary, all future ordinations would be held there, and they have continued in the temporary chapel to the present time.

I lost face that day when the students told me that my brother had overslept. Four of them had to take him, bedclothes and all, and drop him on the floor. Only then was he impressed with the seriousness of the situation. He must have thought he was still at home listening to my mother patiently begging him to get up and go to work. Later that day when we all met the Bishop, and my mother complained to His Lordship about such a son, Bishop Gibbons said: "That may be so, Mrs. Lane, but he is the only one in this room who knows how to genuflect when he kisses a Bishop's ring."

After my ordination and First Mass at Maryknoll, I went to Scranton to say my second Mass at the Venard School, where I had been the first student. It was a delightful and unforgettable experience.

Finally, came the day of the first Solemn Mass at home, in St. Mary's Church, Lawrence, Massachusetts. Father James T. O'Reilly, the Augustinian pastor, preached the sermon. It is still a happy memory that has remained with me all through the years.

In the Diary of the Venard School, these lines appeared among the February notes of that year:

"Two other Maryknollers gladdened us with their presence during the mid-year recess, and with their first priestly benediction as well, —Father Lane and Father Sweeney, both recently ordained at Maryknoll. Such occasions are fruitful in graces, and forecast to the students the great happiness in store for them when their days of preparation are over.

"As Father Lane was the first student enrolled at the Venard when it first began, in its early home on Clay Avenue, Scranton, back in the old 'stone age', the students at once instituted habeas corpus proceedings for a holiday in celebration.

"They won their case with ease, for never again in this wide, wide world will there be another 'first' student at the Venard."

So here we are bringing to a close this period of happy student days, just as we reach the end of another chapter; and for that, as Aesop said, when his visitor stopped talking and went back to sleep, "Thanks be to God!"

22

The New Seminary

". . . We imagine ourselves crossing the Hudson at the Tappan Zee and rubbing our eyes as we note, two miles back, on a height six hundred feet above Ossining, a great pile of gray, with a quaint cross-tipped tower, that breaks, with unusual interest, a beautiful landscape. It is a daydream. . . ."
— James Anthony Walsh, August, 1920

Late one night, after the students were in bed, there was a loud knocking at the front door of the seminary. Someone wanted to get in, and he was in a hurry. He was a stranger, too, because he missed the night bell at the side of the door. The doorkeeper turned on the entry light and looked through the glass. A New York State trooper, big and impressive in his gray uniform and broad-brimmed campaign hat, was standing outside. This happened about a year ago.

A teletype message received a few minutes before at the barracks in Hawthorne had started him on this late evening mission. The trail he was following brought him right to our door. Not many minutes later, the trail ended—in one of our guest rooms! It was a lad we had taken in off the road. He was wanted in another state, but he really was not a bad sort.

"We see your pagoda up here on the hill," the trooper said, "as we cruise up and down the highway, but this is the first time I've been inside."

How many people, I asked myself, have seen our "pagoda up here on the hill" and wondered what was inside. Seen from the Hudson River, or met by motorists on the Briarcliff-Peekskill Parkway, which

249

cuts through this part of Westchester, the seminary is a big pile of field stone, covered with a roof of green tile and topped by a tower with its eaves turned up in oriental style. These turned-up eaves are designed, the Orientals say, to shoot off into space any evil spirits that might try to make an emergency landing on our roof, to send them rocketing away from our happy home. Heavy beams, painted green and Mandarin red, fill in the open spaces of the upper tower, and a copper cross surmounts it all. On a clear day, seen in bright sunshine against a blue sky, the seminary tower would make any passer-by stop to look.

I asked myself also how many people realize the backaches and the heartaches, the toil and the planning, the worries, and—I was going to say the blood—that have been the price of this "pagoda up here on the hill."

Late in the fall of 1919, we dug a deep trench from the boiler room in the stone building on the highway, up to the top of the hill on the newly acquired property, where the seminary was to be built. This was the first step. Before snow fell that year we had spent many hours of manual labor filling in the ditch, after the water mains, the steam lines and the hot water lines had been laid, and after the electric cables had been put in their corner of the trench. "May they all stay put," Father Walsh sighed, "and may the next man who digs a ditch at Maryknoll—bury his troubles in the woods! It is so vexing to have to dig a hole and then fill it again and meanwhile pay so much money for the whole business."

"Don't build now," people told him, "it's foolish." Others told him to go ahead; it was the only right thing to do.

"We can't live in tents all through the winter," Father Walsh said. "Temporary structures cost money, too, and then it is all wasted when you have to tear them down. We are going to build solidly. We have been building solidly, and we are not sorry, because a bird in the hand is worth two in the ice-chest, and perhaps next year things will be even worse."

Right after my ordination in February, 1920, Father Walsh made me his procurator. That term, "procurator," is common in seminaries and monasteries. In the days of the Roman Empire, a procurator was a man who looked after the Emperor's money matters in the far-off provinces. The dictionary says that a procurator is a man who manages the affairs of another; of course, this would not mean necessarily that he doesn't mind his own affairs. In a seminary, a procurator is the one who pays the bills, not out of his own money, fortunately for him. He is the one who worries about when we shall eat and what we shall eat, and sometimes even if we shall eat. His particular domain embraces the butcher, the baker, the mops and brooms, and the candle-stick maker, as well as the plumber, the steamfitter, and the fifty-seven varieties of salesmen. He is supposed to have a worried look, and everyone nods understandingly and indulgently when he rushes about with hair bristling, seeking someone to devour. That was my job for three years and a half.

During this period the new seminary was going up. Father Walsh, naturally, was in charge of all the planning and designing, but with so many other matters to attend to, he had me superintend the carrying-out of his instructions.

To fill a column of his "Home Notes" in *The Field Afar,* Father Walsh wrote about his new procurator: "There is a new procurator at the Knoll, and, with nothing on his mind but some light hair and the idea of procuring as well as preserving, he succeeds in keeping everybody moving. This procurator is fortunate in having no money worries and no creditors to look occasionally in the face. These belong to the treasurer, whose eyesight is too poor to allow him to recognize any other than benefactors.

"The procurator, of course, has his troubles. He finds, as many do, that it is very easy to start things but the 'dickens of a job' to keep them up. He gets the machinery all set up, turns the crank, and discovers a loose nut. He orders a 'certain kind,' and something comes that is 'just as good,' but twice as bad. Perhaps you have had similar experiences, but Maryknoll gives scope to a wide variety, since it includes seven houses, a farm, a central-heating plant, and a water supply. Add to this the responsibility of catering to one hundred and thirty people—plus the canary bird that Algernon Croesus sent when he was leaving for his winter home.

"Catering is naturally the great difficulty for a procurator, who, by all traditions of Catholic institutions, is supposed to be economical to such a nicety as to make him unpopular. Ours at Maryknoll has an unusually patient group of people to deal with, and whatever appears on the table is taken or left without a murmur. It may be a squeal-less porker or a sinewy rooster, an un-fatted calf, or a home-chopped sausage—nothing is ever said, so far as the writer knows, and little is thought, about the lay-out.

"But the great burden is, while seeing a hundred things that need to be done, suddenly to be confronted with the announcement that there is no water—which means an upset all along the line. But the water situation has now improved. The question of supply is no longer serious: our difficulty has been to hitch the supply with our faucets, and with a few thousand dollars we can do this. But who wants to give a water supply to a foreign mission or any other seminary?

"Some years ago, as you know, when we received money from John D. Rockefeller in compensation for the loss of some property that we are glad not to have secured, we sank the cash under the ground, turning it first into pipes that connected our establishment with the 'Cloaca Maxima' of Ossining.

"For a water supply, however, the case is really quite different. There is the symbolism of the commodity, as well as the water itself —'My soul thirsteth after the fountains of living waters.' "

It was decided to build the new seminary with field stone. This is one of the staple products of Westchester. The county is filled with loose stone. Every spring, farmers ploughing and harrowing their fields, reap a new harvest of stones. Since the days of the Dutch, this unfailing harvest of rocks has been gathered up, laid at the sides of the fields, and then, during the off-season winter months, the field stones have been piled orderly, high and wide, to make substantial and picturesque dividing walls, more sturdy and more lasting than the rail fences of New England.

We had a rich supply to begin with on our own property, and there were more stones coming up each year. If this store should be exhausted, there were neighbors all around us who would gladly bequeath us their savings of generations. All we had to do was cart them.

So the architects, Mr. Maginnis and Mr. Walsh—the latter Father Walsh's brother—drew a picture of what the seminary should look like: the foundations would be thick and solid, like the caverns under Monte Cassino and the Convento di San Francesco at Assisi; Roman arches would extend along the ground floor and the main floor, and the upper structure would continue its Roman lines, until it reached the roof, which would have a touch of the oriental.

The first sod was turned for the new seminary on June 29th, 1920. Monsignor John Dunn came from New York, Father James Kelly came from Boston, Father Cashin was here from Sing Sing, Fathers Callan and McHugh left Hawthorne for the day, Father Thomas Phelan made another trip from Brewster, and there were others. Bishop Legrand, of Dacca, India, happened to be here. There were almost one hundred and fifty of us living at Maryknoll then, and for all of us it was the prelude to a new era. For Father Walsh, especially, it was historic: on that day, we blessed our first stone building, St. Peter's and Paul's, which was serving as boiler-room and seminary, and then, the same day, actually started the new seminary.

A few weeks later, the first stone was set on the long concrete footing. It wasn't much of a stone, and the ceremony was very simple, attended only by the laborers and ourselves; but it was a beginning.

I find it a lesson in faith to think back now on that day in the summer of 1920, when Father Walsh looked ahead and saw in vision what we now see in fact. Viewing the seminary tower from some far corner of the farm during my morning stroll, or coming upon it suddenly after leaving a path in the woods, I love to recall the words written by Father Walsh back in 1920 as he watched the steam shovel digging a great hole in our hilltop.

"There is noise on the hill, at least from seven in the morning until well into the afternoon," he wrote. "It is the noise of steam driving a great shovel that is gouging the earth for the foundation of the American Foreign Mission Seminary.

"We like the noise. It sings the song of progress, and at times it thrills us. Even the heavily burdened treasurer does not object, although every puff of steam and every cart load of dirt means an addition to the bills that fall daily on his desk.

"We picture ourselves, our friends, and future generations of priests, walking in another year along the solid pavements already roughly outlined. We think of our missioners asking themselves if ever again they will see the much-loved Knoll, and if, in that happy event, they will recognize it.

"We vision—and the prospect is near—the great refectory, the spotless kitchen, the archives, the crypt under the chapel, replacing the soil now being excavated. Above we see the chapel itself, the simple dignified entrance, the museum, offices, class and conference rooms. And, rising higher, we vision rooms for no fewer than three hundred Maryknollers, with allowance for their guests.

"Our imagination peoples this projected house with every room filled, and we ask ourselves, 'What next?'

"But we do not attempt to answer the question. 'It is enough, O Lord!' When the time comes the question will be met and solved, because this is not the work of men.

"So we daydream again, and we imagine ourselves crossing the Hudson at the Tappan Zee and rubbing our eyes as we note, two miles back, on a height six hundred feet above Ossining, a great pile of gray, with a quaint cross-tipped tower, that breaks, with unusual interest, a beautiful landscape.

"It is a daydream that is already at the beginning of its realization —and the Catholic faithful, priests and laity, will make possible the fulfillment as certainly as they have, under God, prepared for its foundation."

Father Walsh's dream is fairly completed. Two wings remain to be realized. One of them will contain the permanent Chapel.

Already his question, "What next?" has come up, after every room was filled. The question, he said, would be met and solved when the time should come. Its solution brings a smile to the lips of some of us. When the onrush of students overflowed the seminary, we had to use double-decker beds.

Men scoffed at Father Walsh's huge plans in those early days, but in point of fact he underestimated the needs. He designed a building for one hundred and eighty students, and there came a time when we had to crowd in two hundred and fifty-five. This meant that over a hundred future missioners had to take to the double-deckers.

Sometimes the rector is asked: "Do the boys ever fall out of the upper decks?"

"Yes, sometimes," he explains. "When they fall out of the upper, we put them in the lower, and after a while they don't fall out any more."

When we were building and needed solid stones to pave the lower floors and the cloister walks, we turned to the sidewalks of New York. Our contractors remembered the gray and green "bluestone" piled up in lots near the waterfront of New York, after the city had removed them from the sidewalks of lower Manhattan. The contractors got busy, struck a bargain, and soon load after load of the flagstones was brought up the hill and laid in place.

They cover the floor of the rotunda at the main entrance of the seminary. They cover the whole floor of one wing that is given to parlors and offices. They furnish the pavement for the cloistered walk through the arches bordering the quadrangle, and for the terrace walk above the arches. They are the floor of the seminary refectory, and the floor of the students' recreation room.

Hence, we literally pray and play, walk and talk, work, eat, and entertain our visitors on the sidewalks of New York.

While it was a big important start to have Westchester field stones right at hand to begin the building, and to get flagstones from the streets of New York for some of our floors, there were still numberless items of building materials to assemble, put in place, and pay for. So for months and years we lived and dreamed and worked and worried among cement and plaster, terra cotta brick and electric conduits, fittings and couplings, radiators, fixtures, faucets, steam lines and return pipes, wheelbarrows, salamanders, and donkey engines.

Little by little the seminary took shape, but it was five years and longer before some parts of it began to look finished. Twenty years later the west wing was rising. The plan is not yet complete.

Father Patrick Byrne had much to do with planning the building. He had ideas. He knew how to convey them to Father Walsh, and he had ways of convincing Father Walsh when the latter hesitated. Perhaps few people realize the one hundred and one little details of practical value and lasting worth which Father Byrne contributed to the seminary building as it stands today.

Meanwhile, as procurator, I had to give a good part of my day to contractors and jobbers, supply men and an endless train of salesmen. But I also had to take care of the farm. I took my job seriously. For hours I pored over *The Farm Journal,* to find out the latest ways of bringing up pigs and chickens and getting the most for the dollars invested. We installed an alarm clock and electric lights in the chicken coop, to get the hens up at four o'clock in the morning and keep them on the job until the late evening. One by one we discarded various breeds and, eventually, I think, settled on white Leghorns.

We had a herd of Holsteins, but I'm afraid that the balance sheet at the end of the year would not show a great profit for our efforts at milk producing. Brother Xavier, who in his farming days in Vermont had to make a living by it, must have smiled at some of my innovations. He never used the veto, however. He let me learn by experience.

I thought we should try a new breed of pigs, and I settled on the Jersey Durocs. Perhaps I was partial to them because their bristles were reddish, like my own thinning locks. The Jersey Durocs turned out to be another headache. During an epidemic of hog cholera, I accumulated more experience in farming.

William Kaschmitter was put in charge of the incubators and brooders. It was his job to go to the incubator room regularly to check on the heat, and each night he had to set the lamps to provide the proper temperature. One evening, the Seminary Rector, in executing a disciplinary measure, made it impossible for poor Bill to get to the incubators. The next morning all the eggs were thoroughly cooked.

While the new building was going up, we made plans to install a fifty-five kilowatt turbine generator. This would be steam-driven from the boiler room and would give us all the light and power we needed. An engineer would be required to supervise this unit. I found the right man in Tarrytown. He was a Belgian with a big heart and an amazing accent, who understood our English much better than we understood his. He had had long experience in electricity, mechanics, and farming and turned out to be a Godsend to us who, young and inexperienced, found ourselves beyond our depth in the stream of boilers, steam lines, electric motors, horses, cows, pigs, and chickens. He knew everything and could do anything. We called him the "Chief."

His English was devastating. For him, valves were "wallufs," but if in an effort to make yourself understood you too said "wallufs," he would register absolutely no intelligence until you finally said "valves."

One day his truck broke down on the way out into the country. He phoned to the seminary for help. "We are here by the ducks canals!" he shouted into the instrument. That meant nothing to the Brother at the other end of the line. Where in the world were the ducks canals? "Where did you say the truck is, Chief?" he asked once more. "What! So you don't understand English, hein!" he shouted. "By the ducks canals—woof! woof! the ducks canals!" Then it was clear: the truck had given up on the hill near the dog kennels, a road just beyond our farm where the dogs of the Grace Lane Kennels used to bark and bay in dissonance whenever our tower bell rang out.

Planning meals for the ever growing family became a problem, but happily our Sisters assumed the greater part of this worry. Dollars were never numerous, but the Sisters knew how to make a piece of meat and a bag of potatoes go a long way. Father Walsh at that time used to recommend whole wheat as a breakfast food. This became our every morning dish, and Father James Anthony would urge it on our visitors, explaining the nutritive value and calory content of this wholesome dish. We had a standing order with the supply house.

After a time, I thought I noticed watermelon seed and bits of oats in our breakfast food. I investigated and discovered that for several mornings, instead of whole wheat, we had been served with piping hot dishes of "Lay or Bust," a special grain mixture prepared for laying hens. The order had been confused, or perhaps the wrong sacks were used, but at any rate I acquired a bit of undreamed-of fame by this incident.

Recently I came upon an old recipe which we were using for our bread at that time. "BREAD: one-half barrel of flour, one-half pound of yeast, thirty-five quarts of water, two quarts of sugar, one quart of salt, two pounds of lard.—Knead for one-half hour; allow to rise for two hours. This will make forty loaves (two feet long)."

Our Sisters did the baking. They took care of our laundry also, and in their free moments they kept busy with needle and thread to give new life to our old shirts and worn-out cassocks. Sister Anna Maria was a very important member of the family; she had charge of the mending. It happened at times that, after she had repeatedly repaired a shirt or pair of trousers, the patches would seem to be greater than the original piece. She would say: "Tell Brother Aloysius to send over a button, and I'll sew a shirt on it."

Cardinal O'Connell came to Maryknoll in the fall of 1921. I remember him as he spoke to the students. He was standing on the receiving platform of *The Field Afar,* and the students were gathered around him in the open air. "Your priests tell me," he said, "that you do not look upon yourselves as heroes and martyrs, preparing for a career of terrifying hardships, but that with the utmost cheerfulness you are preparing to go to the Orient, as a plain duty, to bring the light and grace of Christ's Kingdom to those who sit in darkness and spiritual death. May this humble and joyous spirit remain here always. . . . May Maryknoll continue to be a glory to America, as it certainly hitherto has been!"

During the winter of 1921-1922 the new seminary was a huge roofless stone shell, with a startling likeness to some bombed-out monument of Europe. Students began to live in it before the roof was on. When it was eventually roofed, more students moved in. One class lived in what is now the library. It was then just a bare fortress of rough stone, steel girders, cement floors and unplastered fire brick. The students called it "All Saints' Hotel." My room was just outside this temporary dormitory. Sometimes an unmonastic din came from within "All Saints' Hotel," and I felt bound in conscience to investigate and restore the peace. This I had to do cautiously, however, because it was the delightful pastime for the denizens of the place to conduct a "fire-drill." This they did by rousing their fire chief, a timid lad of gentle manners, downcast eyes and honeyed accents, and then installing him aboard a huge iron cart which was used by the contractors for hauling stone and cement about the new construction. With this equipage they would take off and rush full tilt the length of the floor space. If you opened the door just as the engine of destruction approached, you might need to be put aboard and rushed to the infirmary.

By June of 1922, the building, consisting of one-half of the main structure and the northwest wing, was alive with activity, though unfinished within. Father Walsh told the story in his Tenth Annual Report:

"Work on the new seminary, begun in June, 1920, was pushed as rapidly as our resources would permit. Under God's Providence these were not sufficient to allow the execution of our original plan for completion by the middle of September. Labor troubles, together with difficulty in securing certain materials, also contributed to delay. On the other hand, the number of vocations to our work, especially to the sisterhood, furnished a problem in accommodations that was solved only by installing the students in the yet unfinished building.

"Despite the absence of plaster, woodwork, finished floors, and specified plumbing and heating fixtures, comfortable quarters were provided by the installation of rough board stairways and doors, temporary plumbing, lighting and heating; and, as the building now stands, but recently under roof, it shelters almost the entire student body.

"Progress on the work of completing the projected structure varies with the monthly financial returns. Every effort is being made, however, to hurry construction, as so many other needs of Maryknoll are crying for attention. On the basement floor, the kitchen and refectory have been practically finished—the former being provided with the usual modern kitchen apparatus warranted by the consequent saving in time and money, while the refectory in its monastic lines well embodies the spirit that the entire building is designed to emphasize—the simplicity, fortitude, and nobility of the apostolic ideal."

The following year, that is in the spring of 1923, we completed our moving from the old seminary into the new building. Father Walsh was the last to leave the old farmhouse. He lingered on long after everyone else had found a corner in the new seminary. At last, as he said, he woke up one day to the fact that, as far as he knew, he and a small mouse were the only occupants of the old house. He had never seen the mouse, but there were evidences of his activity, and also of the mouse's discrimination. The mouse had burrowed into the Superior's old shoes. Imagine its foolhardiness in attempting to step into the shoes of the Maryknoll Superior!

The next night, Father Walsh said, there were two occupants in the house—himself and a cat. But soon he realized that it was time to abandon the place to the cat and the mouse and to the squad of painters who had come to give the farmhouse a new look in preparation for the Sisters, who were getting ready to rush in where the angels no longer cared to tread. So, balancing his traveling bag with a brief case, he sauntered reluctantly away from his old Maryknoll home.

He was hardly out when the Sisters moved in, and the old seminary became their Motherhouse. Thirty-six professed Sisters, for whom the place became "Home Sweet Home," changed its name to St. Dominic's, and later changed it again to Rosary House. The novices were living in St. Joseph's Hall, a rather pretentious title for the converted barn which had been vacated by the students. Their chapel was the small stone building, once a laundry, called St. Martha's.

The Teresians had become the Foreign Mission Sisters of St. Dominic on February 14th, 1920. A complete document on their work and training, together with their history during the preceding seven years, had been drawn up, signed by Archbishop Hayes of New York, and carried to Rome personally by the Apostolic Delegate, Archbishop Bonzano. When word of their full approbation was received from Rome through Archbishop Hayes, the Maryknoll Sisters took their place as a recognized religious community in the Church of Christ. There were forty-four Sisters at that time.

"And what about the future?" Father Walsh wrote on that occasion. "We do not know, but under God's Providence we see the Maryknoll Sisters at work throughout this country helping the American Foreign Mission Seminary in its various activities, whether in the simple round of household duties, in clerical and literary work, or among the Orientals who have found a home in our land: and we see them, too, in the mission field, catechizing, nursing, doctoring. In fact, we set no bounds to their work for the salvation of those countless souls who have not so much as heard the blessed names of Jesus and Mary."

A year later, when their formal novitiate was completed and twenty-one Sisters made their vows in the community's first ceremony of profession, their numbers had risen to seventy-one. Like the students, Brothers and priests, they came from all along the line, from Boston to California, from Canada to Virginia, and from over both great oceans. They had to crowd their numbers into these old farmhouses, the converted barn, and the upper floors of *The Field Afar* building, and put up with these circumstances for ten long years, much to the distress of Father Walsh who said it all reminded him of an excursion boat that turned over at the dock, because it was overcrowded. Eventually, their new Motherhouse rose up through the trees across the highway, and then at last they came into their own.

The seminary, though not yet totally constructed, grew gradually and assumed in general the lines visualized by Father Walsh. It really became a symbol, and it remains in our mind's eye when thoughts turn homeward from mission posts thousands of miles across the seas.

During three years and a half of World War II, when I was detained in various internment camps in Manchuria, my thoughts turned daily to Maryknoll. Under the circumstances, anyone would be a bit homesick now and then. Our mission work was stopped. We had practically no contact with our people. A high fence, and guards with guns, kept the world outside away from us. My thoughts would steal homeward and I would think of Maryknoll. There would come the vision of the gray pile of stone on the hill, the green tile roof, the tower, and the cross, the same vision which Father Walsh saw in his daydream of 1920: "We imagine ourselves crossing the Hudson at the Tappan Zee and rubbing our eyes as we note, two miles back, on a height six hundred feet above Ossinnig, a great pile of gray, with a quaint cross-tipped tower, that breaks, with unusual interest, a beautiful landscape. . . . It is a daydream. . . ."

23

The Mission Letters

"And when our work is done,
Our course on earth is run,
May it be said, 'Well done;
   Be thou at peace.'
E'er may that line of gray
Increase from day to day,
Live, serve, and die, we pray,
   West Point—for thee."
— *Alma Mater* of the United States Military Academy

It has been the practice in recent years for Catholic cadets of the First Class at West Point to make a week-end retreat at Maryknoll just before graduation in June. The Catholic chaplain at the Military Academy, seeing something in common in our two schools of training, wants his young officers to make this final religious contact before they receive their commissions and go overseas.

Not everyone sees this similarity of vocation. The career of a West Pointer is full of glamor, while, to some people, a foreign missioner is a hopeless anomaly, or, to paraphrase their own parlance, he is a benighted fool.

Back in the war days of 1917-1918, Father Walsh developed this comparison. Thousands of young Americans were crossing the Atlantic to fight in France, just when he was getting ready his little corps of four Americans to set up a beach head for a bigger battle in the East.

"In the eyes of the world," he said, "the soldier, or the Red Cross worker, is a hero; the soldier of the Cross of Christ is a fool.

"One leaves home and loved ones for a time, hoping soon to return; the other gives them up for life, expecting no recall.

"A departure that, for the one, may well be a stepping-stone to skill, success, and fame, means for the other, the giving up of every chance of attaining 'rank' at home. . . ."

In the hard, monotonous day-by-day plugging along the path of duty, the life of neither the young lieutenant nor the young missioner has much of lasting glamor,—but if there is any at all, I think it goes with the missioner.

He always has an ideal, something that stands higher and means more than Hill 147, something more precious and promising than a war to end wars, something even higher than his nation's flag, because his ideal is made and completed in heaven. He knows that no matter how few campaigns he may seem to win, none of his hard work is lost. It all counts up, and it will weigh eventually in favor of his cause.

It is not so with the brilliant young army officer. He has acquired the bitter knowledge that his hard work and his courage and his masterful tactics may bring victory in the battle,—but then, that the peace for which he and his comrades who died around him paid such a terrible price, can be lost in the secret bargainings of unworthy statesmen.

Americans are rightly proud of their Military Academy at West Point and its Corps of Cadets. The aim of West Point, besides imparting a liberal education in the arts and sciences with the specialized training needed by a leader in the Armed Forces, is to develop in the cadet qualities of character, leadership, integrity, loyalty, discipline, and a sense of duty, all essential for a commander of men. If we may judge from the young officers who have come to make a retreat at Maryknoll, it is clear that the Military Academy achieves its aim.

It is an experience to hear them sing their "Alma Mater." I have listened and thought how aptly it would express our own ideas. The hymn was written in 1908 by Colonel Reinecke. He was a cadet at that time, and when he actually composed it he was "walking the area." This was a disciplinary sequel to a bit of frivolity in the Yearling Camp that summer. Yearlings used to gather at the Battle Monument to sing furlough songs and to "bay at the moon." To kill time that day, he put together these words, as he marched up and down, and adapted them to the melody of Kuechen's *Treue Liebe*:

Hail, Alma Mater dear,
To us be ever near,
Help us thy motto bear
Through all the years.
Let Duty be well performed,
Honor be e'er untarned,
Country be ever armed,
West Point, by thee,

Guide us, thy sons, aright,
Teach us by day, by night,
To keep thine honor bright,
For thee to fight.
When we depart from thee,
Serving on land or sea,
May we still loyal be,
West Point, to thee.

And when our work is done,
Our course on earth is run,
May it be said, 'Well done;
Be thou at peace.'
E'er may that line of gray
Increase from day to day,
Live, serve, and die, we pray,
West Point, for thee."

In recent years, officers of the Army of Occupation in Japan have come back and told us what they saw our missioners doing. One of the staff at the Military Academy talked all through his dinner telling what he saw in Kyoto, the unbelievable feats which one of our priests was accomplishing to relieve distress among the poor and homeless.

In the same way, word has come back from priests in Japan, in letters written to the chaplain at West Point, telling of the excellent example set by young Catholic officers, recently graduated from the Military Academy and doing a tour of duty in the Far East. Their leadership in things religious makes relatively easy the work of the military chaplain. They set the pace for church-going and right living and they get things done which the priest would find just about impossible to do by himself.

The Army men have told us interesting things about our missioners. Other travelers have brought back accounts of what they saw, and some of them have shown us movies they took at missions in China, Korea, Japan, Latin America, and other places along their line of march. All this makes our men in fields afar seem not so far.

It was not so in 1920 and 1921, and the following years. At that time, what we knew about our missioners had to come from their own letters. Their arrival, their first impressions, difficulties, joys, problems, plans, life and work, sickness—all this had to come to us in their own writings, or in an occasional message from an older European missioner who had been in correspondence with Father Walsh over the years. As each letter came, we tried to fit ourselves into the picture, to imagine what we would do or would not do under similar circumstances. We were all subject to call. It was understood that a new group of priests would leave for the East each September, and there were not many of us available.

We learned about the siege of Kochow. This was reported in American newspapers in September, 1921, but we preferred the account given by Father O'Shea and sent to us direct.

"It's a great life if you don't weaken," he wrote. "We aren't beginning to weaken, so far as we can see. But we've had a lively time here —sort of a 'hot time in the old town' of Kochow, and for the second time in half a year.

"At present, thank God, we're all alive and well, which is far more than could be expected of any individuals going through what three of us have experienced in the past few days. At present also we are hosts, much to our disgust, of the military Mandarin of Kochow, and about thirty of his staff and other hangers-on. At the same time, two other military Mandarins of even rank, Generals Wong and So, are also staying in town, where they are making use of the former headquarters of General Foo, now with us.

"In other words, Kochow has again been captured, and even more skilfully looted than it was in December. And, what is more to us, we also were 'taxed' by the new arrivals—to the tune of my fine white horse and all the belongings of the catechists here gathered for retreat. However, we are doing business as usual, and Father Meyer has just finished his sermon on 'The Last Things' with an unusually impressed audience. But cheer up, say we, for the worst is yet to come, and we know not when nor how.

"When we got back here from Wuchow, we found that the Kwangsi raiders were not far behind us. General Foo was here. He wanted to leave, but the gentry begged him to stay in the hope that his own men would arrive before the Kwangsi soldiers.

"He stayed—and lost, for Sunday morning the Kwangsites attacked in such force as to cut off the two companies which he had across the river, and then surrounded the town where only a hundred-odd soldiers were guarding the wall. The Kwangsites were attacking fearlessly, and at noon Foo came to the conclusion that surrender was inevitable. He sent a messenger, asking me to go and see him at the Yamen. Father Meyer and I went immediately. Two four-inch shells burst near by, and the rifle fire was brisk.

"General Foo and his staff admitted that they were helpless, and they asked us to save unnecessary loss of life and property by going out to see the Kwangsi general and obtain terms.

"At about one o'clock, Father Meyer and I, with Mr. Epiphanius Yip, our catechist, and two aides of General Foo, went to the city wall and tried to get into communication with the Kwangsi soldiers who were sniping from the adjoining houses. Finding this impossible, we went to a more quiet portion of the wall, where Father Meyer descended by making a flying leap for some poles stacked in a lumber yard.

"Waving a small American flag, he went to where the snipers could see him, and was finally passed along to the Kwangsi forces, who received him in a business-like manner. The Kwangsi general said that·the terms were immediate evacuation through the North Gate, with their arms and accoutrement.

"Father Meyer returned about three o'clock, and firing was stopped on all sides. Returning to the compound, he sent Epiphanius Yip to General Foo with a letter given him by General So. Although the Kwangsi general had not told Father Meyer, he and his men had set four o'clock for the end of the armistice.

"When Yip arrived at Foo's yamen, he found him in consultation with two officers from the attacking army. Yip came back to tell us that General Foo had decided to remain, in the hope that he could 'stall for time' until relief came with his forces from Sunyi. This was a surprise; it put us in a false light with the Kwangsi general.

"During all this time, refugees had been coming into the compound with their valuables. We had to refuse a great number of them, because they were military officers. Finally, we got the outer gate locked, with a pile of military baggage on the outside. On Yip's return, some of the officers waiting outside forced their way in with him. Among the things brought in were eight loads of General Foo's personal stuff, accompanied by as many soldiers. Our protest was physical as well as verbal, one of the Fathers skinning his knuckles very badly in an attempt to keep the compound inviolate.

"Just while this local excitement was at its highest, two shells struck the town and firing began on all sides. One of the shells struck the Yamen, and the other just missed it, with the result that General Foo's headquarters became panic-stricken. The soldiers carried General Foo and his staff with them in their wild flight. Where their treasures were, so were their hearts, and they ran wildly to our mission compound.

"Here we had the gate open trying to push out the objectionable baggage. The soldiers, of course, made short work of pushing in. General Foo tried to keep some of them out, but it was in vain, and I told him to let them come—that I could not let in half the company and keep the others out to be massacred. At the same time I upbraided him and made him surrender his side-arms to me."

Here let me interrupt Father O'Shea's letter just long enough to inject a parenthesis. His phrase, "I upbraided him," is a mild understatement. We learned later that when General Foo appeared at the mission gate, Father O'Shea was very provoked with him, first for going back on his word, putting the missioners in a bad light with the attackers, causing the added fighting and destruction, and now for trying to save his own skin by running to the mission. When he came up to the gate, our little "Captain" sailed into him, leading with his left and planting a hard right jab on the astonished countenance of General Foo.

The General lost considerable face; he also lost a couple of teeth. Nevertheless, Father O'Shea and Father Meyer took him in, had him change his uniform for the apron of a house boy, and gave him shelter. When the invading army went through the place later looking for him, they kept the General hidden in a rice bin under four feet of the grain. He got enough air to breathe through a sort of air-line made of connected straws. Later, when the fortunes of war turned and General Foo found himself once more on top of the pack, he started up his printing presses with a new issue of provincial money and sent Father O'Shea five thousand dollars in homemade currency, as a slight token of gratitude. And now back to Father O'Shea's account:

"All this time the firing was coming closer, and as I closed the gate after the last of the Kwangtung men, the bullets were whistling past.

"Having shattered the East Gate of Kochow with a shell, the Kwangsi soldiers poured into the town and made for the Yamen. They were shooting as they came, evidently fearing an ambush, and it was rather squeamish work to hold them up at the mission gate. However, they were made to understand that the crowd within had surrendered unconditionally, and they were just coming in peaceably to take the guns when another party came in over the rear wall from the civil Mandarin's Yamen. Father Wiseman got these to stop firing, but that was about all. Just when the firing stopped and the looting began, it is hard to say; but inside of twenty minutes the compound was a wreck.

"It was certainly due to God's Providence that the loss of life was so slight. Father Meyer, to whom under God most of the credit must go for the prevention of bloodshed, saw only half a dozen dead men; and the later reports were that the victory was almost a bloodless one. Our action in disarming the Kwangtung men on their arrival in our compound certainly saved their lives, for the Kwangsites were savage at what they called the treachery of General Foo in trying to hold out after he had sent us to arrange for the surrender. Had they found him they surely would have shot him down . . ."

At about the same time with this report on the siege of Kochow, a letter came from Father James Edward Walsh and Father Frederick Dietz telling about the fighting around Wuchow, the gateway to Kwangsi Province.

"The American gunboat, the 'Pampanga,' came into port and some of the crew paid a welcome visit," they wrote, "Uncle Sam's boys will remain here to see that his citizens at the Baptist and Catholic Missions, and at the Standard Oil, are not molested.

"On June 20th, the fun began! My, but China is fast modernizing! Please throw overboard your notions of primitive civilization, etc., over here. An airplane—the first that has favored Wuchow—flew over the town and dropped a couple of bombs, causing much consternation and a little damage. Most of the shops shut their doors, and the people ran in all directions.

"Two days later we heard the booming of guns down the river. We lunched on board the 'Pampanga' by invitation and did it in sailor-fashion. The next morning we witnessed a general exodus from the town. In the afternoon, the airplane came again and accentuated the general panic by dropping some more bombs. 'Twas a most unwelcome visitor and gave one a creepy feeling. It also dropped some circulars saying that the people in town would not be molested, and inviting the Kwangsi soldiers to come over to the Kwangtung side with their arms, promising them an extra month's pay in the balance.

"We gladly admitted into our little compound as many as wanted to come. The place was crowded with men, women, children, chickens, dogs, baggage, boxes, and household furniture, and we had indeed as much privacy as a goldfish.

"It's an ill wind that blows no good. With so many people so close to a chapel and a priest, what more natural than to invite them to a talk? So Father Walsh did it, explaining to them our reason for being here, removing a few false notions, and instilling some fundamental religion. The language teacher followed with another little talk.

"We went to the Customs looking for news. The place was a sight. They had given refuge to hundreds of Chinese who were encamped in the basements, on the porches, and over the spacious lawns. The foreigners were playing tennis as usual, and regarded the whole affair much as a joke. It was a joke for them—all in one place, with an American gunboat moored close by and two British gunboats expected shortly; but not a joke for the poor Chinese with vivid recollections of ruthless murder and rapine. They know their soldiery, and have this proverb about them:

> " 'Good steel's not used for nails and trifles,
> And good men do not shoulder rifles.' "

"Added to the usual Sunday crowd at Mass were some sailors from the 'Pampanga.' There were a dozen of them, and about half were non-Catholics. Doubtless it was pure ennui that brought the latter, as time hangs heavy on their hands in a port like this, but they appeared to enjoy everything, even listening patiently to a sermon.

"Our number one catechumen, that is, our most promising prospect for baptism, visited us this Sunday. His wife is a Catholic. He is something of a notable in these parts, and in looks he is a perfect ringer for a Greek athlete of Pericles' time. This brings to mind the old argument about the Chinese descent. Some claim that the Chinese are the same race as the American Indians, and, in fact, there are many theories about it. For myself, I think I have seen on Chinese faces the features of almost every race under heaven. The old Roman type is common; so are Irish physiognomies; and I have seen living images of Leo X, Lord Russell, Jean De Reske, De Valera, Babe Ruth, and Lloyd George twice. Speculation about Chinese relationship to other races is interesting, but doubtless is not profitable. . . ."

Happily, most of these early letters were preserved, published in *The Field Afar,* and later in special volumes of *Mission Letters.* All of them are interesting.

Father Hodgins wrote about his people in Yeungkong: "In our congregation are carpenters, watchmakers, brass-workers, and pigskin-box-makers. Yeungkong does a big business in brass knives and scissors. Our town is still more famous for its pigskin boxes, which it exports to Canton. You can get the real pigskin, but the imitation made of bamboo paper is almost as good and much cheaper. They are lacquered and withstand the white ants and mould and moisture. Our sacristy boxes for altar breads are of this make and are handsomely decorated with a Chi Rho design.

"All the people were at Mass Sunday, because now the catechist visits as many as possible on Saturday night and reminds them of

Sunday. As the people work every day, all days look alike to them."

Mr. Epiphanius Yip, the man mentioned in the story about the siege of Kochow, was invaluable to our newly arrived missioners. He was a catechist, that is, a Chinese teacher who could get right down to the people and explain to them in their own language all that the Church teaches. Knowing the history and teachings of the Church, he could take the message which our priests wished to convey and bring it to the uneducated people in a language, and with figures, which they could quickly grasp. A catechist can reach a greater number of people and cover more ground than a foreigner. Mr. Yip was the best. Father Walsh, at the request of friends in Pittsburgh, gave this brief picture of the man:

"Epiphanius Yip, head catechist for the entire mission of Kochow, is thirty-five years old. He is married, has three children, one of whom he hopes will be a priest. He lives at the mission always, as his duties keep him there. His mother was an Annamite Catholic who migrated here and converted her husband on marrying him. This young man is a clever, well educated, and finished Chinese gentleman. He is in excellent relations with the officials and notable people of the district, and has helped much to put the Church here on a plane of dignity where she enjoys the prestige she should. He is an excellent Chinese scholar, and speaks French."

The Ecclesiastical Review, during 1920 and the following years, published some of the letters of Father Francis Ford and Father James Edward Walsh. I remember this one from Father Ford, in particular. It was written from Yeungkong just about a year after he arrived in China.

"I have just realized the impossible!" he wrote. "Fifteen years ago, when I had as good an imagination as any schoolboy, I dangled my feet in the boys' gallery of our old brick church in Brooklyn and listened to a missioner's talk. He had a grisly beard that contrasted oddly with the 'lace-curtain' surplice he wore, and his gestures were wild. But a few moments of his broken English made my feet hang limp and even the old women beneath me forgot to cough or tell their beads.

"He was Father Conrardy, a fiery enthusiast, and his subject was his lifework among the lepers. He gloried in his love for them and flung the challenge in our faces to show our Catholicity by helping him to build a home for them. It seemed harder for him to beg the money than to do the disgusting work of nursing slowly rotting Chinese men and women, but he traveled Europe and America for funds. With a generous impulse I put a nickel in the basket—five times my usual sum—and the rest of the Mass was spent in repeating to myself Father Conrardy's last words: 'My one ambeesh is to die a martyr.'

"Later, when the mission fever caught America, my pastor frequently invited other missioners to preach; but Father Conrardy was the first I had seen and his face and words remained with me, and soon I began to idealize him and his work, and the Damien of China meant much to me. So last week when the suggestion was made to call at Father Conrardy's Leper Island, I feared a disillusion. Like an old-timer returning to his village in 'Old Home Week' I felt I would be disappointed. I almost preferred to stay at home and nurse my ideal; but the call was too urgent.

"There is little of the stage-setting of Molokai in the approach to the Leper Colony near Canton. No pale green sea, tall palms, and rugged cliffs; no great expanse of ocean to elevate the spirit to the heroism of the life among the lepers. Instead, the swift cold train and a walk of a few minutes on a cinder path bring the island in view— Sheklung, 'Stone Dragon' by name.

"A sampan from the asylum, manned by four lepers, is the first contact with the pest-laden island, and a half hour in its comfortable, though bare, 'cabin' is a quiet prelude that eases one to the disgusting sights to come. I knew I should not meet here Father Conrardy's successor, young Father Deswazieres; but his assistant Father Chau, equally young, would make us welcome. . . .

"Perhaps the one note in common among these two young priests and Father Conrardy is a singularly pure motive in serving God, that brings with it simplicity and a poor conceit of their sacrifice. They are not self-conscious in talking of their work for God; they see it only as His work. And the four Immaculate Conception Sisters from Canada, who care for the women, have the same delicate spirituality that comes from living up to the noblest ideals. But, then, it is somehow expected of womenfolk and we take it for granted in them.

"The work here with seven hundred lepers is too big to size it up in a short visit. We saw merely the surface of the island's life, the happy patients who tried to smile us welcome in spite of the sores that sometimes made the smile a hideous grimace. We saw the rows and rows of low buildings that housed the patients—cheerless, untidy rooms the men kept, in contrast with the neat, clean dwellings of the women. Experience, however, with Chinese villagers has softened criticism into sympathy and the wonder of it is how any order is possible . . .

"We saw the little patches of ground, war-garden size, where each leper was free to plant whatever he wanted, flowers or vegetables; and a several-acre farm where the truck garden lay. Everyone seemed to be at work, except the more sickly, though no one strained himself, and many were the pleasantries that passed from mouth to mouth.

"Life at Sheklung is happy, except for the short periods of fever and pain when a corrupted member ulcerates and drops off, leaving a diseased stump. Certainly the lepers are happier than when, as outcasts, they haunted the roadways of the Province begging their scanty meals. Here their urgent wants are supplied, and they are granted forty cents a month for 'pin money' with a chance to buy cheap luxuries in the colony's store.

"There is nothing morbid on the island. Peace, if not downright cheerfulness, is on every face, and most of them have tasted the solid comfort of the Church's sacraments. All the women and most of the men have asked for baptism, though there is no inducement given them. What a storehouse of merit is there, with sound souls purified in baptism and their sufferings made acceptable to God! They are the Church Suffering on earth and their purgatory is well nigh ended. . . ."

Another letter of Father Ford, which impressed us at home with the vivid picture he drew, was about a visit to Yamaguchi in Japan. He wrote it long after he was settled in Yeungkong. A few miles out in the South China Sea from Yeungkong is the island of Sancian, where St. Francis Xavier died.

"The nearness of Sancian Island keeps St. Francis Xavier ever in our minds over here," he wrote, "so you'll pardon me if I run back over the trip through Japan to speak a little more of Yamaguchi. It was St. Francis' headquarters in his mission work in Japan.

"He stayed longer at several places in India, but Japan was his mission field as the term would be understood today; for here it was not a question of directing the work of his many helpers, as in India, in a Christian atmosphere, but of announcing the glad tidings in a hard tongue to purely pagan auditors. I think we missioners can get more inspiration from his life in Japan than elsewhere. And Yamaguchi was his residence for nine months of the short two years he spent in Japan.

"One of the most pleasant memories of my visit there is the quiet afternoon's talk with Father Cettour. I remember telling you that as we stood waiting for the train, 'some whiskers and a cassock' came walking towards us. That is as much of Father Cettour as I described before, so I want to do him justice to soothe my conscience. He has been twenty-three years at Yamaguchi.

"He told me of the search for the footsteps of the saint, the finding of the well he used and other little sacred spots that in a Christian world would be enshrined as scenes of pilgrimages. The site of the house St. Francis lived in was finally discovered but it cannot be bought now, for the Imperial Government has built an armory adjoining and no structure may be raised within defined limits that include the historic site. We contented ourselves by feasting our eyes on it later.

"In our talk I tantalizingly asked Father Cettour what he would do if he had a thousand dollars. It is a harmless pastime in its way, and Father Faber says even good intentions are meritorious for heaven. He replied that the most urgent work for him would be the starting of a young men's hut on the plan of the Knights of Columbus huts at the front . . .

"Question Number Two was naturally on the language, and he told me a little story of an old woman who for years had lived retired in her house and garden. As a true daughter of Eve, she showed her curiosity to see the foreigner who was in town, and with the boldness of a timid old lady she had herself driven to the lodging one evening. He courteously invited her in and treated her as a grandmother should be treated the world over.

"When she found her breath, she exclaimed: 'Well, well, to think that I should see a foreigner before I die! I am seventy-nine years old and you are the first I laid my eyes on. But how is it that you speak the same language that we do? Are your parents living? How did they let you come so far?' And she rattled on in amazement.

"He told her he had come because he loved the Japanese and that his mother had died since he arrived in Japan and that she had gone to a heaven he wanted his adopted Japanese to go to. The midnight came and went before he had finished talking, for the case was urgent, as the lady was old, and within a month he had baptized her and made her house his chapel in that village.

"Goa, Malacca, and Sancian have their monuments that mark the dwelling of St. Francis Xavier, but Yamaguchi, where he labored long among his 'dear Japanese,' the great historic spot in Japan, is without a token of him. Perhaps God has left it for the present generation to erect a little house that would further His cause the best in these latter days—a K. of C. hut."

In the spring of 1923, Father Patrick Byrne went to Korea to take over a mission field entrusted to us there, and to prepare for the arrival of more priests from Maryknoll. He was in Seoul on Pentecost, when Bishop Mutel ordained four young Korean priests. Then he started north for Pyongyang which was to be the center of our new mission.

"Meantime the night fell, and day broke," he wrote. "This artistic transition brings us to the railway station the morning after Pentecost where we awaited the train from the south, on positively our first appearance of the season in a missionary role.

"Five Korean priests, returning to their charges, helped us into the train, and remained a devoted bodyguard for six hours, or until we reached a bridge over a river the size of the Hudson, and apparently as popular. Here, Father Alexis Kim, in whose territory we were, signaled for lifeboats, and we hurried into our shoes—which everyone takes off in a Japanese train—for we were entering Pyongyang, the largest city in the Maryknoll sector and the logical center for our mission work. In this district there are over twelve hundred Catholics.

"Father Kim, a Korean of middle age, is evidently popular with his parishioners. We stepped from the train into a crowd of white-sheeted figures that created the momentary apprehension of being held up by the K. K. K. A second glance, however, sufficed to reassure us, for though the garb was a flowing white, the faces were both intelligent and kind.

"Introductions followed. We began to bow slowly, profoundly, repeatedly—till all was lost. When we later regained our senses, it was to find ourselves in rickshaws, bowling along at a merry pace through some very merry crowds. The city was 'en fête,' approaching the climax of a ten day celebration in honor of its first street railway system, and there were visitors from throughout the peninsula—the Koreans ever faithful to their composite white; the Japanese relieving the sameness by supplying rainbow divisions, in colors complementary and otherwise.

"The mission compound is a considerable distance from the railroad station, and we improved the opportunity of becoming better acquainted with our new 'home-sweet-home' by converting the hitherto respectable rickshaw into a vulgar 'rubber-neck' wagon.

"Already the second largest city in Korea, with sixty thousand natives and twenty thousand Japanese, Pyongyang continues to push out in all directions. Situated on the west bank of the picturesque Daido-Ko River, and with Mount Daijo a faithful sentinel at its back, it is now reaching a claw, in the shape of a twentieth-century bridge, across the river to the lower land on the east bank, where a large level plain will ease the city's growing pains.

"We left the rickshaws and started to scale the Heights of Abraham—or so they seemed—typical Korean streets with the added advantage of trying to stand on end. However, the ascent, if pleasant, was short and soon led to the royal postern gate in a stone-walled compound on the summit of a knoll.

"Sesame was already open, and we stepped through to face a multicolored dress parade—school boys in black and white lined up on one side, school girls in red and white on the other, with a rear guard of school teachers, parents, Christians in general, and a few stray pagans. It was quite overwhelming, that simultaneous salaam, and we were at a loss for any adequate response until we thought of our kodak.

"At once the atmosphere became tense and jubilant, and for the next half hour, willing trains of boys, girls, and elders were shunted and shifted for suitable poses."

Subsequent letters from Father Byrne told of the other towns in the new Korean mission. He visited some of them. He made a trip to Yeng You, by way of O-Ha. Buying a ticket for this place, he said, made you smile audibly, and then that helped your pronunciation. Later he went north, towards the Manchurian border.

"Next in our line of march was Sin Uiju, on the Yalu River, the northern terminus of the Korean railway. Across the river lies the large Manchurian town of Antung, with many thousands of Koreans in addition to its Chinese and Japanese. Sin Uiju is the northern gateway to Korea and it is growing rapidly—so much so that it is difficult to get official figures of population, which the pastor, Father Paul Pak the Second, reckons at twenty thousand. A small hamlet, you say. Granted, but only three years ago it was smaller still, having but nine thousand three hundred. This is what a Bostonian with real courage would call 'some jump,' but which he would probably designate 'a truly remarkable augmentation.' Be it so! The mission property is easily described. Like peace in Europe, at this writing, it doesn't exist. A church and school are absolutely needed in Sin Uiju.

"We arrived at noon, and having despatched both the delegation and the dinner, set out with the hopeful pastor for a look at what, to his Korean mind, are some choice lots. By Korean mind, we mean a mind that doesn't mind drains, or sewers, or swamps, or anything that's juicy. The American mind, on the contrary, rather inclines to dry land, though this is doubtless a concession to our enervating environment and hyperaesthetic olfactories. At any rate, land must be found soon, as the sailors said to Columbus, and we hope someone can tell us where to find it. Suitable plots that could have been had two years ago for four hundred dollars an acre have jumped to only ten times that price today. We loosened our collar, struck up the strains of 'Over the Hills to the Poorhouse,' and instructed our rickshaw man to take us past the Protestant schools and churches that occupy the choicest positions in town.

"We were sorry to disappoint the zealous young pastor with the elephant ambition and the flea income; with three hundred Catholics and no place to put them. He had heard 'The Yanks Are Coming,' and thought the arrival of Maryknoll presaged the Golden Age for the Catholic Church in Korea, or at least in Sin Uiju.

"It is at Uiju, twelve miles to the east, along the Yalu River, that the first Maryknoll group will make its headquarters while wrestling with the language. The house is a comfortable bungalow, and while the winter is reputed to be so severe in the north that the poor farmers are kept awake o'nights by the chattering of the polar bears' teeth, yet Manchuria across the way tempers its cold winds with coal trains, and stoves which are the only cheap thing in Korea.

"What a contrast with the hard times of the old French missioners, some of whom are still living—for instance, Bishop Mutel, who entered the kingdom at the risk of his life, and lived for years in whatever holes in the ground afforded shelter, at the mercy of any traitor who chose to denounce him. How insignificant are the trifling hardships of today compared with the really heroic trials that tested the stamina of those rugged apostles who introduced the faith! 'Behold we count them blessed who have endured.'

"There have been many martyrs in Korea, heralded to the world; but there have been in greater number those 'unknown saints' of whom the world will never hear—men who, by living for Christ, have done what was perhaps harder than dying for Him; men who have borne 'the burden of the day and the heats' for twenty, thirty, forty years; and who have faithfully blazed the trail for the missioners of today. It is the privilege of Maryknoll to follow where these pioneers have led."

These letters from Father Byrne, Father Ford, Father Walsh, and the others, fed our imagination. We saw ourselves one year, two years or three years later, walking those same trails, baptizing, teaching, ministering to the dying, in the towns and hamlets whose names became familiar to us through these mission letters.

The after-supper recreation at Maryknoll, outdoors in the quadrangle under the star-lit fall and winter skies, was often spent in singing the old songs. Then as now, seminarians aspiring and conspiring to reproduce the close harmony of barber shop quartets, would render—in both senses—the heart songs popular in childhood days. John Murrett contributed much to this musical outlet and helped to make the rendition as painless as possible. His compositions for religious use and for entertainment are ever popular.

It was in those early Twenties that he composed various lyrics, some of which he adapted to already existing melodies, while putting others to music of his own creation. One of the best was "O Maryknoll," sung to a movement in the music from "The Prince of Pilsen." If I recall it correctly, it goes like this:

"O Maryknoll, My Maryknoll, your sons can ne'er forget;
The golden haze of student days is round about us yet.
Those days of yore will come no more, but through each mission year,
The thought of you, so good so true, will make you doubly dear . . .
The thought of you, so good so true, will make you doubly dear. . . ."

24

Hongkong and Manchuria

"Far away!" what does it mean?
Does distance sever there from here?
Can leagues of land part hearts?—I ween
They cannot; for the trickling tear
Says: "Far Away" means "Far More Near."
— Rev. Abram J. Ryan

In the fall of 1923 I was aboard the *SS President Jackson,* crossing the Pacific on my way to Yokohama. My final destination was Hongkong. It had all come about suddenly, and the transition from the busy life of procurator at the new seminary to the role of language student in the Far East was all accomplished within three months.

One day late in the summer, walking along the road, I had met Father Walsh on his way to the office. We went along together, and then, taking me by the arm, he turned to me and said: "Father Raymond, how would you like to go to China?" The question fairly took me off my feet. Of course, I wanted to go to China; that was why I had come to Maryknoll in the first place, but in the rush and routine of this other work since ordination the vision had momentarily faded. I was to relieve Father O'Shea at our procure, or business office, in Hongkong, study the Cantonese language, and help in the direction of the St. Louis Industrial School.

"The heavens weep when angels go abroad." So they say. The night of my departure, I was shown all the attention due to the combined choirs of angels and archangels, thrones and dominations. It poured, by the bucketful and by the hour. On my ordination day, three years previous, we had what I thought was the biggest snowstorm in years, and on this night in October, 1923, the rain was torrential.

The ceremony was inside, in the seminary chapel. I should have been joyous, but various little incidents conspired to upset me. First of all, my old pastor, Father O'Reilly, the Augustinian, had come down from Lawrence to preach the departure sermon. The years had passed since the day he gave me his blessing and sent me off to Maryknoll. I might have realized that he was beginning to age, but that night I noticed it for the first time. In the course of the sermon he had me someplace down in Central America, carrying the cross with Bartolomé de Las Casas, and then he had to spend the rest of the time getting me back to Ossining and on my way to China. When we reached that part of the ceremony where the clergy come forward for a farewell handshake and a word of Godspeed, Father James Anthony put his hands on my shoulders and whispered: "Good-by, old man." This intimate bit from him, with the sudden realization that it was in truth a good-by, started a tight dry feeling in my throat. This grew worse after the ceremony, when I started down the long corridor in search of my mother and brother who had gone ahead to wait for me in one of the classrooms.

I had been planning to say something befitting a missioner who was at last "on his way." My mother had been losing her sight. When I entered the room, she stood up and started towards me, groping her way. This was too much. I broke down utterly. The others in the room that night can tell how I went to pieces and mingled my feelings with the downpour outside. My mother was the brave, strong one. Calmly and gently she put her hand on my shoulder and said: "Don't worry about me, son; I'll be all right."

It was a long, long hour in the train that night, going from Ossining to the Grand Central Station. The picture of my mother, when we said good-by, lingered with me. Father O'Reilly had come along. When we arrived at the Grand Central Station, we said our last "farewell." He went towards the Boston train, with stooped shoulders, and slow of pace. I went to the Penn Station to get my train for the West. I told myself it was probably the last time I would ever see him on this earth. It was so: he died before I returned to the States.

Father John Morris and I were traveling together. We were to meet Father Gleason later. In Chicago Father Edward Broderick showed us the best in hospitality. Father John and I went to South Bend and explained to Father Hudson and Father Cavanaugh that this was our last chance to see Notre Dame play before we sailed for China. Father Cavanaugh found tickets for us, and we watched the famous Four Horsemen and their team run away with the game from Georgia Tech.

Father Morris, who was to join Father Byrne in Korea, helped to make the trip an eventful one. At Los Angeles, we were taken on a visit to Clover Field, the airport, and were invited for a ride in one of the planes. I alone accepted the offer. Just before taking off, I was handed a printed form and asked to sign away all rights and claims for indemnity and compensation in case of disaster, accident, loss of life, limb or property. Father Morris asked me what kind of wood I would prefer for my coffin. Then he and the others escorted me to a demolished plane beside the hangar, in which the pilot had been killed the week before.

I was attired in correct flying costume which helped to hide my shaky knees and gave no clue to the sinking sensation in the pit of my stomach. In a moment we were in the air. It was a two-seater training plane, a "crate" if ever there was one. I sat on a parachute, with a loose strap around my waist, through which I would have slipped out very nicely if the plane took to tricks. Lieutenant Schonhauer took me up four thousand feet and then cruised above Santa Monica Bay, out over the ocean and back again through the mountain peaks. We were up about a half hour. I don't know how often I said the Act of Contrition or how many pious ejaculations I made. But the crucial moment came when I least expected it. Hovering at four thousand feet, the pilot throttled the engine down almost to a standstill, and turned to ask me if I would like to loop the loop. I simply pointed to the ground, with a pleading expression in my eyes. He took me literally: during the next few seconds, the fields and the ocean and the mountains came up and whirled around me. It was marvelous how the whole bay could rotate through the air without spilling a drop, and when the universe leveled off once again I learned that we had dropped three thousand feet. It was a relief finally to feel the wheels touching the runway.

We visited San Francisco and sailed from Seattle. There, with the aid of a friend's long coat, we hustled Patsy up the gangplank and into our cabin. Patsy was an Airedale which we were bringing to Father Byrne. Being a sociable critter, Patsy liked company, and when he was alone in the cabin he set up a long, mournful wail. This was all right during the excitement of leaving port, but as we moved out to sea and things aboard ship became quieter, his constant yelping was getting us into trouble. We had to hand him over to the cabin boy who took him below, and he made the rest of the trip to Yokohama in steerage. "Just because," as Father Morris said, "he wouldn't keep his mouth shut."

One of our traveling companions was Captain Robert Dollar. He was eighty-one years old at that time, one of the greatest shipowners in the United States. He was making a globe-circling journey to establish a round-the-world freight and passenger service. He was a great old sailor, never missed a meal,—or anything else aboard. At eighty-one, he was full of activity and enthusiasm and, barring accidents, looked as if he would live on to be a hundred years old.

As we entered the port of Yokohama, we began to see some of the destruction wrought by the terrible earthquake two months previous, when almost one hundred and fifty thousand lives were lost. Fortresses at the harbor entrance were just piles of twisted and broken concrete, all tilting at crazy angles and looking as if some great giant had placed a mammoth crowbar underneath and lifted them into a jumbled broken heap.

The sea wall and the docks were shapeless masses of broken concrete blocks and twisted steel. We left the boat, intending to go by train to Kobe. I went to the Imperial Hotel at Tokyo and was there only a few minutes when the place started to rock and shake. I rushed to the window and, finding that barred, hurried out of the room and on to a sort of roof terrace where a crowd of foreigners had already gathered. Telegraph poles were rocking back and forth, describing weird arcs; wires were snapping; and the whole earth seemed to billow under my feet. I must have looked frightened, but the hotel boys assured me that the danger was passed. Damage had been done somewhere, no doubt, but the tremor of that day was a mere quiver compared with the terrible disaster of September first.

I changed my mind about taking the train to Kobe and returned to the boat where my traveling companions greeted me with cheers and mild jeers. Father Morris, as I learned later, was in a railway station at Yokohama when the quake occurred. He had asked for a ticket and when he looked up to the window again to get his change and the ticket, the clerk was gone. Then he noticed the station had been abandoned and newsstands were rocking. He picked up his bags and fled in terror. The Japanese standing outside greeted him with smiles and chuckles as he shot through the door, just about thirty seconds too late if the station had fallen. At any rate, Father Morris and myself missed our rendezvous, and we did not meet again until we were in Korea.

At Kobe, I met Father Fage. For years he had been in correspondence with us at Maryknoll and had welcomed all our missioners on their arrival in the Far East. This was the beginning of a long happy friendship, which ended only during World War II when American planes bombed Kobe and destroyed the section in which Father Fage's church was located. His body was found later in the ruins, kneeling at the altar rail together with the aged parents of Monsignor Furuya, our Japanese mission superior at Kyoto.

I said good-bye to Father Fage and took the train for Shimonoseki to get the boat for Pusan. The mention of Shimonoseki always makes me smile. Father James Anthony loved to plan your trip and give you tips on how to travel, what to do when you arrived, and where you might find friends and shelter. His sense of planning made him familiar with maps and timetables, and he would outline your journey for you. Some people, like one of my companions in Manchuria, found this tiring; they would rather fix their own time, and what great matter if they missed a train now and then.

Father Walsh was outlining the various laps in Father Mac's journey to the East. He looked up the trains, found the time for his departure at Harmon, the arrival in Chicago, the train for Seattle, the day of the boat's sailing and the boat's name, and then the arrival at Yokohama. "Then," he went on, "the train from Tokyo will take you to Kobe and Osaka and then right down to Shimonoseki. . . ." "Oh," interrupted the other, "and isn't that a nice word— Shi-mo-no-se-ki! I like that, Shi-mo-no-se-ki." And he repeated it over and over again with a soft purling brogue rich with the dew of Ballaghadareen. That ended the planning. Father Mac had to map his own way from Shimonoseki to Mukden.

At the customs house we had been asked: "Have you any tobacco?" and forthwith replied: "Yes, we have no tobacco." We had been warned about customs beforehand and instructed by Father Byrne and Father Cleary, who had an experience at Kobe worthy of the record. The officials questioned the right of two big apples in Father Cleary's satchel, and while they retired to discuss the question and fix the levy, Father Pat ate both apples. This complicated matters seriously for a brief moment, but the officers decided that apples in the clergy were not dutiable, and so the poor missioner was richer by the few cents which he did not have to pay, and by the apples which he ate.

I was getting nearer to Korea. I said my rosary alone on the hurricane deck that night as the boat pulled away from port. The moon was bright, and the Japanese mainland plainly visible. I thought of Francis Xavier and his journey through these parts, and wondered at his courage and zeal, prompting him to set out for the Orient, when the land and the people were scarcely known, and travel was so long and arduous. We of this latter day hardly deserve the name of missioners, in comparison with those soldiers of Christ.

In the cathedral at Seoul I finally caught up with Father Morris. He accused me of, and I blamed him for, the mishap that made us lose each other in Yokohama and Tokyo. He said that after he ran out of the railway station in Yokohama he took a rickshaw to go to the church. He had all his baggage with him—and piled it in his lap —a suitcase, a satchel and Patsy, the Airedale, in a crate on top of them all. The rickshaw man slipped, sending Father Morris and his baggage spilling into the street. The Japanese rickshaws are high, and when Father Morris came to rest, Patsy was under him. No bones were broken, he said. This reminds me of the time I visited Cardinal O'Connell. Entering the study of His Eminence and failing to make the proper reconnaisance, in my embarrassment and rush to kiss his ring, I knelt down and sank my knee into the ribs of a poodle asleep at the Cardinal's feet. The yapping of the dog made an inauspicious beginning for the interview.

Everything in Korea was interesting. I couldn't help thinking of the martyrs who gave their lives for the Faith in this land. At Maryknoll we had read the life of Just de Bretenières, and the story of how the Koreans themselves brought the Faith to their country from missioners in Peking. The people in their loose white garments, the oxcarts, the "jiggys" on the backs of men carrying loads of rice and kindling and produce—all were just as I had imagined.

As Father Morris said, in Korea we got a cold reception. He referred to the unheated churches and poorly heated houses. In Korea, he said, thermometers are used to measure the cold, not the heat. Father Byrne, who met us in Seoul, was looking for pipe and fittings to bring to the mission at Uiju. He had met a representative of the American Radiator Company on the train one day and through him had obtained a supply of radiators. He was waiting for us to help him install the heating plant.

Father Byrne took us to Uiju. We went in an ancient Ford, converted into a carry-all and used as a public utility by the Northern Korean and Yalu Motor Transport Company, Inc., or some such concern, with an impregnable franchise. It was an old Model T Ford, with a third row of passengers injected in the middle. Father Morris and I occupied the place amidships. Father Byrne was in back, seated atop a packing case filled with pipes, fittings, and Stillson wrenches. The road was narrow, and shortly after darkness fell, we were in a head-on collision in which we lost our two front wheels.

I was cold all the time in Uiju. At night I piled on more and more blankets, until Father Morris said I would need a periscope to see the clock. Four of us, Father Byrne and Father Cleary, Father Morris and myself, worked all day hooking up the radiators and connecting the boiler. Father Byrne and Father Cleary had installed the system some days before, not realizing that the threading of the Japanese nipples would not match the threading of the American fittings. When they turned on the water, every coupling leaked; in fact, the water poured out and squirted out as if from a hot spring. We had to dismantle the whole system and begin all over again.

Father Morris was beginning to settle down to a quiet life of study, which he found infinitely more consoling and satisfying than the years he had spent in America, going from parish to parish collecting for the missions. He became Mok Sin Poo, by his new Korean name. Father Byrne was Pong Sin Poo and Father Cleary was known as Kil Sin Poo. Patsy, the Airedale, began his new life's work in Korea, chasing fleas. He worked in night and day shifts, and before I said good-bye to continue on my journey, he was already getting nervous and had a distracted look. Father Byrne had to call twice to get his attention. He seemed to be always listening for a flea.

The rest of the trip was full of incidents, too numerous to describe since this is not primarily a travelogue. I visited Mukden, Tientsin, took the Blue Express for Shanghai, said Mass at St. Joseph's Hospital where Mr. Lo Pa Hong and Mr. Tsu served the Mass, and there caught up with Father Gleason, who had come on a Canadian boat. Together we sailed for Hongkong, and our ship entered the harbor at dawn on the morning of December 19th. A message from shore told us to hold our peace and wait in patience. We were watching at the top of the gangplank, when a familiar voice called up from the maze of small boats in the water far below the deck of our liner. Away down in a small sampan—it seemed a tremendous distance below us—we saw the cassocks. The portly "Captain" O'Shea jumped from boat to boat, just as sprightly as in the days when he piloted the good ship "May Queen." After him came Fathers Ford and O'Melia, Brother Michael and Brother Albert. It was a happy ending to the long trip.

In Hongkong, one of my first visits was to Happy Valley Cemetery, to the grave of Father Price. In his will, Father Price had asked that his heart be removed and sent to France to rest beside the tomb of Bernadette. I am certain that if he ever foresaw all the trouble this simple request was to cause, he would never have made it. Years later, in Manchuria, I met the priest who carried out this apparently simple assignment, which turned out to be a complicated affair. He said there was no end of permissions to be obtained and papers to be signed before the heart could be taken from Hongkong, and then the same formalities had to be gone through all over again to get the heart into France. Ultimately, Father Price had his way, and his heart rests today in a small niche close by the crystal and gold casket, or reliquary, which encloses the precious remains of his beloved Saint Bernadette.

The religious order of which St. Bernadette was a member has opened a school in Kyoto, where our Maryknoll missioners have been at work for many years. This surely would have delighted the heart of Father Price; who knows—maybe he arranged it? The Mother General of these religious, the Sisters of Charity of Nevers, stopped at Maryknoll not long ago on her return trip from Japan. She brought us a notable relic of St. Bernadette. She told us how, as a young Sister, she had seen Father Price at prayer in their chapel at Nevers. She spoke, too, of his vigils, made with the special permission of the Mother General, when he spent entire nights in the cemetery chapel near the spot where Bernadette was buried. That was before her canonization. Truly, the protégée of Our Immaculate Mother took very good care of her own protégé, Father Bernadette.

I spent two years in Hongkong. I wonder sometimes how so many things could have happened in those two short years. My principal work was to look after the purchases for our missioners and to manage our general business matters at the procure. Brother Michael and Brother Benedict assisted in this work. St. Louis Industrial School was another charge which I carried, with the help of Brother Albert and Brother Martin. Every day I studied Cantonese, and took occasional lessons also in Portuguese. On Sundays, I preached twice for Father Spada at the Holy Rosary parish, following the yearly outline of sermons drawn up by our old professors, Fathers Callan and McHugh. Once a week, I went to the convent of our Maryknoll Sisters in Kowloon to give a conference.

Ch'an Chuk-shaan, leader of a notorious outlaw band, kidnaped Father O'Melia and Father Rauschenbach in a raid on Sancian Island. When word came to us, I tried to get action through the United States Consulate in Hongkong. After days of delay, the SS Sacramento was ordered to the island with a rescue party. Meanwhile, wireless messages referring to the kidnaping had been picked up by a Chinese gunboat patrolling the South China coast, and the skipper at once set out for Sancian.

He arrived there shortly after our two priests had escaped from their captors, just when they had reached the opposite side of the island and were looking without success for a boat to take them to the mainland. The Chinese warship spotted them and took them aboard. This was hours before the American gunboat reached the place. It was a feather in the skipper's hat, and I saw to it that he was made the hero in a long story published in the Hongkong papers.

The Hongkong strike was going on at that time. For a year or more it dragged along, making everyone uncomfortable. The idea was that no Chinese should work for a foreigner. Fortunately, our boys remained on the job and were not molested. Feeling was running high, however, and we were advised to remove our priests and Sisters from Yeungkong. This was more easily said than done. Again, I had difficulty in getting a United States gunboat to go for them. Impatient with the delay, I appealed to the Governor of Hongkong, and he at once despatched his launch to Yeungkong. The launch reached the entrance to the Yeungkong harbor, but there was an unforeseen delay owing to tides: the boat's fuel was running low, and so the commander decided he would have to return. We learned later that our priests and Sisters had already set out on a Chinese junk, were almost to the harbor entrance, had seen the launch and tried to signal to the British sailors, but to no avail. When the launch sailed away in the direction of Hongkong, they had to go back to their residences in the town.

Finally, an American gunboat arrived from Swatow. It went to Yeungkong and took off our Sisters. The officers turned over their quarters to the Sisters and did everything to make the trip easy and comfortable. A mishap attended the boat's approach to port, and it could have ended in tragedy. The gunboat was towing a tender in which there were two sailors ready to man a machine gun in the event of any hostile action while the boat was at its mooring. A projecting rock suddenly appeared through the waves in the path of the gunboat, and the pilot swerved quickly to avoid it. The turn was so sharp and so sudden that the small boat in tow was swamped.

The commanding officer decided that they could not risk the danger of overturning the launch by returning to pick up the sailors, who were washed into the bay. They struck out for shore. It was a long swim. One arrived at night outside the city gates. He was let in and brought to the mission. The other finally touched land at some distance from the town and was taken in by a friendly Chinese family. He got back to his shipmates the following day by Chinese junk, greeted with wild cheers, as one returning from the dead.

The Governor of Hongkong and the Secretary of the Colony were always friendly. We had been asked to take over the construction and the direction of a student hostel near Hongkong University. This promised to be a worth-while venture. One of our priests, Father Drought, was engaged to teach at the University. He would likewise be in charge of the students outside of class hours. A spot was picked out, near the University. It was the site of an old fort, and there was a disappearing gun with its mounting still there when we were planning the building. Blue prints were all ready, and we were about to start construction when suddenly the whole plan was dropped. This was part of the unhappy outcome of a project regarding a hospital in Kowloon, on the mainland.

The administration of the Colony had asked our Maryknoll Sisters to staff the hospital. Finding properly trained nurses in sufficient numbers had always been a problem for the authorities. Someone explained it this way: nurses came from England to work in the hospital, but as soon as they found a husband they got married and left.

When it was announced that our Sisters were to take over the hospital, a tempest arose and rocked the sides of the teapot. The Governor was besieged by indignant subjects of His Imperial Britannic Majesty, who voiced their disapproval. In the newspapers we were attacked with scathing letters to the editor, and we learned that we were guilty of two capital crimes: we were Catholics and we were Americans. Moreover, we were guilty, on our own confession, of the insufferable presumption of acceding to the Governor's request regarding the hospital. To save the Colony from infiltration by American papists, one devout Christian in Kowloon made a house-to-house canvass to secure signatures for a formal protest. I believe that the opposition was not numerous, but it was noisy and it caused distressing embarrassment for the Governor.

The contract had already been signed. Our Sisters were ready to begin work. The Governor could not very well go back on the agreement, but he foresaw difficulties. Père Robert felt that the Sisters should take the initiative and withdraw. There were good reasons, however, for not withdrawing. Still, it had been a gesture of friendliness on the part of the Governor to ask us in the first place; to leave him now to stew in a tempest which none of us had foreseen would hardly be a friendly return. At the Governor's request, the Sisters withdrew from the hospital, and later we gave up the Industrial School and dropped all plans for the hostel.

In less than a year, the Sisters were asked again to take over the hospital, and the man who had led the opposition in Kowloon, good repentant and forgiving Christian that he was, became the leader in promoting the Sisters' cause. The policy was fixed, however, wisely or unwisely, and Father Walsh decided that to save us from similar controversies in the future, which might have a deadening effect on our initiative and leave us with a complex of being thwarted and frustrated, it would be wiser to concentrate our efforts on the China hinterland.

One day, late in 1925, a cablegram came from America, telling me to pack up and report at Mukden. Maryknoll was taking a new mission field in Manchuria. I was to go north, begin the study of a new language—Mandarin—and make preparation for the later arrival of newly ordained missioners. My previous trip through Manchuria had been during the winter. I still thought of it as a bleak country,— treeless, drab and cold; but there were souls there to save, twenty or thirty millions, and that was our business. Bishop Blois was waiting for me in Mukden. I was to be under his direction, studying the language and learning the first steps of mission work in the land which the Chinese call their Northeast.

In Hongkong I used to get some recreation playing ball with the Hongkong Baseball Club. Brother Michael and I would make for Happy Valley every Saturday afternoon during the baseball season, peel off our cassocks and get into baseball uniforms. Pious fans, of European extraction and tradition, took exception to this evidence of modernism. A complaint went to Rome. In due time, Father Walsh at Maryknoll received a mild suggestion that it might be better for everyone concerned if Father Lane would get his recreation in some other way.

When I left Hongkong for Manchuria, there was a note about my departure in the newspapers, with the not-too-accurate comment that the Hongkong Baseball Club was losing "a pillar of strength." This item was dutifully translated and copied into a certain bulletin which circulated among European clergy circles in the Far East. When I arrived at Mukden, Bishop Blois had it in his hand and read it to me. Thus, you might say, I started my missionary career in Manchuria, with two strikes against me.

Bishop Blois was strict, but not so strict with us as he was with his own French missioners. He had a genuine personal interest in each of our men. He was fatherly. His advice was sound. He was generous with us and helpful in a thousand ways. During the dark days of World War II, he looked after our missions and helped us, who were in internment camps, to keep alive. He was a father, friend, and good neighbor for twenty years, until his death in May, 1946. One day, as he was setting out to visit a sick priest, a Russian military vehicle overturned his carriage. It affected his heart, and some weeks later he died. I was at that time in Dairen, capsulated by our Russian "liberators" and the Chinese Communists, and I was unable to attend the funeral of my old friend and counselor.

All my mission years in Manchuria were spent close to Bishop Blois and the other French missioners of Mukden for whom I developed a deep affection and esteem, and with whom I was associated in countless experiences,—some thrilling, some tragic, and many amusing. But this is all part of another story, for here we must limit ourselves to the early days of Maryknoll, of which we have just about reached the end.

25

Windows on Yesterday

*"Adieu, Maryknoll! A Dieu! To God! In His Hands
thou art secure, and under the protecting favors of
her who mothered the Saviour of men, all will be well
with thee. . . ."*

— James Anthony Walsh

If you stand, in the evening, on the cloister terrace at Maryknoll to
watch the sun go down in the hills beyond the Hudson, you may
wish for the art of a Turner or a Whistler to record in colors a
majestic panorama proclaiming the existence of God and His glory.
The scene rearranges its splendor from instant to instant, until at
last a film of red and purple and gray slowly moves over it and then
disappears as night settles down over the world.

Lingering with the sunset to watch the last pastel blendings grow
dim, you will see the sky change to a deep blue, studded here and
there with a bright star. You will see also the flashing of an airway
beacon, many miles away on the peak of a hill across the river, just
where the sun went down. Rotating in quick bright flashes, the signal beam sweeps hundreds of square miles in its orbit. This final
chapter will be like that beacon: in a few quick flashes it will sweep
over the years that have intervened since the early days, letting the
light rest momentarily on certain memorable scenes.

One of these memorable events was the consecration of Bishop
James Edward Walsh. In 1927, he became our first Maryknoll Bishop.
The ceremony was on Sancian Island, in the chapel that marks the
spot where Saint Francis Xavier died while waiting in vain for a
chance to enter China.

Linked with the consecration of Bishop Walsh is the death of Father Daniel McShane. He alone was absent from the ceremony, for, unknown to the other missioners, he was too ill to travel and was at his little mission in Loting, dying from smallpox. Like Father Price, he had no Maryknoller with him during that last illness, until word reached Hongkong, and then Father Rauschenbach hurried back to Loting in time to give Father McShane the last sacraments and be with him when he went to God.

Father McShane had caught the infection from a dying babe. The infant was number two thousand four hundred and eighty-three on the list of little ones taken into the orphanage by Father McShane during his seven years in Loting. They buried him in the front yard of the mission. His last letter, scribbled in pencil, reached Hongkong the day he died:

"I'm over a week on my back with smallpox. Thank God, I did not go down to spread it to the others. Please tell Bishop Walsh I'm trying hard to offer my sufferings for his many new responsibilities. I give him everything I have. God love him and dear Father Superior, my mother and brother and sisters. Tell them I'm praying for them. I hold no grudge against anybody. I am thinking of the Sisters and Brothers also. Doctor Dickson has been especially kind to me. Can't retain the least food, and the heat is intense. God's blessed will be done. No mail seems to be coming this way. Pray for me."

In 1929, the first General Chapter of Maryknoll helped Father Walsh to realize that his boys were growing up. From that time, he relinquished to younger hands and less busy minds many of the details which, till then, he had continued to direct personally. A younger man took over the students and became rector of the seminary. This was myself. Someone else assumed responsibility for money matters. Another had the burden of official drummer, going on the road to make friends and explain why we went to China and Korea.

In 1933, Father James Anthony Walsh was made Bishop. The Pope chose this way of giving recognition to his work and of honoring Maryknoll. The ceremony of consecration was in Rome, in the chapel of the new Propaganda College on the Janiculum, and the date was June 29th, the very day—over a bridge of twenty-three years—on which Father Price and Father Walsh had been authorized to return to America to start a foreign mission seminary.

Again as in 1910, all the bells in Rome were ringing to herald the day of Rome's heroes, Saints Peter and Paul. Friends came from America: Archbishop McNicholas was there and, with him, Bishop Vehr of Denver. Bishop Dunn and Monsignor (later Bishop) McDonnell of New York, Monsignor Cashin, friend of Sing Sing days, Monsignor Duggan of Hartford, friend of Brighton Seminary days, Father Joseph Bruneau of Saint Mary's Seminary, Baltimore, and many others were with him in Rome that day. Mother Mary Joseph was there, and so also were the Maryknoll priests studying in Rome.

Cardinal Marchetti, Vicar of Rome, was at the ceremony. Cardinal Fumasoni-Biondi, the "Red Pope" of the Church's world-wide missions, presided as consecrator. He was assisted by Archbishop McNicholas and Bishop Dunn.

It was a beautiful day, full of symbolism. The chapel in Rome's Papal Seminary for the Missions, dedicated to the Epiphany—"The Manifestation to the Gentiles"—presented an unforgettable sight. The walls of the apse, a rich mosaic of unbroken gold, and the yellow curtained windows, poured down saffron to mingle with the cherry of the prelates and the scarlet of the cardinals. In the student body there were thirty-two different nations—omnes gentes. Except for Father James Kelly, of Boston, who was assistant priest, all the ministers at the altar were from the Far East and included seminarians from the Maryknoll missions in South China, Korea and Japan, who were studying in Rome. The choir, one of the finest polyphonic choirs in Rome, was likewise a mingling of many nations, and their music gave forth a harmony of blended voices that were gathered from lands widely diverse, and, in worldly affairs, in some cases, mutually hostile.

Pope Pius XI received Bishop Walsh and gave him a pectoral cross, a gift which he made to every Bishop consecrated in Rome. "And as a mark of special esteem for the cause you represent," the Holy Father added, "I also give you this ring," and he gave our Bishop a beautiful cameo mounted on gold.

Before he left Rome, Bishop Walsh spoke one Sunday at the American Church in the Holy City. This is Santa Susanna's, staffed by the Paulist Fathers. It was the Feast of the Precious Blood, and he chose for his text a sentence from the office of that day, words written by Saint Augustine: "What He gave, He gave for all." He said that his Titular Diocese, Siene in Egypt, was once a flourishing Christian area, but today is only the figure of a tragedy. The faith in Siene and in many other dioceses of northern Africa is dead; dead, quite evidently because its possessors, as Saint Augustine said, refused to realize that faith kept for the possessors alone cannot live, that faith must glow with charity, and charity must expand or die.

There were other events during those years, including the extension of our work to the Philippines, Hawaii, and Japan, and my return to Manchuria as superior of our new mission at Fushun.

Meanwhile, the Teresians, who had become the Maryknoll Sisters and were officially known as the Foreign Mission Sisters of Saint Dominic, found it hopeless to try any longer to squeeze into our castoff wooden dwellings and into the tiny halls above *The Field Afar* offices. Out of necessity, they put up a large Motherhouse, across the road from our farm.

In the 1920's, they had convents on the West Coast and in China, Korea, the Philippines, and Hawaii. During the following decade, as their numbers grew, they multiplied their works in those places. They also started a cloistered branch of the Maryknoll Sisters, whose life work, like that of Saint Teresa of Avila and Saint Theresa of Lisieux, would consist of prayer and penance, vigils and fasts, to beg God's direct help on the suffering millions and on the missioners who went among them.

In more recent years, the Sisters have branched out to Panama, Nicaragua, Bolivia, Chile, East Africa, the Pacific Islands, and Ceylon. The little group of six hard-working happy ladies whom I met at Saint Theresa's Lodge on my arrival in 1913, has grown to a community of a thousand, at work literally all over the world. They are conducting schools, hospitals, dispensaries, and are engaged in social service and the training of native young ladies to be Sisters. They have become doctors, registered nurses, masters of arts, school principals, settlement workers, novice mistresses, dentists, medical technicians, office workers, domestic workers, artists, writers, secretaries, bookkeepers, photographers, needleworkers—in fact, they are doing everything that serves and helps to "teach all nations."

In 1936, Bishop James Anthony Walsh died. He had been ailing for two years. In the summer of 1934, he went to Bavaria for treatment at Father Kneipp's Sanatorium. He was better for a time, but, as winter approached, he fell ill again. The following Easter he was greatly improved and was back at his desk. Late in the summer, he felt himself losing strength, and only with a supreme effort was he able to consecrate Bishop Francis Ford in September.

He said his last Mass on December 5th, 1935. He hoped that he would not spoil the holidays for everyone by taking his leave just before Christmas. He held on until the spring. Easter of 1936 was for him a day of intense suffering and agony. Two days later, his pain left him, and the lividness of struggle departed. Archbishop McNicholas, who was with him during those last days, said that he who had literally been the leader of a flying squadron to save souls, was no longer interested in action. His day was done. There was only one thought—that of meeting God. The perfect end was at hand. Limp and white, like one who has used up all his strength and has no more, he passed away, April 14th, 1936. His last words were, "Jesus, Mary and Joseph."

He lay in state in the seminary chapel. The Office of the Dead was chanted, and Mass was celebrated the next morning. In the evening, the coffin was conducted to the Motherhouse of the Sisters, and there the same prayers were offered. After the Mass sung by the Sisters, the funeral cortege moved down the highways to New York City. At the door of Saint Patrick's Cathedral, it was met by priests of the Archdiocese. Here, once more the Office of the Dead was chanted over Bishop Walsh, and the next morning Catholic America took over from Maryknollers the duty of doing final honor to his memory.

Cardinal Hayes, three Archbishops, fifteen Bishops, five hundred priests, hundreds of Sisters and a Cathedral overflowing with the laity attended the funeral Mass celebrated by Archbishop (later Cardinal) Mooney. That night, back at Maryknoll, Archbishop Murray of Saint Paul blessed the grave in the little cemetery at the edge of the woods, and the Father of Maryknoll was laid to rest in the shadow of a rustic cross. Later that same year, the body of Father Price was brought back from Happy Valley Cemetery in Hongkong so that we might have the two founders resting side by side in our God's Acre as an inspiration to the seminarians and a reminder of the beginnings of Maryknoll.

When Bishop Walsh saw the end drawing near, he wrote farewell letters for all his Maryknollers,—a letter to the Sisters, one to the Brothers, a letter to the students. Here is the letter to his priests:

"Dear Priestly Sons in Christ:

I make no distinction since we are all missioners. Whether our daily tasks are in the home land or on the field, we are of one heart and one mind, pledged to the evangelization of the world, with special interest in the people entrusted to our care by Rome.

I write in the expectation of my own departure, this time, with God's grace, for the life that changes not. You have been my comfort, my pride and my joy. I am fully aware that while much credit has been given to me, because of my position in the Society, my work would have been a failure without the help you have so generously given me.

I have known my limitations and you have borne with them. God certainly uses the weak for His Divine purposes. But, after all, our work is His work and you will make no mistake if you look to Him for guidance. All that He seeks from you is generosity and ready willingness to use the opportunities—or meet the difficulties—which will inevitably present themselves.

I have often urged you to appreciate what is good in other societies than ours. Keep up this spirit, but watch closely that loyalty shall be a shining virtue in your life—loyalty to the Society, to your Superiors, to one another. That we may be one in Christ, is my prayer.

Keep me in filial remembrance and know that, if God finds me worthy, I will be your helper until we meet merrily in heaven.

Affectionately in Christ,
JAMES ANTHONY WALSH
Titular Bishop of Siene
Superior General"

Bishop James Edward Walsh of Maryland, one of my seminary companions, became Bishop James Anthony Walsh's successor, chosen at the General Chapter held in Hongkong, in 1936.

Still vivid in my memory is the kidnaping in 1937 of Father Jerry Donovan, and his death amid Red bandits. Jerry was a lively little carrot head, just starting philosophy, when I was procurator at the seminary. After his ordination in 1928, he taught the youngsters at the Venard, our college in Clarks Summit, Pennsylvania, for a few years, and then he came to us in Manchuria. On October 4th, 1937, we had a celebration at our seminary at North Fushun in honor of Saint Francis of Assisi, the seminary's patron. Father Jerry was there; he was in charge of the adjoining mission. The next day, while the people were gathering in the afternoon for October devotions, he was taken out of the chapel at the point of a gun and led off to the hills.

Four months of hoping and praying and nerve-wracking waiting followed. We tried to do some bargaining with the bandits, but it failed. In February, Father Jerry's body was found, lying frozen in the snow, many miles to the northeast. Father Quirk flew to Huai Jen with the American Consul, to identify the body. The next day the Japanese military brought the coffin to our center house at Fushun, and we saw Jerry on his return—a broken, twisted body, still frozen, a few tattered clothes, a ragged cassock, a torn white shirt with the cuff links still in place, his eyeglasses with the nose-piece broken, the rope that had been about his neck, and the stick used to twist the rope. All put together, they told a tragic but thrilling story.

Father Francis Connors died the following year, also in February. Back in student days he had been one of the giants of manual labor and was our boss road-builder, laying out the driveways and service roads in Roman style with a heavy foundation of field stone.

After ordination he was in South China. With Father Joseph Sweeney, he devoted his life to the lepers. From childhood he had to cope with a chronic handicap, a muscular obstruction of the intestines. After an operation, which had eventually become unavoidable, he took a sudden turn for the worse and in less than a day slipped away to his reward. His tombstone has the inscription: "There met him lepers."

My nomination as Bishop came in 1940. I made a quick trip to the States to be consecrated in my old parish church, Saint Mary's, in Lawrence, where I had once been an altar boy. Bishop James Edward Walsh presided at my consecration, assisted by Bishop (later Archbishop) Cushing and Bishop McCarthy of Portland. I had been back in Manchuria less than a year when the war came.

December 8th, 1941 was a memorable date for us in Manchuria. Word came of the attack on Pearl Harbor. Plain-clothes men, employed by the Japanese, came to see us and to find out how much we knew, what we were thinking. "They will be back tonight," someone said. They came back, long after dark, with guns and a truck. We were put in jail.

The next day, our Maryknoll Sisters, who were still free, took care of many things for which we had not been given time. They sent the young native novices and the seminarians off to their own families. They made provision for the orphans and the old folks. Lest the Blessed Sacrament left in the tabernacles be desecrated by pagan hands, they distributed the sacred hosts to their own community and to the faithful.

Then followed three long years and eight months of internment, with no word from Maryknoll or home, and no way of sending messages home. Only twice during that period could we feel that our unwritten messages would reach their destination; that was when some of our missioners went home by exchange on the Gripsholm. Father McGurkin remained with me in prison camp during the entire period of the war.

The Feast of the Assumption of Our Lady, August 15th, 1945, lives forever in our memory. We had a secret radio which brought news of what was happening. Russia had been let into the war against Japan. There were some long night hours that we spent in damp, mosquito-infested bomb shelters. The Japanese guards disappeared. On the morning of the 15th, a Manchu guard came into our dining hall. He was not a Christian but, having lived with us for two or three years, he had come to know our Church calendar. He wrote on the blackboard a series of Chinese characters signifying something like this: "On this day of Holy Mother Going-up-to-Heaven Festival, you are free men again."

The frightful mass withdrawal of the Japanese from Manchuria, or rather their attempted withdrawal, was beginning. Trucks, trains, and strings of open coal cars were jammed with fleeing Japanese. Several successive days of torrential downpour soaked the roads and the families en route. A feeling of catastrophe was in the air. Women and children and old folk died by the tens of thousands, some from exposure, some from undernourishment, and the rest from spotted typhus. Japanese escape in those days was hopeless. Russians were coming in to take over the towns and run the railways.

Thousands of Chinese had been taken from their homes below the Great Wall to work in Japanese labor camps in northern Manchuria. These people began the long overland trek to their homes. Many died on the way.

We left our place of internment at Szepingkai (pronounced "Sipping Guy"), and started for our mission at Fushun. We were under Russian escort. Ordinarily, it is a two-hour ride to Mukden. It took us a day and a half. We reached Mukden at midnight and walked into a nightmare. The city was ablaze with bonfires made by the Russians and Chinese, who had been looting the Japanese department stores. There was machine gun fire that would strike terror to the stoutest heart. Nearly all the lights in the railway station had been destroyed, and in the darkness Russian soldiers were robbing, not only the Japanese, but also the Chinese and Korean refugees returning from labor camps. It was a sickening sight.

We waited in the station for daylight to come, and by the craziest of contrasts a group of Russian boys carrying Tommy guns gathered around us to sing American songs in Russian. One of them was from the Ukraine and he did a native dance, in his battle boots. Another had discovered a guitar in one of the Mukden stores. He had it with him and played it marvelously well; he whistled and danced at the same time. He had been with an orchestra in Prague before the war. We sang Kate Smith's favorite song, "God Bless America!" to which they generously applauded. We added a few of Stephen Foster's. A big lad, whose parents died in the siege of Leningrad, leaned on his machine gun and sang "Rose Marie" in Russian. His boyish face, with a spit curl escaping under his dirty cap, his pug nose and freckles and blue eyes, made an engaging picture as he sang for us there in the dim light of the station. It gave you a different light on the boys that made up the Red Army.

We found fifteen hundred American G.I.'s, who had been taken from the Philippines, Wake, and Guam, crowded into a few sheds on the outskirts of Mukden. It was there we learned that General Wainwright had been detained at a secret prison camp only a few miles from our place of internment to the north.

It was also from the soldiers there that we learned the details of the death of Father William Cummings. He had been ordained at Maryknoll in 1928, and was working in the Philippines when the war broke. He remained on Bataan with the American soldiers and with them made the death march to the sea. He and the boys were put aboard a prison ship. They described the horror as they lay on the beach waiting to be led away. An American bomber squadron swept down to strafe the beach and blast the boats. They saw their own United States planes swoop down; they saw the bomb bays open, the bombs drop, and they saw the death and havoc wrought around them. The flyers, of course, believed they were attacking a Japanese fighting force.

On the way to Formosa, and from there to Japan, Father Bill and the boys were locked in the hold, in almost complete darkness, with insufficient water and practically without food. The hatch was held by a guard with a machine gun. They heard the planes pass overhead, saw their shadow cross the open hatch, heard the bombs strike and crash, and they were kept down in the hold at the point of the gun.

Father Bill, already wounded and weak, calmed the men who were nearly crazed from sufferings and tension. He became weaker and weaker. One night he died. He had had the Blessed Sacrament with him; before he died he entrusted the pyx to one of the Catholic boys. "If we had only had a little water, we might have saved him," they told us at the prison camp in Mukden. They buried him at sea, somewhere between Formosa and Japan.

News came to us later about Father Sandy Cairns. He was on Sancian Island when the war started. An enemy patrol came ashore one day and took him away with them. He was never seen or heard of again. We have had rumors and conjectures, but no definite information of where or how Father Sandy came to his journey's end.

Little by little, we learned the complete story of other Maryknollers who died during the war. Father Leo Peloquin died at the International Hospital in Kobe, Japan, in June 1942. He had been in Korea for almost twenty years, during which he successfully opened several mission stations and supervised the construction of mission buildings for our priests and Sisters. Father Peloquin had not been well; he had suffered a number of heart attacks. During the months of tension preceding the outbreak of hostilities, he was subject to the very stringent travel restrictions placed on foreigners, and was thus obliged to make a hard journey by foot over the mountains, when he should have been resting quietly in a hospital. Later, as an enemy national, he was prevented from traveling when he needed hospitalization. Six months after Pearl Harbor, when the first exchange of the war was being effected, he set out with his fellow missioners to be repatriated. He had another heart attack on the trip from Seoul to Kobe; he died in Kobe and was buried there.

Father Leo Sweeney, also with a long record of pioneering work in Korea, died of a heart ailment after he reached America. He was the younger brother of Father Joseph Sweeney. His schools in Chinnampo were the pride of Korean parents and the joy of the youngsters.

South China, Maryknoll's first mission field, has taken a heavy toll in the lives of our missioners. Of the thirty-five priests, fourteen Brothers and thirty-three Sisters who have died since Maryknoll was founded, more than one third labored in South China. Several of our priests lie buried there. There we have the most difficult climate; opposition in the South seemed always the most bitter; and there have been repeated setbacks. In South China, perhaps more than anywhere else, do the words of Bishop Byrne apply: "Men who, by living for Christ, have done what was perhaps harder than dying for Him."

Father Otto Rauschenbach met a violent death early on the morning of May 14th, 1945, in the market town of Kai Laam, when the bullet from the gun of a bandit entered his heart. He had been in the missions of South China for twenty years. He was just about to set out for the States on a long-deferred furlough. There was a little delay in the arrangements, while he was at Loting, so he decided to go back to his people to say Mass for them once more; otherwise they would not be able to get to Confession and Communion for the Feast of Pentecost. The other missioners tried to dissuade him, on account of the presence of bandits and Japanese troops in the district. There was real danger. Souls needed him, he decided, and that was enough reason for facing any danger. The Christians buried him near the spot where he died.

Just before the war broke out, cutting off all our contact with Maryknoll and home, Father Rauschenbach had an article in *The Field Afar*. It was called "Iodine Sunset" and it gave a good illustration of that constant search for a way into the people's heart. It illustrated the unceasing trying that eventually brought success to our South China missioners' labor, where missionary labor has been hardest.

"Conversions come through contacts," he wrote. "Generally, the more contacts, the more conversions. Hence, every mission activity has this as its ultimate aim. But no mission activity throws the missioner into greater contact with every member of the family than does dispensary work. Father, mother, brother, sister, all—at one time or another—have pains and aches, chills and fevers, and even more serious complaints.

"Our very first convert in this new field was such a contact . . . . The case of the official's son was similar, though more serious. In his case we had to enlist the assistance of the Little Flower. Net results: the patient himself, his mother, and two sisters were brought into the Church. . . . The principle we work on is to give the patient something, even if it is nothing more than a couple of aspirin tablets or some soda mints. The sick feel better when they leave us, and, as Dr. Walsh says, 'take the cure while it cures.'

"But just one more word: why must a missioner assume the role of physician of the body as well as of the soul? Simply because, if we do not, it will not be done. When Our Lord sent His apostles to preach to the whole world, did He not say something about curing also?"

It was almost a year after the war ended, before regular mail came to us and we learned what Maryknollers had gone through in other parts of the East during the war days. We read about our priests and Sisters in the Philippines, the prison of Santo Tomas, the huge prison camp of Los Baños. We heard about their miraculous deliverance when General MacArthur was retaking the islands. There was street fighting in Manila. Many non-combatants were being killed. The retreating enemy was shooting down innocent Filipinos. The guards at Los Baños were showing bad temper.

At seven o'clock on the morning of February 23rd, 1945, American paratroopers of the Eleventh Airborne Division dropped out of the sky over the camp. They came down shooting. At the same time, Filipino guerrillas had surrounded the camp. They closed in and overpowered the Japanese garrison. Some of the American soldiers had rosaries around their necks. The rescue came on the second day of a special three-day prayer of the Sisters. The prisoners, over two thousand all together, were hurried out of the camp and escorted safely to a fleet of armored amphibian trucks that had crossed Lake Laguna de Bay to bring them to safety behind the American lines.

One of the Sisters described the American lads dropping from the skies: "They looked like angels, their delicate rayon parachutes as wings ruffled in the early morning breeze!" Of this rescue at Los Baños, General MacArthur wrote in his report: "Nothing could be more satisfying to a soldier's heart than this rescue. I am deeply grateful. God certainly was with us today."

The war ended in August, 1945. I was in Manchuria for almost a year after that, at Fushun until Christmas, and then at Dairen. That was during the Russian occupation. Never to be forgotten are those days with the Russians.

We had hour-long discussions with Captain Sogolov, an electrical technician with the Subaikal Motorized Army. This army was sent to Fushun to dismantle the giant electric power plant built by the Japanese. Captain Sogolov, a strict adherent of the Soviet code of etiquette, invited himself to live with us. He talked by the hour, in Russian, and was determined to make himself understood, and equally determined to understand our replies to his one hundred and one questions. Our contributions were expressed in a new sort of Esperanto, made up of newly acquired Russian words, bits of

German, French, American slang, and plenty of pantomime. Whenever his wordy descriptions brought blank looks to our faces, he acted them out and at times did everything but stand on his head to put across his idea. He was a gentleman, through and through, when he was sober.

With Captain Sogolov was Alexander, his aide-de-camp, likewise invited by the captain to live with us. Alexander was a good boy, because all of God's children are good. But Alexander was also a bad boy, because, taken from his home when only a youngster, he had been brought up in a barracks on the Soviet principle of mass education. For Alexander, you know, belonged to the state, not to his family, and apparently the only rule of right and wrong that Alexander learned was, "Don't get caught at it!"

I couldn't help liking Alexander, with all his roughness. He was eighteen years old. He carried a Russian submachine gun, the magazine of which looked like the film box of a movie camera. He wore heavy cleated campaign boots, and he would come pounding in on our clean floors, calling "Papa! Papa!" That was for me. "Papa" in Russian must mean everything from Pope to Bishop, and on to Father. It was the signal for me to dig out a bar of chocolate, a pack of cigarettes, or a left-over biscuit. He found a pal, a little terrier that we had in the yard. He tried to tell me about his own little dog which he had to leave home on the farm, back in Russia near Kazan. His mother was still at home—he hoped.

It took mountains of patience and self-control to smile when Alexander would swing the machine gun from his shoulder, point it at a cloud or at one of our shacks, and proceed to unload the bullets with a terrifying racket, or when he and his pals would come into our sitting room, put a Russian polka on the victrola, and cavort about the room in their spiked boots. Still, I liked him.

Then there was Captain Berganov. He was in charge of a mechanized unit, consisting of a fleet of American-built Studebaker trucks, all six-wheelers. His mission was to haul the loot to the loading platforms at Mukden. He seemed to enjoy his visits with us. He was polite, respectful, a good disciplinarian. He kept his drivers and guards out of our house.

One day, after several hours of work at the power plant, he

stopped at the house for a short visit. Out again, he started up his trucks and made ready for the return to Mukden. Then he came back into the room. He closed the door, made certain there was no one around, reached into his breast pocket and pulled out a wallet. He took from it a handkerchief, and from the folds of the handkerchief, a little crucifix. His mother had given it to him, he said, when he was leaving home in the Ukraine, when he was first called to the service. She was a good Christian—he had told us about her before—keeping up her religion in secret. It was her prayer, of course, that her son would remain good. He carried the crucifix with him wherever he went with the Russian forces, all through the Finnish campaign, the German campaign and into Hungary, and then during the long trek across Mongolia and into Manchuria. That was the first time anyone else had seen it; he would never dare show it to his fellow army officers. I learned in those days that not all the officers and men of the Soviet army were registered members of the Communist Party.

There were many nightmares during those months following the war. We missed one of the worst: it was the night Russian soldiers broke into our center mission at Fushun. We had not yet returned from the internment camp. They carried off clocks and clothes. One of the soldiers went off with my frock coat, which had been given to me five years before by Bishop James Edward Walsh who explained that it was the proper dress for a bishop and I should wear it. I have had a suspicion that I might find it some day among the Russian delegation at Lake Success.

There was tragedy that night when, to escape the soldiers, a little Chinese Sister jumped from an upper window, and then, with her back broken, crawled through the weeds and mud until the danger passed. She has been a cripple ever since that night.

I remember another terrible night. Just before Christmas that year, I started out for Dairen, taking with me some of our Manchu Sisters, who were to look after our school and dispensaries formerly staffed by our Maryknoll Sisters. The Russians were keeping the country closed, allowing no one to come in. We waited hours for the train in the station at Mukden. Things looked very bad. Drunken Russian soldiers were moving about in groups, some with guns drawn. They had robbery and worse things written in their faces. After about an hour of terrible anxiety, two young men approached us. Both were Russians, and one spoke good English. They asked if they could be of help to us. I explained our plight, and they made themselves our bodyguard. At least five times, during those six hours of waiting for the train, they argued with our would-be molesters and turned them away. When the train came, they helped us with our mountain of baggage and found us seats. At Dairen they told the station guards: "This is the American Consul and his staff," and they saw us safely to the mission. Later, they told me they were Soviets, and that they came from Harbin; but that night they surely looked like Guardian Angels.

Six months I was in Dairen, during which I gained experimental knowledge of Russia's unilateral system of interpreting the Yalta and Potsdam agreements. One day in June, I was in the dentist's chair. The doctor had been probing into some root canals, and he had my mouth filled with packing and plaster to get an impression for a partial plate. A messenger came in from the United States Consulate. A boat had come from Shanghai, on instructions from the Secretary of State, to take me out of Dairen and start me back to America for Maryknoll's General Chapter. It was the SS *Ring Splice,* a freighter operating with the Fifth Fleet.

There were delays at first by the Russian harbor master, because he did not want the ship to come into port. I was given four hours to get ready and get out. That night there were more delays, when the same harbor master would not let the vessel leave port. Finally, we sailed. Many things happened on that trip to Okinawa, and again aboard the SS *Bronx* on the journey to San Francisco, but all that does not belong in this story. At the General Chapter my fellow Maryknollers gave me the task of being Maryknoll's third Superior General.

Meanwhile, during the war, our missioners, who had been unable to go to the East, had found open doors in Central and South America and were getting ready to go to Africa. To find them, or write to them, I had to get out an atlas and learn a whole new list of names— Huehuetenango, Malacatancito, Ixtahuacan, Carrillo Puerto, Isla de Cozumel, Cochabamba, Riberalta, Chillan, Pemuco, Talca, Temuco,

Galvarino, Arequipa, Puno, with many others, and then Tanganyika with Musoma, Kowak, and so on. I made a memorable journey of several months' duration through all our missions in Latin America, and in 1950, I visited our infant mission in East Africa.

A quick trip to the South, which I made since starting this chapter, gave me an opportunity to thank the people of North Carolina for their gift of Father Price to Maryknoll. The occasion was the fiftieth anniversary of Monsignor Irwin's ordination. In earlier chapters I told of Father Michael Irwin's visits to Maryknoll, during which he would tell us about the experiences he and Father Price had in the missions of North Carolina. The golden jubilee celebration was held at New Berne, Father Price's old parish. Bishop Waters of Raleigh was there. Monsignor O'Brien, also a comrade in the apostolate with Father Price and perhaps the one who remembers him best, was present, as well as Monsignor Freeman, at whose home both Bishop Gibbons (later Cardinal) and Father Price frequently stayed. Father Price's nephew, Mr. Charles Price, was there, too. These people, gathered at a spot so full of associations and memories of Father Price, helped me to garner many precious details regarding Father Price's years as an apostle in the Tar Heel State.

In 1950 came the war in Korea. Father Patrick Byrne had been made a Bishop in April, 1949, and sent by the Holy Father to Seoul as Apostolic Delegate. When the Red troops of the north invaded the south, Bishop Byrne and Father Booth became prisoners of the Reds. No news came. When Seoul was retaken three months later, we learned something about what our missioners went through, although meanwhile they had been carried off to the north with the retreating Red armies. Survivors told about the poor food given to Bishop Byrne and his companions, the calculated mistreatment, the daily ordeal of questions with the constant threat of immediate death, their failing health and the sufferings of their eighty-one year old French companion, Father Villemont. Our hopes grew dimmer and dimmer as the Americans advanced with the Southern Koreans, taking back the country from the invaders and finding no trace of Bishop Byrne or Father Booth.

Recently, I re-read this letter written by "Uncle Pat," as he called himself, when he first went to Korea over a quarter of a century ago:

"What a contrast with the hard times of the old French missioners, some of whom are still living—for instance, Bishop Mutel, who entered the kingdom at the risk of his life, and lived for years in whatever holes in the ground afforded shelter, at the mercy of any traitor who chose to denounce him. How insignificant are the trifling hardships of today compared with the really heroic trials that tested the stamina of those rugged apostles. . . . There have been many martyrs in Korea, heralded to the world; but there have been in greater number those 'unknown saints' of whom the world will never hear— men who, by living for Christ, have done what was perhaps harder than dying for Him; men who have borne 'the burden of the day and the heat' for twenty, thirty, forty years. . . . It is the privilege of Maryknoll to follow where these pioneers have led."

I mentioned Alexander, the good little Russian from Kazan, who became the bad little boy with the Soviet army in Fushun. Many of the officers and men, especially the M.P.'s, knew that he lived with us. They knew that we called him Alexander, though that was neither his first name nor his family name. Late one Sunday evening, about six months after the war ended, during a quiet after supper recreation with our Manchu seminarians, the doors opened suddenly, and a squad of Russian M.P.'s came into our living room. They were headed by a polite young officer who spoke German and, of course, Russian. "Where is Alexander?" he asked. Captain Sogolov and Alexander had departed days before, and we thought that they must be hundreds of miles away on the road back to Russia. Apparently, not. They said that Alexander was in the neighborhood and was wanted. To our naive question, "What has Alexander done?" his reply was simply: "Something serious."

They were invited to look around the house, but the young officer took our word for it. We had not seen Alexander in weeks. They went out quickly. A moment later, one of our Chinese teachers came in, burning up with curiosity. What had happened, he wanted to know; he had been outside when the trucks drew up; our house had been surrounded with armed sentries while the patrol was in our living room.

It does not take army vehicles many minutes to cover three miles on roads that are in fair condition. The squad was soon at our mission on the north side of the river and made a similar raid, with the same results.

"Where is Alexander?" I wish I knew. I don't know what he did, nor whatever became of him. I had tried to be kind to him, but, when he departed, the job was not yet complete. Now, when I read about Communist armies marching here and moving there, I find myself thinking about Alexander,—thinking about the ten million Alexanders, who have been called from their homes, dragged away from their mothers and fathers and sisters, from their rabbits and puppy dogs, to carry a gun and spill their blood for dialectic materialism and other things about which they know nothing and care less, and which, if they are educated, they abhor. Alexander was not interested in the ascendancy of the proletariat and all the cruel crimes committed with that as an excuse. He wanted to be back on the farm with his mother and father and his puppy.

"Where is Alexander?" I think that will be one of the first questions I will ask, if, after my course is run, God finds me worthy and calls me to His everlasting Kingdom of happiness and peace. Perhaps Alexander will be there in the happy crowd with Father Price and Bishop Walsh and the Sisters, with Father McShane, Father Jerry, Father Sandy, Father Bill Cummings, Brother Henry, and the rest, on that day of days when "we all meet merrily in Heaven."